Ending Apartheid

Turning Points Series List

General Editor: Keith Robbins
Vice-Chancellor Emeritus, University of Wales Lampeter

THE END OF THE OTTOMAN EMPIRE, 1908–1923
A. L. Macfie

THE PARIS COMMUNE 1871
Robert Tombs

THE BOMB
D. B. G. Heuser

THE FALL OF FRANCE, 1940
Andrew Shennan

THE GREAT TREKS
Norman Etherington

THE OIL CRISIS
Fiona Venn

GERMANY 1989
Lothar Kettenacker

ENDING APARTHEID
David Welsh and J. E. Spence

Ending Apartheid

David Welsh and J. E. Spence

Longman
is an imprint of

PEARSON

Harlow, England • London • New York • Boston • San Francisco • Toronto
Sydney • Tokyo • Singapore • Hong Kong • Seoul • Taipei • New Delhi
Cape Town • Madrid • Mexico City • Amsterdam • Munich • Paris • Milan

Pearson Education Limited
Edinburgh Gate
Harlow CM20 2JE
United Kingdom
Tel: +44 (0)1279 623623
Fax: +44 (0)1279 431059
Website: www.pearsoned.co.uk

First edition published in Great Britain in 2011

© Pearson Education Limited 2011

The rights of David Welsh and J. E. Spence to be identified as authors
of this work have been asserted by them in accordance
with the Copyright, Designs and Patents Act 1988.

Pearson Education is not responsible for the content of third party internet sites.

ISBN: 978-0-582-50598-8

British Library Cataloging in Publication Data
A CIP catalogue record for this book can be obtained from the British Library

Library of Congress Cataloguing in Publication Data
Welsh, David, 1937–
    Ending apartheid / David Welsh and Jack Spence.
        p. cm. — (Turning points series)
    Includes bibliographical references and index.
    ISBN 978-0-582-50598-8 (pbk.)
    1. Apartheid—South Africa—History.   2. South Africa—Race relations—History—
20th century.   3. South Africa—Politics and government—1984–1994.   4. Government,
Resistance to—South Africa—History—20th century.   5. Nationalism—South Africa—
History—20th century.   6. Social change—South Africa—History—20 century.
I. Spence, J. E. (John Edward)   II. Title.
    DT1757.W44 2010
    968.06—dc22   2010019794

10 9 8 7 6 5 4 3 2
14 13 12 11

Set in 9/13.5pt Stone Serif by 35
Printed and bound in Malaysia (CTP-VP)

For Sue and Virginia

Contents

Acknowledgements

The authors would like to express their gratitude to Professor Keith Robbins for inviting us to write this book. He was wonderfully patient and a very skilled editor. Our thanks are also due to the Department of War Studies at King's College, London for research funding.

****

Jack Spence would also like to thank Robin and Anne Titley for their help in the preparation of this manuscript. The authors are grateful to all who helped with the production and publication of this volume: Mari Shullaw; Laura Blake; Kathy Auger; Belinda Latchford; Mary Nisbet; Josie O'Donoghue; Jayne Peeke; Hazel Clawley. Several librarians were kind enough to find sources for Jack Spence in particular: Susan Frank; Mary Bone and Malcolm Madden (Chatham House); Andy Jack and Tyrone Curtis (LSE); Anita Brady and Paul Chandler (Royal College of Defence Studies, London).

David Welsh thanks Catherine Welsh for her assistance.

Publisher's acknowledgements

We are grateful to the following for permission to reproduce copyright material:

Extract on p. 177 from 'The international community and the transition to a new South Africa', Evans, G., *The Round Table*, 83, Issue 330, 1994, reprinted by permission of the publisher (Taylor & Francis Group, http://www.informaworld.com).

In some instances we have been unable to trace the owners of copyright material, and we would appreciate any information that would enable us to do so.

Foreword

Keith Robbins

The notion that, at a certain point, 'history' turns, is deeply embedded in popular consciousness, and even in the minds of many historians. At such a moment, it is frequently said, history moves in a direction which is conspicuously 'different' from what has hitherto prevailed. A new world, perhaps a strange one, is born: wars are won and lost, rulers fall from power, administrative systems collapse, boundary walls fall down, empires disintegrate, natural resources become exhausted, 'new worlds' are discovered, and so on. In some instances, the 'turning points' may appear very obvious to contemporaries, but in other cases it is only with hindsight that the 'end of an era' becomes evident. It is also by no means always apparent that a particular event or development is in fact a 'turning point' at all. Some may be sceptical about the very notion of a radically different 'before' and 'after'. Further, believers in the inexorable grinding of deep processes of social or economic change may find it absurd to bother so much with the behaviour of humans, individually or collectively, at specific points in time.

The series in which this book takes its place lays down no doctrinal requirement on authors. Contributors have been free to make use of the 'turning point' concept as they choose. That said, it is obvious that the issues tackled all have about them some aspect of drama or crisis. *Ending Apartheid*, as a topic, fits naturally. It too raises all the usual deep questions. While it existed, there were many views expressed about how and when apartheid would end. Some suspected that it could only be ended at the conclusion of a full-scale internal war and by the replacement of one complete 'system' by another. Others supposed that it was not inconceivable that it would end through a change of heart. It was further argued elsewhere that it would peter out as it became steadily more apparent that it simply could not work in the way in which theory dictated that it should. It just could not be delivered. These arguments, and others, were put forward for decades both within and outside South Africa. They shaped how people thought and acted.

What was never clear, of course, on any scenario in relation to its demise, was *when* it would occur, or perhaps, to put it another way, how one would know whether or not it was in fact 'ending'. To attempt to answer how it might end, one might have to know when it had begun, and that might not, on examination, be straightforward.

There was a further conundrum. Who were the 'actors' in this story? It might appear, at one level, that the answer was clear. 'Apartheid' was a matter of South African history. So it had begun and so it would end. 'Outsiders' neither should nor could effectively 'intervene' in the country's internal affairs. 'Outsiders' could not understand the cultural and political dynamics, black and white, which were involved. The cry that South Africans would come to a 'solution' by themselves came from quarters which had very different views on what that solution should or would be.

There was a very different alternative perspective. 'Apartheid', it was said, was not *just* a South African question. It was a matter of fundamental human rights and there should be no constraint on the part of any external body – be it the United Nations, the Commonwealth of Nations, the World Council of Churches – in acting to try to bring it to an end. Ending apartheid was a matter for the 'international community'. There was no longer any substance in South African government complaints about 'interference'. What 'acting to try to bring it to an end' might be, however, was another matter: Boycotts? Sanctions? Disinvestment? Assistance to insurgents? Here were ample matters to debate and decide far away from South Africa.

Just as these two broad viewpoints can be identified, so can two broad kinds of historical interpretation. One, perhaps particularly in South Africa, has concentrated on what happened inside. Its focus has been so keenly placed upon internal politics and leading personalities, in all quarters, that the 'Outside role' can sometimes seem little more than 'noises off'. On the other hand, there have been those, perhaps particularly outside South Africa, who have highlighted the international dimension, either in the form of governmental or intergovermental action within the United Nations or the Commonwealth, or in the guise of pressure put upon governments by such bodies, in Britain, as the anti-apartheid movement.

'Ending apartheid', therefore, has too often only been approached from one angle or perspective. The benefit of this book is that both ways of looking at the issue come within the same volume. They have been written by two authors whose academic backgrounds, within the study of politics, have led to different foci in their research. Neither the material written up to and including Chapter 5 by Professor Welsh, nor that written in Chapter 6 by Professor Spence, is presented as a simple explanatory alternative. Ending apartheid was a complicated intermeshing of the internal and the external. It was never wholly one nor wholly the other. Readers must work out for themselves, in the light of what is presented, where, when and how pressure fused so that apartheid could not survive. Both authors have shared what they have written with each other but they have written as individuals. Their writing, moreover, grows out of a long personal and professional association. The duality in the book is further reflected in the fact that Professor Welsh is based in South Africa and Professor Spence in the United Kingdom. That one man is an 'insider' and the other (now) an 'outsider', however, should not be taken too far. Professor Spence was born, brought up and passed his early career under apartheid. There is, therefore, in this book a fusion of experience, expertise and location which makes it a unique assessment of 'ending apartheid'.

Few of those, inside or outside, who speculated on how apartheid would end, guessed that it would in fact end in the way it did. Its ending was not quite the cataclysmic, even apocalyptic, moment which some had forecast. Individuals and their communities, this book seems to suggest, edged themselves, painful bit by painful bit, to a solution. Each side, or perhaps one should say the many sides, accepted, on the one hand, that however acceptable apartheid had once been, or had been portrayed to be, it could no longer be sustained and, on the other, that however oppressive and demeaning it had become, it could not, for a good many years at least, be overthrown militarily. The way in which it did end, therefore, grew, grudgingly, out of these reluctant recognitions all round. South Africa did have a new beginning but the past did not disappear overnight. It is for this reason that an epilogue, still reflecting on both internal and external developments written by both authors and then joined, is pertinent. Dismantling apartheid did not cause to vanish deep questions relating to the functioning of democracy and the rule of law in a country of multiethnic and multicultural diversity, not to mention continuing disparities in wealth and education. New goals were set, new institutions devised and new frameworks fashioned, but even the manner of ending apartheid, achievement that it was, has left an awkward legacy of 'example' which has proved difficult to handle globally, on the continent of Africa, and even inside the country itself. Not everything, at this particular turning point, turns out to be quite as our authors had anticipated, or at least had hoped. Few turning points, in their aftermath, ever do.

Prologue: The dramatis personae

South Africa is a society of considerable diversity. Conventionally the population is divided into four categories: African, Coloured, Indian and white. None is internally homogeneous: Africans incorporate nine ethnic clusters; the Coloured people are of varied origins, including the descendants of slaves and the progeny of mixed white/slave marriages or liaisons, as well as other permutations; the Indians are mainly Hindu, traditionally speaking several languages, with a smaller Muslim minority; the whites include Afrikaans- and English-speakers, the latter category containing a small but significant Jewish minority.

The aboriginal inhabitants were the San (so-called 'Bushmen'), stone age hunter-gatherers, and the Khoi (so-called 'Hottentots'), who were pastoralists. Bantu-speaking Africans had settled in what was to become South Africa as early as 2,000 years ago, contrary to assertions by white politicians that Africans and whites arrived in the territory at approximately the same time. White settlement began in 1652 when the Dutch East India Company established a revictualling station at the Cape. The settlement survived, in spite of the Company's initial reluctance to consider it permanent. Its numbers were augmented by the arrival in 1688 of approximately 180 French Huguenots, who were assimilated into the original group, leaving little more than French surnames, some beautiful farmsteads, and the ability to produce wine.

After the final annexation in 1806 of the Cape by the British, the English-speaking white segment increased with the settlement in 1820 of 4,000 on the turbulent Eastern Cape frontier and a comparable number, by Byrne settlers, in 1849 in what had become the British colony of Natal. Many more arrived after the discovery of diamonds and gold in the last third of the nineteenth century.

Elements of the original Dutch settlement penetrated the hinterland during the eighteenth and nineteenth centuries, coming into conflict with indigenous African polities. The Great Trek (1836–8) was a significant exodus into the hinterland of Eastern Cape Afrikaners (and their black servants), mainly in consequence of their refusal to accept the principle of equality before the law for all races laid down by the British colonial authorities. The Great Trek was one of the founding heroic events that were celebrated in Afrikaner nationalism's social charter.

Three Trekker republics were established: Natalia (taken over by the British in 1843), the Orange Free State and the South African Republic, more commonly known as the Transvaal. The tightening grip of British imperial control in the last quarter of the nineteenth century, accelerated by the discovery of minerals, and imperial rivalries in the Scramble for Africa, led inexorably to the Anglo-Boer War, 1899–1902, which was to have a profound effect in shaping modern South Africa and accelerating the growth of Afrikaner nationalism. After the war the defeated Trekker republics were declared British colonies, both attaining self-government not long thereafter. In 1908 agreement was reached among white politicians on the unification of South Africa: Union came into being in 1910.

Racial discrimination had long been entrenched in South Africa. By the early decades of the eighteenth century the earlier relative fluidity of race relations in the Cape had been eclipsed by a clear system of racial stratification and the presumption of racial inequality had taken root among whites. The constitutions of both Trekker republics were based squarely on a colour bar; and in the British colony of Natal, a tortuous system of voter qualifications meant that only a handful of Africans ever qualified for the franchise, while legislation in 1896 completely excluded Indians.

In the Cape Colony, however, a somewhat different system was put in place in 1852 when representative government was granted: the franchise would be non-racial, though restricted to males who met relatively low income or property requirements. Although the qualifications were changed in 1887 and 1892, the principle of a non-racial franchise was retained and, despite fierce opposition, was incorporated in the constitution of the new Union. But the constitution provided that only whites could become members of parliament.

By 1900 all of the indigenous societies of southern Africa had been brought under white rule. A combination of conquest, appropriation and, in some cases, 'treaties' involving the cession of land by uncomprehending African leaders, had resulted in the loss of much of the land to which Africans had historically laid claim. 'When the white man came, we had the land and he had the Bible; now we have the Bible and he has the land' runs a rueful Xhosa saying.

Landlessness, the imposition of taxes and, in some cases, forced labour spelled the end of self-sufficiency for African communities: labour on white-owned farms and, later, on the mines was necessary to make a living. Limitations on the right of Africans to acquire land outside of designated reserves were imposed in terms of legislation enacted in 1913.

By 1910, as the new state came into being, white domination was firmly established. In succeeding decades a spate of discriminatory legislation flowed from the all-white parliament. There was a substantial cross-party consensus that segregation was the right policy for dealing with the 'native problem'. Moreover, the roots of Afrikaner nationalism, already evident in the late nineteenth century and given a huge stimulus by the Anglo-Boer War, were set to flourish: its principal vehicle, the National Party (NP), was founded in 1914, and soon became a formidable political force.

The consolidation of white rule over African societies had meant the smashing of primary resistance. The defeat in 1879 of the Zulu by the British army had signified a milestone in the imposition of white control: no other indigenous army could remotely match the power of the Zulu army. Africans, however, were adapting in various ways to their new circumstances: some were converted to Christianity and received education in the mission schools; some became migrant labourers on the mines and elsewhere; others had little option but to work on white farms, in some cases on land that had ancestrally been theirs. The nucleus of a small class of clerks, teachers, preachers, transport riders and artisans was also forming. Landlessness, poverty and the quest for better opportunities would be the driving force behind the great townward movement of Africans. Identical forces were propelling Afrikaners from the *platteland* (countryside) to the towns and cities. Indeed, the urban centres would be the major scene of the conflict between white and black.

Despite the huge disparity in power, the consolidation of the white-controlled Union of South Africa did not occur without African protest. Indeed, small groups of proto-nationalists had sprouted in various parts of the country, as had newspapers. Hopes that victory by the British in the Anglo-Boer War might herald a new deal for Africans were dashed.

In 1912, an effort was made to unify African organizations by the formation of the Native National Congress at a conference held in Bloemfontein. Among its objects was:

To encourage mutual understanding and to bring together into common action as one political people all tribes and clans of various tribes or races and by means of combined effort and united political organization to defend their freedom, rights and privileges.

It would be a long struggle for the African National Congress (ANC, 'African' replaced 'Native' in 1923). Its studied moderation, even seeming subservience, would achieve little over the succeeding decades, during which it appeared from time to time to be overshadowed by more militant organizations. But it managed to survive, and by 1948 when the narrative of this book begins there could be little doubt that it was the premier political organization among Africans.

In contrast to the struggling existence of the ANC, the NP went from strength to strength, but it suffered many vicissitudes in its quest for Afrikaner unity: a damaging split in 1934 effectively broke that unity, until a more radical generation of leaders was able to restore it in the 1940s.

The significance of demographic factors will become apparent in this book. Table 1 provides census data from the year of the first census in 1911 until 1996.

TABLE 1 Population by race according to census results 1911–96

Year	African	Coloured	Indian	White	Total
1911	4,018,878	525,466	152,094	1,276,319	5,972,757
1921	4,697,285	545,181	163,594	1,521,343	6,972,757
1936	6,595,597	769,241	219,691	2,003,334	9,587,863
1946	7,830,559	928,062	285,260	2,372,044	11,415,925
1951	8,560,083	1,103,016	366,664	2,641,689	12,671,452
1960	10,927,922	1,509,258	477,125	3,088,492	16,002,797
1970	15,340,000	2,051,000	630,000	3,733,000	21,794,000
1985	24,901,139	2,881,362	878,300	4,961,062	33,621,863
1996	31,127,631	3,600,446	1,045,596	4,434,697	40,583,574

Within the white population Afrikaans-speakers outnumbered English-speakers in the approximate ratio of 60:40, a fact whose relevance will subsequently become apparent.

Terminological tangles

The appropriate nomenclature for South Africa's racial categories is a minefield. Bantu-speaking Africans were originally called (by whites) Kaffirs, which was derived from an Arabic word for infidel. It is now regarded as highly offensive, and public utterance could result in a criminal charge. Thereafter, Africans were officially termed 'natives', then 'Bantu' (actually the Xhosa word for people), appropriate in scholarly circles only in respect of those African languages that share a common grammatical structure. Next, Africans were termed 'blacks', which was an improvement on past labels, but created confusion when the Black Consciousness movement of the 1960s and 1970s (which is described in the text) opted to refer to Africans, Coloureds and Indians collectively as 'blacks', 'black' in this usage denoting common status as the victims of discrimination, rather than skin colour, which in any case varied quite widely across and within the three categories, especially among Coloured people. Opting for the term 'black' reflected a desire for oppressed people to unite, but also to repudiate the term 'non-white' or 'non-European' since there were understandable objections to be labelled as the negative of whites.

In this book, 'black' is used to denote all categories previously labelled 'non-white', i.e. African, Coloured and Indian people.

Afrikaners experienced similar changes: originally, they were termed 'Dutch' or 'boers' (meaning 'farmers'), but the term 'Afrikaner' came into increasingly common usage during the nineteenth century, a process that went hand in hand with the development of the Afrikaans language, which was derived from Dutch, with the incorporation of a number of words from Malay (spoken by many slaves) and English. Afrikaans became the language of the common people, as well as a majority of Coloured people. After some years of tension, involving the continued use of Dutch in church and state, Afrikaans was eventually accorded recognition as an official language in 1925. It was the medium through which Afrikaner nationalism expressed itself and the emblem of its aspirations.

CHAPTER 1

The rise of apartheid

As many as 80 per cent of Afrikaners supported the National Party's appeal to nationalism in the election held on 26 May 1948. Together with its smaller ally, the Afrikaner Party, the NP managed to win by the narrowest of margins – five seats. It was a surprise, not least to the Nationalists themselves.

The defeated United Party government, led by Field Marshal Jan Smuts, had been complacent. Its cabinet, with few exceptions, had been lacklustre. It had vacillated on the fundamental issue of racial policy, appearing to recognize that major changes were needed but not having the will to push them through. A further consideration, exploited by the NP, was that Smuts, who was 78 years old, would be succeeded by the relatively liberal J.H. Hofmeyr, who was also the most effective member of Smuts's cabinet. Then there was the issue of 'swamping' by Africans who streamed to the cities during the wartime years, at the same time supposedly depriving white farmers (80 per cent of whom were Afrikaners) of labour. There was also the supposed threat of being swamped by immigrants from Britain, who were being encouraged by Smuts. This, the NP reckoned, could 'plough the Afrikaners under' by eliminating their majority in the white population.

A critical issue in racial policy was the status of urban Africans: successive governments had followed the recommendation of the Transvaal Local Government Commission of 1921 that:

. . . it should be a recognized principle of government that natives – men, women and children – should only be permitted within municipal areas in so far and for so long as their presence is demanded by the wants of the white population. (Para. 267)

Smuts himself recognized that this principle flew in the face of the reality that increasing numbers of Africans were urbanizing and putting down roots in the cities. The Natives Laws Commission, appointed in 1946, reported in 1948 that:

> ... the idea of total segregation is utterly impracticable; secondly, that the movement from country to town has a background of economic necessity – that it may, so one hopes, be guided and regulated, and may perhaps also be limited, but that it cannot be stopped or be turned in the opposite direction; and thirdly, that in our urban areas there are not only Native migrant labourers, but there is also a settled, permanent Native population. (Para. 28)

The UP accepted the findings of the Commission and would have acted on its recommendations had it been returned to power. What difference this would have made to the nature of the conflict is impossible to say; but creating stable urban living conditions for urban Africans and limiting the migrant labour system could have prevented some of the hardships that apartheid was to inflict.

The NP was quick to repudiate the findings of the Commission, and to incorporate them into its propaganda that UP policy would result in the 'swamping' of towns and cities by Africans. Its own programme reinstated the earlier policy that urban Africans were 'temporary sojourners' – the phrase that came to be officially used – and, moreover, did so with a vengeance.

Few outsiders knew what apartheid meant, but it was apparent that it would entail a far harsher enforcement of discrimination than previously. A party commission, chaired by Paul Sauer, a closer colleague of D.F. Malan, the NP leader and future Prime Minister, produced a report that spelled out what was intended, but without providing any detail of how the recommendations were to be achieved. It made, in summary form, nearly 30 policy recommendations, virtually all of which would be implemented. Given the absence of any supporting details, the report could hardly be described as a 'blueprint'; but it did represent a crystallization of much of the thinking of pro-Nationalist organizations, the Afrikaner churches, individual scholars and think-tanks, including the *Afrikaner Broederbond* (AB), an influential secret society of mostly elite, male Afrikaners.

In the early years of its rule, the NP insisted that apartheid was essentially a continuation of South Africa's traditional policies. In many respects this was partly true since for most of the apartheid legislation there had been at least partial precedents enacted by previous governments, and none had questioned the overriding principle that white supremacy was to be maintained.

Before analysing the unfurling of apartheid, it is necessary to examine the NP and its role in Afrikaner nationalism. As D.F. Malan described it, the Party was 'organised Afrikanerdom' in the political sphere; but it was no ordinary party:

We occupy a central position in our Afrikaner community life [volkslewe]. If we split, then our entire people split in all directions, as costly experience has taught us time and time again. . . . We can make or break the volk.[1]

In the early 1940s, when Malan made these observations Afrikanerdom was, in fact, divided: it had split in 1934 when the NP's first leader (and Prime Minister from 1924 to 1939), General J.B.M. Hertzog had split the NP from top to bottom by fusing it with Smuts's South Africa Party to form the United Party, which, in turn, had split in September 1939 on the issue of South Africa's participation in the Second World War, to which many Afrikaners, including Hertzog and Malan, objected. In the 1940s, the supposedly reunited NP, led by Malan, faced a major challenge from an extra-parliamentary paramilitary 'movement' called the *Ossewa-Brandwag* (OB, the Oxwagon Sentinel), many of whose leading figures were sympathetic to Nazi ideology. It claimed a support base of nearly 400,000. Malan stood firm, rejecting the OB's repudiation of the parliamentary system and insisting that the fight for control of the country must eschew violence. By 1945 the OB was a spent force and, despite a bad beating in the 'khaki' election of 1943, Malan's NP could legitimately claim to be the pre-eminent political force of Afrikaner nationalism.

Although the UP had gained big victories in the 1938 and 1943 elections, strong currents of a resurgent nationalism were flowing beneath the surface. The celebration of the centenary of the Great Trek in 1938 occasioned a huge outpouring of Afrikaner emotion, and the narrow (13 votes) margin by which parliament opted to go to war in 1939 angered many: the decision appeared to confirm that South Africa remained tied to Britain's apron-strings. As important, Afrikaner preachers, teachers, professors and community leaders, many no doubt inspired by the AB as well as politicians, were crucial elements of the surge. Moreover, many of the Afrikaner supporters of Smuts, so-called *Bloedsappe*, were dying off or answering the siren call of nationalism. Perhaps 30 per cent of all Afrikaner adults were either *Bloedsappe* or followers of Hertzog, who, in the eyes of militants, had betrayed the cause by joining forces with Smuts. In the 1948 election the major focus of the campaign would be to bring these UP supporters into the NP fold.

Afrikaner nationalism was more than the NP, despite its central position in Afrikaner community life. Other spheres were, ideally, seen by nationalists as constituting an organic whole, a totality committed to furthering the cause. The spheres represented different activities or interests. Among the most important were:

1 The churches, of which the Nederduitse Gereformeerde Kerk (NGK) was by far the biggest. Critics often unkindly jibed that the NGK was 'the NP at prayer', which contained some truth since the Church provided theological legitimation of apartheid. Moreover, the churches encapsulated Afrikaners in an Afrikaans environment that had been of critical importance in ensuring that urbanization did not cause individuals to drift away from the *volk*.

2 Universities and schools were of importance in ensuring that students were educated in an Afrikaans environment, in their mother-tongue. Educational institutions were anchored in the life of the community and, therefore, important agents of socialization.

3 Business: it was recognized that political power without economic power meant a dangerous imbalance. Hence concerted efforts to redress the huge gap in wealth and income between English-speakers and Afrikaners by harnessing Afrikaner purchasing power and establishing companies that were rooted in the community.

4 Trade unions with a specifically Afrikaner orientation were either created or, as in the case of the Mineworkers' Union, taken over. The critical issue was to prevent the leakage of Afrikaner workers into organizations that emphasized class, rather than ethnic, solidarity.

5 The press was of inestimable value as a source of news of interest to the Afrikaner community, but also for putting across the NP view to its readers. *Die Burger*, a Cape Town daily founded in 1915, served this role faithfully, and wielded considerable influence among its readers. It is no great exaggeration to say that for much of the apartheid era press and Party were in a symbiotic relationship.

The image of organic unity among the spheres suggested that cooperation was harmonious. This was only partly true: competition within spheres was common. Rivalry between Cape- and Transvaal-based firms and newspapers could be acrimonious, and competition among churches for congregants was not unknown. One of the principal functions of the AB was to achieve coordination, as well as to ensure that 'right-minded' people were appointed to key posts in the spheres, as well as in the civil service and other institutions such as the South African Broadcasting Corporation.

Apartheid literally means 'apart-ness', but in what respects did the new programme intend to force people apart? In 1947 the Sauer Commission had emphasized that total separation of the races, even if an eventual ideal, was practically impossible to implement. Consideration had to be given to the country's needs and interests, with due care to avoid disruption of agriculture, industries and general interests. Indeed, it was stressed, every effort should be made to curb the movement of Africans from white-owned farms. As far as possible the number of so-called 'detribalized' urban Africans was to be frozen and henceforth preference would be given to migrant labour.

As it unfolded, the NP's rule until 1990 comprised three broad and over-lapping phases:

1   1948–58: The consolidation of Afrikaner power; establishing the legislative framework of apartheid, including tightening areas where segregation was supposedly failing or imposing it where it was not in place; and taking steps to impose restrictions on black opponents.

2   1958–66: This was the period of Dr H.F. Verwoerd's premiership which featured the proscription of the main African political organizations and a major extension of security legislation. International opprobrium increased, especially after the shootings at Sharpeville in 1960 (described below). Verwoerd sought to defuse international hostility by offering a 'new vision', with apartheid now re-branded as 'separate development'.

3   1966–89: The steady erosion of the apartheid ideal, accompanied by the dawning recognition among key strata of NP supporters that the policy was unworkable. P.W. Botha (Prime Minister from 1978 to 1982, State President from 1983 to 1989) made some significant reforms but could not bring himself to abandon the apartheid paradigm. A major split in the NP occurred in 1982 as a result of a new constitutional system.

Shocked at its defeat in 1948, the UP consoled itself with the belief that the NP's victory was a temporary aberration that would be corrected at the next election. After all, many more votes had been cast for the UP than the NP, but distortions caused by the single-member first-past-the-post constituency system and a weighting in favour of rural seats had given the NP victory.

For their part, the Nationalists realized the precariousness of their position, and determined that the chances were that it would be a long time before it ever relinquished power. The historical paranoia of Nationalists was that the perfidious English would seek to compensate for their numerical deficiency vis-à-vis Afrikaners by the enfranchisement of increasing numbers of black voters and large-scale immigration from Britain. What was required was limitation on the numbers of immigrants and the insulation of 'white' politics from potential black voting power.

The first decade of Nationalist rule saw determined efforts to achieve the latter: legislation enacted in 1946 to give Indians limited representation (three white MPs) – a provision that was boycotted by the Indian community – was repealed; immigration was severely limited and the residential requirements for eligibility for the franchise were extended; six parliamentary seats were accorded to white voters in South West Africa (now Namibia), all of which were easily won by the NP in constituencies that contained far fewer voters than those in South Africa; the removal of Coloured voters from the common roll in the Cape Province; and finally, in 1958, the voting age was reduced from 21 to 18, in recognition of the higher birth rate among Afrikaners than English-speakers.

The most urgent of these measures was the neutralization of Coloured voting power in terms of a right that qualified male Coloured people had enjoyed since 1853. Their voting power had been diluted by the countrywide enfranchisement of white women in 1930, and the abolition of qualifications for white voters in 1931. Nevertheless, there were 17 Cape constituencies where, in close-run contests, even the small number of Coloured voters was potentially decisive. Moreover, since only an estimated one-third of eligible Coloured males had registered as voters, the expansion of their numbers could spell disaster for the NP.

The problem was that the clause in the constitution (the South Africa Act of 1909) that supposedly protected the Coloured common roll vote was 'entrenched' (together with a provision for language equality between Afrikaans and English), and could be repealed or altered only by a two-thirds majority of a joint sitting of both Houses of Parliament. This procedure had been followed in 1936 when the common roll voting rights of Cape African males had been abolished, and replaced by the allocation of four (white) seats to be elected on a separate roll – a provision which the NP also sought to abolish, and succeeded in doing in 1959.

For five years the NP mounted a long – and squalid – campaign to force through legislation to destroy the Coloured common roll vote. The effort began in 1951, but the legislation was declared invalid by the highest court in the land, the Appellate Division of the Supreme Court, which found that the constitutionally prescribed method had not been followed. The NP, insisting that parliament was sovereign and its will could not be thwarted by constitutional limitations, thereupon enacted the High Court of Parliament Act in 1952, which provided that in constitutional matters parliament could sit as a court. This, too, was declared invalid by the Appellate Division. Further efforts to obtain a two-thirds majority failed. Finally, in 1955, the Gordian Knot was cut by two radical measures: by enlarging the Appellate Division and requiring that in cases where the validity of an act of parliament was at issue, a quorum of 11 judges was necessary, 6 of whom had to support a judgment; second, the senate was 'packed' with NP supporters. Since most of the newly elevated judges and all of the new senators could be relied upon, the road was now clear for the enactment in 1956 of legislation validating the original Separate Representation of Voters Act of 1951. Provision was made for Coloured (including Indian) voters in the Cape to elect, on a separate roll, four white MPs.

What Nationalists described as the cornerstone of apartheid's statutory basis was a system of racial classification embodied in the Population Registration Act of 1950. It was to be the definitive categorization of people into racial categories that would determine their status in society. According to the Minister of the Interior, Dr T.E. Dönges, the legislation was necessary to enable apartheid legislation to be implemented in, for example, schools, cinemas, sporting facilities and a variety of public facilities and amenities. It would also prevent 'mixed' marriages between whites and members of other racial groups (prohibited by law in 1949), as well as curb violations of the Immorality Act, which was amended in 1950 to make sexual relations between white and Coloured a criminal offence. (Sexual relations between whites and Africans had been a criminal offence since 1927.)

'Racial' classification depended on appearance, general acceptance in a community, repute and descent. It is unnecessary to delve into the attempts to find a consistent basis for classification, which is attested to by the many subsequent amendments that sought to pin down the elusive quality of a person's 'race'. For the great majority of people, 'racial' identity was fairly obvious, but in an area like Cape Town where miscegenation had been occurring for 300 years, heartbreaking problems could arise: variations in skin colour within a single family could result in light-skinned individuals 'passing for white', while darker siblings had to remain 'Coloured'. Some leading families in the Western Cape who were 'white' faced anxious times, fearing that they might be subjected to a racial witch-hunt, or, conceivably, to blackmail.

Apartheid depended on keeping racial differences in sharp focus; and the Population Registration Act was one of the principal instruments for achieving this goal. Another major instrument was the Group Areas Act of

1950 whose aim was no less than the racial zoning of every city, town and village in the country. Enforcement began in 1957 and continued into the early 1990s. Residential segregation was not a new principle: it had been applied to stop alleged Indian 'penetration' of white areas; and legislation of 1923 had required Africans to reside in segregated areas. But the comprehensiveness of the Group Areas Act and its inclusion of Coloured people was new. Few other apartheid laws caused more distress, as communities were destroyed and, as in Cape Town, their inhabitants were required to move to new settlements, often far removed from their places of work. The destruction of community bonds often has the consequence of raising crime rates, and the new settlements were no exception.

Despite official assurances that the law could be enforced 'equitably', the major burden fell on Coloured and Indian people, only comparatively few whites having been affected. The claim that the measure was required to prevent racial friction, was shown to be hollow. Even more bitterness among 'disqualified' (i.e. those forced to move) people was caused when it became clear that the compensation offered to them in terms of a complex scheme was inadequate. In many cases white greed played a part in zoning desirable residential areas occupied by Coloured and Indian people as white Group Areas.

The Nationalists commonly invoked the argument that apartheid was required because 'racial contact caused racial friction'; ergo separation was necessary. In fact the imposition of myriad regulations requiring separate entrances to public buildings and other facilities; racial separation on public transport; prohibition of 'mixed' restaurants, hotels, beaches, cinemas, sports and so forth had less to do with eliminating racial friction than with reinforcing inequality and sharpening the perception of racial division.

These forms of separation that went under the general rubric of 'petty apartheid' were popular among a large segment of the white electorate. Petty apartheid was carried to ludicrous lengths, including the separation of white and black blood by blood transfusion services, and separate cemeteries. Undoubtedly the most remarkable example of petty apartheid was the blasting of a separate entrance for 'non-whites' to the famed Cango Caves, near Oudtshoorn. Every 'Whites Only' sign reminded blacks of their subordinate status and reinforced the humiliation that was an intrinsic part of it.

The critical issue confronting apartheid planners was coping with the African majority, especially those in the 'white' urban areas. The underlying principle was the view that urban Africans were 'temporary sojourners', whose roots lay in those parts of the country designated as 'native reserves'. As far as possible, the numbers of 'detribalized' urban Africans should be frozen.

According to calculations made by the Tomlinson Commission in 1955, there were, based upon the 1951 census, approximately 1.5 million Africans in the urban areas, including 314,000 families who were permanently urbanized. Overall, 27.1 per cent of the African population were resident in urban areas, 42.6 per cent in the reserves, and 30.3 per cent on white-owned farms.[2]

The Tomlinson Commission had been appointed by E.G. Jansen, Minister of Native Affairs from 1948 to 1952. Faced with the enormous task of translating the NP's broad ideological goals into achievable policies, Jansen floundered, thereby inciting the ire of hardline Transvaal Nationalists, who wanted immediate, strong-arm measures. The (all-white) Commission produced a massively detailed report, mostly about the carrying capacity of the reserves but also containing some demographic projections that made uncomfortable reading for apartheid zealots.

The higher projection, accepted by the Commission as a more realistic representation of the population's growth by 2000, produced the following:

Whites: 4,588,000
Africans: 21,361,000
Coloured: 3,917,000
Indian: 1,382,000

The figures meant that whites, who constituted 20.9 per cent of the total population in 1951, would shrink to only 14.7 per cent by 2000. Possibly, immigration could somewhat raise the figure.

Having reviewed the possibilities of intensive development of the reserves and made some fairly radical proposals – such as the replacement of communal land tenure with individual tenure – the Commission reached the conclusion that if the tempo of development it recommended were maintained, the percentage of the African population absorbed by the reserves would increase to 60 per cent of the total African population after 25 years, and would amount to 70 per cent by the year 2000.[3] Even on this optimistic projection however, some 6.5 million Africans would remain in the 'white' areas, exceeding the white population, whose numbers were in any case most unlikely to reach the 6.15 million that increased immigration might enable it to achieve.

The message was clear: even on the most optimistic assumptions made by the Commission, Africans would continue to outnumber whites in the 'white' areas by a significant margin; and if the Coloured and Indian categories were added, the white population's demographic deficit would amount to some 6 million. In short, there could be no credible basis for apartheid: as its critics had consistently argued, white and black were irrevocably linked.

Jansen had been replaced as Minister of Native Affairs by H.F. Verwoerd, a former professor and newspaper editor. He would prove to be apartheid's master-builder. Verwoerd, who had opposed the work of the Commission from its inception, rejected some of its major recommendations, that white capital be permitted to invest in the reserves, that individual land tenure be instituted, and that £104 million be spent on development over the next decade. Verwoerd operated on the assumption that he knew better: it had been unnecessary for his predecessor to establish the Commission since he and his officials had all of the information required at their disposal.

His response to the critics who pointed to the demographic deficit bordered on fantasy. It also foreshadowed a gigantic and inhumane exercise in social engineering. First, according to Verwoerd, of the 6.5 million Africans who would remain in the 'white' areas, some 4 million would be mostly on white-owned farms 'where the problem of apartheid presents no difficulty to us and where apartheid is maintained locally'. This meant that in the semi-feudal conditions on the farms racial inequality was firmly maintained. The comment underlined Verwoerd's conviction that the essence of apartheid was racial inequality.

Second, Verwoerd argued that Africans in the 'white' areas would resemble *gastarbeiters*, who originated from the poorer parts of Europe and worked in Western Europe, but retained citizenship of their home countries. It was obviously a disingenuous analogy. Third, Verwoerd argued that it was an incorrect assumption that the same Africans would be permanently domiciled in the 'white' areas, since it was his intention that the labour force would be migrant workers who oscillated between the reserves and their places of employment. In other words, the 6.5 million would be a constantly shifting mass of people, supposedly anchored in their respective reserves of origin.

Despite rejecting the Commission's recommendation that white capital be allowed to invest in the reserves, Verwoerd made the recommendation that white-owned enterprises should be allowed on the borders of the reserves, enabling African employees to commute on a daily or weekly basis from their homes. Border industries would turn out to be a major strategy of apartheid's planners, but also one that failed.

Verwoerd recognized that if apartheid were to have any credibility there must come a time when the flow of Africans from the reserves to the 'white' areas would be reversed. He believed that 1978 would be the *annus mirabilis* when it would begin. How this date was arrived at was never revealed: possibly it had been cooked up by Verwoerd and some of his equally zealous officials. Despite its basic improbability (and the scepticism of some of his colleagues), the ideological fiction was maintained throughout Verwoerd's premiership, being dropped only after his death.

The instrument for regulating the movement of Africans in the 'white' areas has traditionally been the pass laws. They served three functions: to limit the influx of Africans into the 'white' areas; to tie Africans down to particular employers, notably farmers; and to provide a mechanism for allocating labour to particular sectors, notably agriculture and mining, whose wages were significantly lower than those in the commercial and industrial sectors. The system had been a vexatious one for Africans for decades prior to 1948.

The advent of apartheid would bring a dramatic tightening and extension of the scope of what was now officially termed 'influx control'.

Legislation of 1952 provided that all South African-born Africans, on reaching the age of 16, would be required to possess a reference book, in which would be recorded the individual's personal particulars and details of his employer, and proof of payment of taxes. Women's reference books differed slightly, but in principle the new and draconian form of the pass laws would be extended to them.

The law governing influx control was enacted in 1952 and further amended in 1955 and 1957. It provided that no African could remain in an urban area for more than 72 hours unless he or she:

1   had resided there continuously since birth; or

2   had worked there continuously for one employer for 10 years, or had been there continuously and lawfully for 15 years and had continued to reside there, and was not employed outside the area, and while in the area had not been sentenced to a fine exceeding £50 or to imprisonment for a period exceeding six months; or

3   was the wife, unmarried daughter, or son under 18 years of age of an African falling into classes (1) or (2), and ordinarily resided with him; or

4   had been granted a permit to remain, by an employment officer in the case of workseekers, or otherwise by the local authority [a power subsequently removed from local authorities].

Failure to produce a reference book on demand (after February 1958 for men, and after February 1963 for women) by an authorized official, including police officers, was an offence. Failure to comply with one of the categories listed above was also an offence and could result in imprisonment or a fine, and being 'endorsed out' (the official term) from an urban area.

Legislation such as this could be enforced only by a continuous dragnet that involved stopping people or raiding their homes to check that their documentation was in order. It amounted to institutionalized harassment and contributed to the pervasive sense of insecurity among urban Africans. It broke up families and forced people to become migrant workers, which, of course, was one of its principal aims. For many, life in the impoverished reserves forced them to take their chances by illegally (in the technical sense only) entering the urban areas where the possibility of obtaining a job was greater, even if it meant that sooner or later they would be arrested and convicted. Despite this, illegal entry was, in economic terms, a risk worth taking. By 1986, the year in which influx control was abolished, more than 17 million people had been arrested since the inception of the system – and this was probably an underestimate.[4]

Influx control was enforced with particular ruthlessness in the Western Cape, which had been deemed to be a Coloured Labour Preference Area. Ostensibly the aim was to protect Coloured people from African competition. The area in question, called the Eiselen Line after the senior official in Verwoerd's Department of Native Affairs, was demarcated in 1955 and covered a huge area of the Cape Province, from south of the Orange River on the west coast to Knysna on the east coast.

A corollary of freezing the number of town-rooted Africans was a range of other measures aimed at emphasizing their status as temporary sojourners:

- limiting the scope of African businesses to little more than small convenience shops (and confining them to African townships);
- the phasing out of sub-economic (i.e. subsidized) housing;
- the abolition of the right to lease property on a 30-year leasehold basis;
- the requirement that 'nie-plekgebonde' (not locality-bound) institutions such as certain types of hospital, old-age homes, and homes for the disabled must be transferred to the reserves;
- the limitation after 1959 on the development of secondary and vocational schools; henceforth these had to be established in the reserves;
- from 1968 onwards the reduction in the building of housing, in favour of hostels for single male migrants;

- from 1954 onwards a requirement that township housing be allocated on a strictly ethnic basis;

- all freehold ownership of properties acquired by Africans (well before 1948) was removed, freehold symbolizing a status of permanence that contradicted official policy; and

- urban representation of traditional chiefs was instituted in a further effort to maintain or revitalize the links between urban people and their supposed ethnic homelands.

Overall, the aim was to ensure that urban areas were as harsh and as unwelcoming as possible. Efforts by more humane local authorities, such as Johannesburg, which was controlled by the opposition UP, to mitigate conditions ran counter to the official outlook. A belief that some of the major authorities, also controlled by non-NP councils, were sabotaging national policy, led inexorably to the steady removal of any local authority responsibility for African affairs. This process culminated in 1971 with legislation that vested all control in Bantu Affairs Administration Boards, which were essentially creatures of the central government.

Apartheid left a baneful legacy with which post-1994 government has had to cope. Verwoerd believed that the impact of apartheid on society would be so great that no future government would be able to overcome it. His contention may or may not turn out to be true; but in the field of African education Verwoerd's legacy has continued to be a major problem for contemporary South Africa. The Bantu Education Act of 1953 embodied many recommendations of a commission, headed by W.W.M. Eiselen, that investigated the state of African education.[5]

Prior to the implementation of the legislation most of the provision of African education had been in the hands of missionaries, who functioned under the overall aegis of provincial education departments. Nationalists disapproved of missionaries, other than those from the Afrikaans churches, regarding them with suspicion as part of that anti-Afrikaner force which fuelled their historic paranoia. On a number of occasions Verwoerd inveighed against mission schools and Fort Hare University College (established under missionary auspices in 1916) for producing 'Black Englishmen'. African education had to be removed from these anti-Afrikaner hands and aligned with the aims of apartheid. This entailed bringing the entire system under the control of the central government.

Verwoerd's aims were spelled out with astonishing frankness in a speech delivered in 1954 that acquired instant notoriety:

It is the policy of my department that education should have its roots entirely
in the Native areas and in the Native environment and Native community. There
Bantu education must be able to give itself complete expression and there it will
have to perform its real service. The Bantu must be guided to serve his own
community in all respects. There is no place for him in the European community
above the level of certain forms of labour. Within his own community, however,
all doors are open. For that reason it is of no avail for him to receive a training
which has as its aim absorption in the European community while he cannot
and will not be absorbed there. Up till now he has been subjected to a school
system which drew him away from his own community and partially misled him
by showing him the green pastures of the European but still did not allow him
to graze there.[6]

It was hardly surprising that virtually every representative African organization, educational or otherwise deplored the speech, which was still being
flung back in the Nationalists' faces decades later. The majority of African
parents held the belief that decent education was the key to the upward
occupational mobility that most of them had been denied. There was, however, a perverse truth in Verwoerd's views: an examination of the educational
backgrounds of senior figures in the ANC, then and previously, would have
revealed that the majority were products of mission schools and, in a number
of cases, Fort Hare. The scope and quality of African education before 1953
left a great deal to be desired, mostly because of inadequate funding, but
at least it was not yoked to an ideology that was premised on inequality.
Now, under the new dispensation, full rein could be given to neutralizing
the danger of what D.F. Malan had once called 'an overwhelming majority
of civilized and educated non-whites who wish to share our life-circumstances
with us and who struggle in every respect for equality with us. . . .'[7]
    Several aspects of the new system should be noted.

Funding

Initially, the amount payable to African school education from the central
treasury was pegged at R13 million per annum plus four-fifths of the general
tax paid by Africans, together with loans from the Bantu Education Account.
African communities were required to finance part of the cost of construct-
ing new schools or additional classrooms, and also to pay for additional
teachers. By 1975–6, a crisis period in African education (see pages 41–2),
the per capita per annum disparities in the provision of school education
remained huge:

Whites: R644-00
Indians: R189-53
Coloured: R139-62
Africans: R41-80

The paucity of funding, despite its expansion in the 1970s and 1980s, had other predictable consequences: the poor physical condition of school buildings and facilities and overcrowded classrooms. Comparison of teacher: pupil ratios in 1975 provide another indicator of educational inequality:[8]

White: 1:20.1
Coloured: 1:30.6
Indian: 1:26.9
African: 1:54.1

Another telling indicator is the level of qualifications among teachers: in African schools slightly over 11 per cent of teachers were professionally qualified with a degree (1.68 per cent) or with matriculation (9.53 per cent); over 70 per cent were professionally qualified but with only junior certification (Standard 8) or Standard 6; nearly 15 per cent had neither matriculation nor other technical qualifications. In white schools, by contrast, 95 per cent had professional qualifications, including nearly 30 per cent with degrees (1973 figures).[9]

Numbers

The number of African pupils increased dramatically after 1954: between 1955 and 1975 the growth suggests a veritable explosion – despite the absence of provision for compulsory education, as was the case for whites.

1955: 1,005,222
1975: 3,697,441 (representing over 72 per cent of all African children of school-going age)

An increase of well over 300 per cent looks impressive, but the global figure conceals the fact that the expansion in numbers was largely at the primary level; fewer than 1 per cent made it through to the senior secondary level.

It was not surprising that education was the flashpoint of the uprising of June 1976. Together with the pass laws, it was the most inflammable issue affecting Africans. The Soweto Uprising was a turning point in the decline of apartheid. It is considered below (pp. 89–92.).

Apartheid and the economy

An economic colour bar had been a feature for decades prior to the advent of apartheid. Ad hoc legislation, notably in the mining industry, a 'conventional' colour bar (i.e. not enforced by statute), denial of access to apprenticeships, and limitation on the acquisition of skills combined to ensure that it was difficult, especially for Africans, to break out of unskilled categories of work. Trade unions for Africans, while not illegal, were not statutorily recognized and could not participate in the statutory bargaining machinery established in the 1920s. White workers had demonstrated their muscle, and by the 1920s their unions were firmly established.

The rapid urbanization of Afrikaners during the twentieth century and the ability of Afrikaner nationalism to keep them within the Nationalist fold had been an important factor in enabling the NP to win a number of urban seats in 1948, reducing their dependence on rural constituencies. For years prior to 1948, Nationalist politicians and writers had warned of the twofold danger that Afrikaner workers would be induced to align themselves with class-based organizations and that industry and commerce, which were largely in the hands of English-speakers, would undercut Afrikaners by employing blacks at lower wages.

The memories of the poor white problem, and the aggravating effect of the Great Depression and the equally great drought of the early 1930s, were fresh in the minds of Afrikaners. In 1932 the Carnegie Commission had found that 300,000 whites, mostly Afrikaners, were 'very poor'. This (conservative) estimate indicated that nearly one-third of all Afrikaners lived in severe poverty. The Commission had warned that:

Long-continued economic equality of poor whites and the great mass of non-Europeans, and propinquity of their dwellings, tend to bring them to social equality. This impairs the tradition which counteracts miscegenation, and the social line of colour division is noticeably weakening. (Para 67)

Urban Afrikaners constituted nearly 50 per cent of the Afrikaner group. They were the 'new Voortrekkers', said D.F. Malan in 1938, who stood 'defenceless on the open plains of economic equalisation'.[10]

Although by 1948 the poor white question had largely been overcome, views like those cited remained strong in the NP. Its strengthening Afrikaner working-class support base had to be given additional protection.

Much of the statutory and conventional economic colour bar was carried over in 1948 and expanded thereafter. The linchpin in this phase was a provision enacted in 1956 for 'job reservation'. The legislation created a government-appointed industrial tribunal able to investigate particular situations and make recommendations to the Minister of Labour who could thereupon declare that certain categories of work could be reserved for particular racial groups. He was also empowered to grant exemptions. Although 'job reservation' eventually affected few black workers, the possibility of its being invoked created uncertainty among employers, making them reluctant to invest much time or resources in training them.

In a later phase of apartheid African trade unions would exert considerable pressure on the apartheid state; but in the earlier phases, until the 1970s, they were restricted in various ways. First, as noted, they were not recognized; second, their right to strike was prohibited – a continuation of earlier measures; and third, their organizers, who included a number of white radicals, were harassed by the state and employers. The Suppression of Communism Act of 1950 not only banned the Communist Party of South Africa, but gave the Minister of Justice wide powers to 'list' members of the Party, and, in terms of a swingeing definition of communism, powers to restrict the activities of communist and non-communist opponents of apartheid. The Minister's exercise of these powers could not be challenged in the courts.

The legislation signalled the beginning of a process whereby the executive armed itself with authoritarian powers that were not amenable to legal challenge. Over time such executive powers would corrupt much of the legal system by seriously curbing civil liberties and corroding the Rule of Law.

By 1958 the NP had largely succeeded in its preliminary goals. Electorally, it had gone from strength to strength, winning increased majorities in the 1953 and 1958 elections. In the latter election, it had won a majority of the actual votes cast for the first time, while winning 103 seats to the United Party's 53. For the UP the writing was on the wall: a protracted process of erosion was under way. The Nationalists could also congratulate themselves on having dealt firmly with black opposition, arming themselves with greater powers in the process. Thumping ANC-inspired protest proved to be electorally popular.

The retirement of D.F. Malan in 1954, and his replacement by J.G. Strijdom, a hardliner who spoke the language of *baasskap* (literally 'boss-ship'), represented a shift in the NP's centre of gravity from the mellower climes of the Cape to the tough politics of the Transvaal. Strijdom had once defined apartheid as meaning that 'he did not have to sit next to a native on a bus'. By 1958 he was a sick man, seeing out the election but dying in August of that year.

Strijdom was succeeded by H.F. Verwoerd, the hardliner whose uncompromising implementation of apartheid had enhanced his popularity with the NP caucus that chose the Party's leader. Despite its profoundly anti-democratic record as the party of apartheid, the NP's internal politics was surprisingly democratic. Verwoerd had found himself up against two other strong candidates for the leadership, C.R. Swart and T.E. Dönges, the leaders of the NP in the Orange Free State and the Cape, respectively. Moreover, Verwoerd won only in the second round of voting, defeating Dönges.

In the Prime Ministerial office Verwoerd's zeal, dynamism and intellectual ability gave him an authority that was unmatched by either his two predecessors or successors. He was never wracked by self-doubt and prided himself on being made of granite. He was also zealous in his oversight of cabinet colleagues and their departments, especially those concerning African affairs to which he had appointed ideological acolytes. Verwoerd was also ruthless in dealing with those who stepped out of line, whether NP MPs, who differed publicly with policy, Dutch Reformed Church clergy whose faith in the immutable truths of apartheid showed signs of wavering, or think-tanks like SABRA (the South African Bureau of Racial Affairs), a group of mostly Cape-based pro-Nationalist academics, who questioned official policy regarding the Coloured people. Even the doyen of Afrikaner entrepreneurs, Anton Rupert, was slapped down for daring to contemplate establishing a factory in which apartheid rules would not apply. Even his chosen Minister of Bantu Administration and Development, M.D.C. de Wet Nel, was given a (private) dressing down for suggesting that the targeted *annus mirabilis*, 1978, was unlikely to be achieved.

As noted, Verwoerd was not fazed by the demographic issue. He refuted the opposition argument that the economic integration of the races was so far advanced that separation was impossible. Apart from taunting the opposition with the argument that economic integration would in time be followed by political and social integration, he invoked a remarkable piece of intellectual legerdemain to show that they misunderstood what 'integration' actually amounted to. The following quotation gives the key to Verwoerd's ability to build logical constructions on the foundations of bogus premises:

We say that when a Native drives a tractor on a [white] farm, he is not economically integrated. . . . Merely because he helps the farmer to produce, is such a Native who operates a tractor integrated into the farmer's life and community? Of course he is not, because the concept of integration relates to people, and here we do not have people whose activities are becoming interwoven.

They will only become interwoven in this way if the other forms of integration, namely equal social and political rights, result from these activities.[11]

In other words, there was a fundamental difference between labour that was interchangeable and, hence, easily removable, and labour that was so interwoven with the white community that it could not be removed, even if the state wanted to do so.

Verwoerd's insistence that Africans in the 'white' areas not be permitted to rise 'above the level of certain forms of labour' dovetails with his views on what constituted 'integration'. The quotation also shows how fundamental to Verwoerd's thinking the perpetuation of inequality was, and also why he insisted that there was no distinction between 'petty' and other forms of apartheid: the (absurd and hurtful) separate entrances, separate lifts and myriad other forms of petty apartheid were deemed necessary because the cumulative effect of infractions could blunt racial perceptions and eventually bring the apartheid edifice down.

The second phase of apartheid is associated principally with Verwoerd's efforts to put a positive gloss on apartheid: reserves, now called homelands, would be prepared for self-government and even, it was eventually conceded, independence. The vision of freedoms awaiting Africans in their homelands had been part of the original policy laid down in 1947. Verwoerd sought to implement the new version of apartheid, now designated 'separate development'.

The foundations of policy had been laid in 1951, with the enactment of legislation that granted additional powers to chiefs or traditional leaders. In the Nationalists' view traditional authority structures were to be the basis of political development in the homeland. Chieftainship was to be the pivotal institution. Chiefs had long been recognized as minor cogs in the administration of rural areas: they were responsible for the administration of customary law, for the allocation of communal land, settling minor disputes and other duties, subject to the oversight of the Native Commissioner. The Nationalists insisted that chieftainship embodied the essence of traditional democracy. There had been truth in this contention: traditionally, chiefs were not autocrats who could ignore the wishes of their people – as the Xhosa saying had it, *'Inkosi yinkosi ngabantu'*, meaning that 'a chief is a chief by the people'.

White rule and the alienation of much traditionally occupied land, however, had removed the basis for popular sanctions on the exercise of chiefly power; and chiefs were now more beholden to the white authorities than their people, though many sought to straddle potentially divergent interests.

The terms of the legislation, the Bantu Authorities Act, provided for a hierarchy of authorities, tribal, regional and territorial. The principle of ethnic separation was to be rigorously enforced so that each of the initial eight territorial authorities established by 1970 encompassed a specific ethnic group. It was an article of faith among Nationalists that every African, apart from a few deracinated townspeople, owed their primary tie to one or other ethnic group: African nationalism was a fiction, encouraged by agitators.

The political aim underlying Bantu Authorities was obvious: the socio-economic progress of Africans was possible only through the vehicle of traditional institutions. As Verwoerd explained in 1952:

[I]t is clear that the key to the true progress of the Bantu community as a whole and to the avoidance of a struggle for equality in a joint territory or in common political living areas lies in the recognition of the tribal system as the springboard from which the Bantu in a natural way, by enlisting the help of the dynamic elements in it, can increasingly rise to a higher level of culture and self-government on a foundation suitable to his own inherent nature.[12]

In 1959 Verwoerd unveiled the first instalment of separate development, intended partly as an attempt to provide moral justification for his government's policies, and partly to persuade increasingly hostile international opinion that South Africa was now embarking on a process of decolonization and self-determination similar to that of other colonial powers in Africa. The Promotion of Bantu Self-Government Act established the framework for the future constitutional development of the homelands. It also abolished the small parliamentary representation of Africans (by whites) as being inconsistent with the proposals for separate development contained in the legislation.

Self-government was to be guided by whites as trustees, and might possibly lead to sovereign independence for an independent homeland that opted for it. Verwoerd declined to lay down a timetable for future constitutional steps: evolution would depend on the progress made by each. It was, he said, 'the beginning of an emancipation movement in nations who are still backward in the sphere of government'.

As far as the critical issue of land was concerned, Verwoerd stuck firmly to the traditional white view that 'each group, White or Black, always inhabits the area which it has occupied' – a proposition with no historical validity. His comment clearly implied that no further land was to be made over for African occupation, which would be restricted to the reserves demarcated by the Land Act of 1913 and that of 1936, which 'released' additional land to be added to the reserves that would eventually total 13.7 per cent of the country's land area. Why should minorities who had more land be obliged to surrender land to neighbours who have less, Verwoerd wanted to know?

Verwoerd also believed that the British High Commission territories of Bechuanaland (now Botswana), Basutoland (now Lesotho) and Swaziland ought to be taken into the reckoning of land distribution, as had the Tomlinson Commission previously. But they remained under British control: were this not the case approximately 50 per cent of the land south of the Limpopo River (South Africa's northern border) would have been in African hands. His contention ignored the large-scale loss of land that these territories had suffered in the nineteenth century. It had long been an aspiration of South Africa to incorporate them, indeed provision for this possibility was included in the original South Africa Act of 1909. Their inhabitants, however, were implacably opposed to the idea, and their wishes were respected by the British government.

It galled the Nationalists that the High Commission territories, as poor as most of the homelands and hardly less economically dependent on South Africa, were being prepared to take their place as sovereign, independent states, recognized as such by the international community, but no such recognition was to be accorded to those homelands, colloquially known as Bantustans, that later became independent: Transkei (1976), Bophuthatswana (1977), Venda (1979) and Ciskei (1981) (TBVC states).

Verwoerd's acknowledgement that white supremacy could not continue in the circumstances of the modern world marked something of a break with the past, even if the areas to fall under African control were severely limited in size and potential. Since roughly half of the *de jure* citizens of the homelands were actually resident in the 'white' areas, any analogy with the European Common Market, where political independence coexisted with economic interdependence, was ludicrous. Few Africans, apart from some opportunists who saw benefits for themselves in the Bantustans, were taken in by the vistas of freedom proclaimed by Verwoerd. Africans, after all, had participated just as much as whites in the creation of modern South Africa. Why should they now be denied their birthright by being required to exercise their political rights only in relation to the political structures being established in the homelands? The freedom on offer was essentially illusory.

There was a further major problem with the viability of homelands: their fragmentation, a legacy of nineteenth-century efforts by white governments to break up large concentrations of African communities in the interests of security and easier access to labour. Little was done to address the problem until 1975 when plans were produced to consolidate the homelands.

With the exception of miniscule Qwaqwa (size: 48,234 hectares), all of the other homelands were fragmented to greater or lesser extents, ranging from KwaZulu, with 48 blocs of discrete territory, Bophuthatswana, with 19, Lebowa, with 14, Ciskei, with 19, to Transkei, with two. Moreover, there were numerous 'black spots', usually small blocs of land acquired in freehold by small groups, that lay outside the homelands surrounded by white-owned land. There were 157 such 'black spots' near KwaZulu, all of which would have to be removed by government fiat. Even the proposals of 1975 did not offer complete consolidation into single blocs: KwaZulu would consist of 10, while only Ciskei, Qwaqwa and Swazi would be single blocs. The proposal was yet another case of wishful thinking: the process would be monstrously expensive, cause huge disruption, and require millions of people to be forcibly moved. By 1981 those responsible for overseeing consolidation concluded that the task was impossible.

The year 1960 turned out to be one of mixed blessings for Verwoerd and his government: it began badly when, in February, Harold Macmillan, the British Prime Minister, delivered his 'Wind of Change' speech in the House of Assembly in Cape Town: it was a courteous, but firm reminder that 'some aspects' of South Africa's policy were unacceptable in the modern world. Verwoerd, no doubt anticipating some anodyne observations from Macmillan, was stunned, but delivered an impromptu response that was a courteous but firm rebuff. The 'Wind of Change' speech was nevertheless an important reminder to those who cared to absorb it that South Africa's isolation was increasing rapidly.

Worse was to follow: on 21 March 1960 at Sharpeville, police opened fire on a crowd of Africans protesting against the pass laws, killing 69 and wounding 189, many having been shot in the back while fleeing. The protest had been organized by the Pan-Africanist Congress, which had broken away from the ANC (see page 73). Further protests occurred in other parts of the country in consequence of the Sharpeville shootings, notably in Cape Town where several people were killed. Over 80 people were estimated to have been killed in riots and other demonstrations that accompanied the countrywide stayaway protests.

The government's response was immediate and severe: a state of emergency was declared in terms of which public meetings were banned and 11,500 people of all races were detained in a major round-up of the 'usual suspects'. Furthermore, both the ANC and PAC were banned.

It was a crisis of considerable magnitude that brought international protest raining down on the South African government, and withdrawal of foreign investment. Verwoerd, however, was not to be deterred, insisting that the great majority of Africans were law-abiding.

As protests gradually dwindled and calm seemed to be restored, further drama occurred: when speaking at an exhibition in Johannesburg on 9 April, Verwoerd was shot at point-blank range by one David Pratt. Miraculously Verwoerd survived, no doubt strengthening his admirers' belief that he was under special protection from God. (Pratt was found to be mentally unfit to stand trial and was detained in a mental hospital where he subsequently committed suicide.)

During Verwoerd's recuperation, the senior minister, Paul Sauer (who chaired the NP's internal commission on race policy in 1947), acted as Prime Minister, and took it upon himself to deliver a plea for reform, declaring that 'the old book of South African history was closed . . .'. While no deviation from policy was intended, Africans must be given hope 'and not feel that they are continually being oppressed'. There should be major changes in the enforcement of the pass laws, Africans should be allowed to buy 'European' liquor, attention should be given to raising African wages, and major development of the homelands should be commenced.[13] He made no suggestion for changes in the political dispensation.

Verwoerd was displeased, informing Sauer and others that announcements of major shifts in policy were his prerogative. The relationship between the two men deteriorated. None of Sauer's suggested reforms was implemented – except for a lifting of the ban on selling liquor to Africans. By May 1960, Verwoerd was back at the helm, telling parliament that there was no reason to depart from existing policy as a result of the disturbances. Indeed, the enforcement of policy became harsher: far tougher security laws were enacted, and the security police, whose principal task was to hunt down 'agitators' and those who tried to continue underground the activities of the banned ANC and PAC, were strengthened.

For the NP, the good news in 1960 was attainment of the long-awaited republic: in a referendum held on 5 October white voters (including those in South West Africa) were asked 'Are you in favour of a Republic for the Union?' Over 90 per cent of the electorate voted in what was a rancorous campaign that largely, though not entirely, split along Afrikaner/English lines. The result was a narrow victory – 850,458 to 775,878 – for a republic. Many of those who voted 'no' did so more out of anti-Nationalist sentiment and attachment to the monarchy than repudiation of apartheid.

Verwoerd had campaigned for a republic that would remain a member of the Commonwealth, though a fair number of his supporters had wanted that link severed, too. Their wishes were granted when a number of members of the Commonwealth, notably Afro-Asian states and also Canada, made it clear at the Commonwealth Conference in March 1961, that South Africa would not be welcome. To avoid the humiliation of expulsion, Verwoerd withdrew South Africa's application to retain membership. He returned from London to a tumultuous welcome at Johannesburg airport, declaring that 'we have freed ourselves from the pressure of the Afro-Asian nations who were busy invading the Commonwealth'.[14]

Becoming a republic was Afrikaner nationalism's most cherished aspiration. Now, Verwoerd said, it was time for Afrikaners and the English to stand shoulder to shoulder as a 'white nation'. The subtext was that the white supremacist regime would be more vulnerable if whites remained divided. To demonstrate his good faith Verwoerd promised that the English language would remain constitutionally protected alongside Afrikaans. Moreover, two (undistinguished) English-speaking politicians were appointed to the cabinet.

The rapprochement brought some political gains as increasing numbers of English began to support the NP, perhaps as many as 25 per cent in the 1966 election. But there was also a cost: some radical Nationalists feared that the consequence might be a dilution of pristine nationalism. What seemed possible was that thumping an ethnic Afrikaner drum was now less likely. But did it matter if the republic had been achieved and the status of Afrikaans was secure? It was more important that whites stood together.

As Verwoerd had made clear, there was to be no relaxation of the rigour with which apartheid was enforced in the aftermath of the disturbances of 1960. Apart from beefing up the security police, the government armed itself with dramatically increased powers to cope with alleged subversion. It was the continuation of a long tradition of using the law as an instrument of racial domination. As Albie Sachs argued, the need to reconcile the theory of juridical equality with the practice of racial inequality gave the legal system a contradictory character that persisted throughout the apartheid era.[15]

Tougher laws had been enacted in the early 1950s, but those adopted in the 1960s went far beyond anything previously known. The situation had changed since Sharpeville and the banning of the two liberation movements and their respective decisions to embark upon campaigns of violence (limited in the case of the ANC). Verwoerd appointed B.J. Vorster as his Minister of Justice in 1961, giving him a wide remit to stamp out subversion. Vorster had been a senior officer in the neo-Nazi *Ossewa-Brandwag* during the war years and had been interned by the Smuts government.

The expansion of the scope of security legislation had four dimensions: the creation of new offences with stiffer penalties, including the death penalty; a widening of the ambit of the definition of various political crimes, such as sabotage and terrorism; increasing the onus on the accused to prove their innocence; and an increase in the use of detention without trial. The combined effect of the new legal dispensation was to leave the rule of law in tatters, abandoning the principle of *habeas corpus*.

Compounding these developments was the steady change in the political complexion of Supreme Court judges: many of the new appointees shared the same ideological presuppositions as the NP. It became increasingly the practice that political trials were allocated to relatively small groups of judges in each provincial division, whose 'executive-mindedness' could be relied upon. Countering this trend and, in some cases, mitigating its consequences, were a number of outstanding advocates (barristers) who were prepared to defend those accused of serious political offences. In virtually all of the major political trials from the 1950s onwards the accused enjoyed the services of good counsel.

The most notable innovation of the post-Sharpeville era was the dramatic extension of the periods for which detained persons could be held without being charged. The expansion of periods of detention was: 1961: 12 days; 1963: 90 days (with possible redetention); 1965: 180 days (supposedly for potential state witnesses); and 1967: indefinite periods (for those suspected of terrorism). Detention was in solitary confinement, with no access to lawyers or reading matter other than a Bible. Torture of suspects and even potential state witnesses became a routine technique in inducing detainees to confess. To their eternal shame, the courts invariably dismissed defendants' claims that they had been tortured, believing instead the security police's denials. It was hardly surprising that by the time that the detention laws were suspended in 1991 no fewer than 73 detainees had died while in detention, some committing suicide, others allegedly as a result of accidents, and others literally beaten to death, the most notorious of which was the killing of Steve Biko in 1977 (see pages 42–3).

Detention without trial became a formidable weapon in the hands of the security police. According to the Human Rights Committee's estimates, between 1963 and mid-1988 21,863 persons were detained in terms of security laws, and a further 56,723 in terms of regulations imposed during states of emergency in 1960 and between July 1985 until 1988/9. The compilers assert that only 2 to 4 per cent of all detainees were convicted of an offence.[16]

A further weapon in the security force's armoury was the widespread use of informers (of all races). Over time informers infiltrated not only the liberation movements in exile and domestic political organizations, but communities noted for their activism, universities, newspapers and even foreign organizations with an interest in South Africa. Some were undercover police officers, many were ordinary citizens who believed that they were doing their patriotic duty (for payment), and others were the hapless victims of intimidation who had been threatened with dire consequences unless they cooperated with the police.

Verwoerd's premiership came to a dramatic end when he was assassinated on the floor of the House of Assembly in September 1966 by a deranged parliamentary messenger. Shock at the horrifying circumstances of his death was mingled with relief, not least among some quarters of the Afrikaner nationalist movement. 'He thought for the whole country,' it was commonly said by Nationalists, but his autocratic and vindictive ways were resented by those who had experienced them.

Another acrimonious contest for the leadership followed. Just as Verwoerd's term as Minister of Native Affairs between 1952 and 1958 had catapulted him into prominence, so John Vorster's role as the tough Minister of Justice who had initiated draconian security laws stamped him as the winning candidate, despite his junior status in the cabinet, and residual suspicions regarding his wartime *Ossewa-Brandwag* connection. Eventually, the withdrawal of potential rival candidates ensured that he was elected unanimously.

Vorster was entirely different from Verwoerd in personality and style. He was no intellectual and his premiership would be substantially devoid of any creative response to the mounting crisis that was engulfing South Africa. But he was possessed of a certain native cunning and a capacity for political infighting. Nothing whatever suggested that he might depart from the rigours of Verwoerdian orthodoxy. He was, unlike Verwoerd, less inclined to be vindictive and intolerant of internal critics. Moreover, also unlike Verwoerd who completely dominated his cabinet, Vorster gave his ministerial colleagues substantially more freedom of action, acting more, as has been said, like a 'chairman of the board' than an autocrat. While it is an exaggeration to describe the advent of Vorster as a 'Prague Spring', his less hegemonic style would open the way for divisions inside the NP and within the wider Afrikaner nationalist movement. Under Verwoerd Afrikaner nationalism had reached the zenith of its solidarity; under Vorster hairline cracks soon started to appear.

Verwoerd had created the template for apartheid, as well as bureaucratic leviathans, the Departments of Bantu Administration and Development and of Bantu Education, both headed by M.C. Botha, a wooden reactionary and an ideological acolyte of Verwoerd's. The apartheid juggernaut appeared to have gained an unstoppable momentum. With the parliamentary opposition in disarray, increased English-speaking support for the NP, and the black opposition seemingly routed, there was every reason for the NP to feel confident. Moreover, the economy had recovered rapidly after Sharpeville and GDP grew at an annual average of 5.7 per cent in the 1960s, while both domestic and foreign fixed investment rose appreciably. Underneath the apparently calm waters, however, currents that would later cause turbulence were beginning to swirl.

Another characteristic of Vorster was the absence of Verwoerd's dogmatic omniscience; in fact he was showing signs of pragmatism, even flexibility, that would shock the ultra-rightwingers who were beginning to raise their heads above the parapet. Being conservative, he said of the NP, did not mean that it would stand still or stagnate; and he caused concern by saying to a group of NP MPs that separate development/apartheid was a method of maintaining Afrikaner identity, and not an immutable dogma.[17] It was interpreted as a sign by ultra-rightwingers, now called *verkramptes*, that Vorster was going soft on fundamental principles.

Cautious moves by Vorster to permit a multiracial rugby team from New Zealand to tour South Africa were negated by his refusal to allow Basil D'Oliveira, a Coloured exile from South Africa, to tour with the England cricket team in 1968. He had not been chosen for the original squad, but was subsequently included when one of the team dropped out through illness. Vorster refused to allow this, saying that it was an attempt to make political capital out of sport. The England cricket authorities thereupon cancelled the tour, and subsequently announced that no future tours would be undertaken until South African teams were chosen on merit. It was a major step in the sporting isolation of South Africa, which proved to be one of the most effective forms of international sanctions.

Vorster's so-called 'outward policy', initiated in 1967, sought to achieve détente with black Africa, much of which was implacably hostile to apartheid. His hope was that dialogue would achieve 'understanding' of South Africa's policies; but the few leaders of African states that were prepared to talk to Vorster hoped that dialogue would assist in breaking down apartheid. The hope of establishing diplomatic links with Africa yielded a poor harvest: only Malawi agreed. Even Botswana, Lesotho and Swaziland, although essentially economic hostages to their powerful neighbour, declined to establish formal diplomatic ties. In short, apartheid was an unsaleable commodity.

One outcome of the outward policy caused further rumblings of discontent among *verkramptes*: the arrival of African diplomats, who would be treated as diplomats from any other continent, violated South Africa's colour bar, they maintained. In the event, only Malawi took the bait and established relations, but even this was enough to raise *verkrampte* hackles. It became an article of faith among them that even the smallest cracks in the colour bar would create momentum for more.

Vorster showed no signs of relenting on the main thrust of apartheid: there would be no more land allocated to homelands; there would be no political rights accorded to Africans in the 'white' areas – they could exercise their political rights in their respective homelands, regardless of where they actually lived; and, following Verwoerd's line of argument, the numbers of Africans in the 'white' areas were not the most important issue since what mattered was the maintenance of inequality. He did, however, refuse to be bound by the *annus mirabilis*, 1978, the date by which, according to Verwoerd's fantasy, the flow of Africans to the 'white' areas would turn around.

Meanwhile the machinery ground on, with the focus now on homeland development. Efforts were made to induce industrialists to locate their enterprises adjacent to homeland borders that enabled African workers to commute on a daily or weekly basis. Verwoerd had declared this policy to be the most promising solution to the problem of bringing development to the homelands, preferable to allowing white industrialists to operate inside the homelands, which would create a kind of 'economic colonialism'.

Warnings to industrialists that they should not establish labour-intensive enterprises in existing industrial complexes had been made since 1950. In 1967 the Physical Planning and Utilization of Resources Act empowered the state to impose controls over the establishment or extension of factories in particular areas. The intention was to put a ceiling on the number of enterprises that required significant numbers of African workers in existing industrial complexes. Between 1928 and 1967, according to the Minister of Bantu Administration and Development, the ratio of African to white workers in all South African industries had more than doubled. In the border industries, however, the ratio would not be restricted.

Neither border industries nor the restriction on employing more African workers in the existing industrial areas achieved their aims. Despite generous support from the state, few industrialists were tempted to locate or relocate themselves to remoter border areas. The consequence was that most border industries were established close to those existing industrial complexes that were adjacent to homelands, as in Durban, East London and Pretoria. In several cases existing urban townships were incorporated into abutting homeland areas. By 1975, according to official figures, some 90 per cent of applications from industrialists to establish or extend factories in areas controlled by the Physical Planning legislation had been granted, and the number of Africans affected by refused applications was 82,183.[18] It was clear that border industries were employing only a small percentage of Africans entering the labour market annually.

Nevertheless, Nationalists claimed some satisfaction with figures that suggested a decline in the percentage of Africans living in the 'white' areas: whereas in 1960, according to census statistics, 38 per cent lived in the homelands, compared with 48 per cent in 1970. The hard demographic fact, however, was that only 25 per cent of people living in the 'white' areas were, in fact, white. The increase in the percentage of Africans living in the homelands was attributable far less to development, including border industries, than to the relocation of 'surplus' people and the removal of approximately one million residents from 'black spots' that had been cleared. In some cases entire urban townships were disestablished and relocated in 'homelands', thereby creating the statistical illusion that the percentage of homeland dwellers was rising. In fact, rather than becoming vibrant centres of development as 'national units', as the ethnically based homelands were officially termed, they were dumping grounds in which stagnation, poverty and corruption reigned.

A further significant step was legislation enacted in 1970, the Bantu Home-lands Citizenship Act which held out the prospect that every African in South Africa would eventually become a citizen of a homeland, whether or not he or she had been born there or had long since lived outside a homeland. The legislation was premised on the assumption that in due course all of the homelands would become sovereign independent states (which turned out not to be the case). It was made clear by Dr C.P. Mulder, the Minister of Plural Relations and Development (yet another designation of Bantu Administration and Development) in a parliamentary speech in February 1978:

If our policy is taken to its logical conclusion as far as the [African] people are concerned there will not be one [African] man with South African citizenship. . . . Every [African] . . . will eventually be accommodated in some independent new state in this honourable way and there will no longer be a moral obligation on this Parliament to accommodate these people politically.

Much of Vorster's emotional energy in the first few years of his premier-ship was expended on coping with divisions that had emerged in the NP. The focal point of the tension was the mobilization of a seemingly strong *verkrampte* element centred on Albert Hertzog, a somewhat eccentric figure, who had been appointed Minister of Posts and Telegraphs and, in that capacity had fought a battle to prevent the coming of television to South Africa. Hertzog, the son of a former Prime Minister, had long been associated with a shadowy Pretoria-based group, the *Afrikaner-Orde*, which represented ultra-rightwing sentiment. He had also been intimately involved with the Afrikaner trade union movement, notably the Mine Workers' Union, which he had 'rescued' from control by English-speaking workers. Vorster dropped him from the cabinet in August 1968.

The *verkramptes* claimed to be faithful to the ideological legacy of Verwoerd. Vorster, they alleged, was whittling away that legacy, by permitting 'mixed' sport, allowing black diplomats, welcoming Roman Catholic immigrants, and seeking a *toenadering* (rapprochement) with English-speakers. In a parliamentary speech, delivered on 14 April 1969, Hertzog declared that the culture of English-speakers was sated with liberalism and that only Calvinist Afrikaners could be trusted to save whites from obliteration.

Outside parliament the conflict was raging even more fiercely, notably in cultural and literary circles. The *verkramptes*, who were actively white-anting Afrikaner associations, alleged that much of the recent wave of Afrikaans literature reflected 'spiritual decay' and a weakening of Afrikaner defences against liberalizing forces. Conflict in the ranks raised the ominous possibility of *skeuring*, a split in the NP and the wider Afrikaner nationalist movement. The Afrikaans press, or mostly that part of it owned by the Cape-based *Nasionale Pers*, and particularly the big Sunday newspaper, *Die Beeld*, devoted large amounts of space to the conflict, flushing out *verkrampte* activities wherever they could. The story was not only intrinsically newsworthy, it also made for copy that was avidly read by Afrikaners.

The *verkramptes'* attacks on supposed policy adjustments were thinly veiled attacks on Vorster himself. They were not aiming at hiving off to establish a new party; the aim was rather to capture control of the NP and other spheres of Afrikaner nationalism. Vorster realized this and decided to smash the tendency comprehensively before it had time to establish itself as an organized force: four MPs were forced out of the NP. In October 1969, the dissidents, led by Hertzog, formed the *Herstigte Nasionale Party* (HNP, Reconstituted National Party) at a meeting in Pretoria.

Vorster responded by bringing forward the general election by a year to give the new party little time to establish itself. What followed was one of the most rancorous campaigns in South Africa's electoral history. The HNP contested 77 seats, mostly in the Transvaal and Orange Free State. Its candidates were pitted against the might of the NP's formidable machine and the full force of the powerful pro-NP press. It was not surprising that the HNP was decimated: only 10 of the candidates managed to win over 1,000 votes, mostly in smaller towns in the Northern Transvaal. Overall, their share of the votes cast countrywide was 3.5 per cent – it was a comment on the state of white thinking that the moderately liberal Progressive Party won slightly fewer votes, though the redoubtable Helen Suzman retained her seat to continue her lonely battle against the ravages of apartheid.

Vorster, anxious to wipe out the HNP, was equally anxious to see how much support it had among Afrikaners. It was less than 10 per cent, small, but disquieting since it was apparent that many more Afrikaners had sympathy for the HNP, but its crude, streetfighting style had put them off. The spiritual leader of the *verkramptes* had not even joined the HNP. This was Dr Andries Treurnicht, whose record suggested that he was one of Afrikanerdom's golden sons: a provincial rugby player, a clergyman of the Nederduitse Gereformeerde Kerk and a former editor of its newspaper, and then editor of the Pretoria daily, *Hoofstad*. He had also risen in the ranks of the *Broederbond*, becoming a member of its executive council in 1963, deputy chairman in 1970, and was to become chairman in 1972.

The founders of the HNP had confidently anticipated that the urbane Treurnicht would join them, but, to their ire, he declined. He became an NP MP in 1971, easily defeating Jaap Marais, the HNP's deputy leader, in a by-election in Waterberg, a *verkrampte* stronghold. Treurnicht's stature ensured that his rise in the party hierarchy would be rapid: in a move with fatal consequences he was appointed Deputy Minister of Bantu Administration and Education early in 1976. His responsibilities included oversight of African education in the 'white' areas. He would be a key player in the blunders that led to the Soweto Uprising in June 1976.

The rise of the *verkrampte* movement had a wider significance than a relatively small split. It signified that underlying changes in the Afrikaner community were beginning to have political consequences. By the 1970s, some 80 per cent of Afrikaners were urban. High economic growth rates, especially in the 1960s, had largely wiped out remaining white poverty, diffused higher living standards, and accelerated the growth of thrusting Afrikaner entrepreneurs. Afrikaners were better educated and more widely travelled than ever before; in short, the process of *embourgeoisement* was under way. These developments also meant that the Afrikaner community was becoming internally more diversified – and less amenable to accommodation within a single nationalist movement. Class differences had always been a feature of Afrikaner society but they had largely been contained under the rubric of ethnic solidarity. The virtual elimination of white unemployment and the diffusion of greater prosperity concealed the widening of the income gap among Afrikaners. It was no coincidence that *verkramptes* and their (puny) press inveighed against *die geldmag* (the money-power) and pointed accusing fingers at leading Afrikaner tycoons, notably Anton Rupert, for allegedly reneging on apartheid aspirations.

There was some truth in the allegations: Rupert had never been an enthusiastic supporter of apartheid, despite being a true-blue Afrikaner; and a number of other leading members of the business community chafed against some of the restraints caused by apartheid, and limits on their markets caused by their identification with Afrikaner nationalism. But if there were differences within the government, they were taken up privately and discreetly.

At the other end of Afrikaner nationalism's internal spectrum were the *verligtes* (enlightened ones), a heterogeneous collection that included some MPs, a number of academic and other intellectuals, and various professional people. If there was any linking thread among them it was that, generally speaking, they were better educated than the *verkramptes*. They also enjoyed the support of much of the Afrikaans press. But there was no overarching association or movement uniting them. There were several *verligte* concerns: the slow pace of homeland development; the humiliation inflicted on black people in the name of petty apartheid; and the anomalous status of the Coloured people. They, too, believed that the most effective strategy was to work for change within the NP. Other Afrikaner intellectuals, so-called *oorbeligtes* (over-enlightened ones), scorned them, insisting that they had not rejected the apartheid paradigm and were concerned merely with cosmetic changes.

The question of fitting the Coloured and Indian categories into the apartheid scheme of things was problematic: they had no homelands, and the Coloured people were biologically and culturally akin to Afrikaners. In Verwoerd's time the Coloureds had been deemed 'a nation in the making' – which was a nonsense. They were an intermediate category in the racial hierarchy, subject to racial discrimination that was severe (notably in the form of the Group Areas Act and myriad petty apartheid regulations), though not as severe as that imposed upon Africans. Their political rights in the Cape had been whittled away, culminating in the eventual removal in 1956 of their right to vote on the common voters roll, and its replacement by the right to elect two white representatives to the House of Assembly.

Historically, most Coloured political aspirations were directed at inclusion in the dominant category. Mohamed Adhikari writes:

If the ultimate aim of much of Coloured political organization was acceptance into the dominant society, then most of the day-to-day politicking was a narrow concern with the advancement of Coloured interests. Thus, though there was an assertion of nonracial values and protest against discrimination, there was also an accommodation with the racist order and an attempt to manipulate it in favor of Coloured people.[19]

It is worth noting that many Coloured people held similar racist stereotypes of Africans to those held by whites.

There were small groups of radicals, mostly better-educated people, who joined the Communist Party, the South African Coloured People's Organization (an ally of the ANC), and the Non-European Unity Movement.

In 1968 the Coloured Persons' Representative Council was established: 40 of its members were elected, and 20 nominated by the government. Its powers were strictly limited, which meant that elections were poorly supported. It survived until 1983, when a new constitutional system, the Tricameral Parliament, came into existence – causing in the process a far more serious split in the ranks of the NP than that of 1969 (see below).

For the NP, the political accommodation of the Coloured and Indian minorities posed a problem. The abolition of Coloured voting rights was due solely to NP fears that Coloured voters represented an anti-NP voting bloc and, moreover, one whose size could grow. By the 1960s *verkramptes*, including a few in the NP, were demanding a Coloured 'homeland', also a nonsense since white and Coloured lived, subject to Group Areas, closely intermingled in towns and villages, as well as on farms. Coloured 'reserves' were few in number, scattered and small in size and, consequently, wholly inadequate as a potential homeland.

In 1973 the government appointed a commission, chaired by Professor Erika Theron of Stellenbosch University – a staunch but by no means uncritical Nationalist – to inquire into all matters concerning the Coloured people. The Commission's membership of 20 included 6 Coloured people and a spread of political views. In 1976 it produced a voluminous report, whose key recommendation was that Coloured people be directly elected in the central government and other levels of authority. It concluded also that the Westminster system of government might have to be altered to meet the circumstances of South Africa's diversity. The government rejected the recommendation, as well as that proposing abolition of the Mixed Marriages and Immorality Acts. For the time being the issue of accommodating the Coloured and Indian categories remained unresolved. It would be a major irony that precisely this issue would trigger a major split in Afrikaner nationalism in 1982 that played no small part in accelerating the erosion of Afrikaner nationalism.

By the early 1970s more pressing matters confronted Vorster's government. The seeming quiescence of black opposition for much of the 1960s had given way to greater militance as the Black Consciousness movement made its presence felt. Of equal significance were the large-scale strikes of African workers that occurred in 1973, particularly in Natal. These were the harbingers of a powerful new focus of mobilization, independent trade unions. Moreover, there were stirrings in nearby territories: the *coup* in Portugal in 1974 led quickly to the independence of its colonies, Angola and Mozambique; revolt against the illegal white regime in Rhodesia was intensifying; and from 1974 the South West Africa People's Organization (SWAPO) stepped up its campaign against South African rule in South West Africa. All of these conflicts had reverberations among Africans in South Africa. For Vorster the danger was that the *cordon sanitaire* separating South Africa from hostile black Africa was coming apart.

The South African government had not formally recognized the illegal UDI regime, but it had supported it materially, refusing to participate in the sanctions campaign, and permitting its ports and rail links to be used by the Rhodesians. South African security personnel had also been deployed inside Rhodesia to assist the Rhodesian forces in their conflict with the guerrilla movements.

At a meeting in Cape Town on 16 February 1975, however, Vorster told a shocked Ian Smith, the Rhodesian leader, that South Africa's support would end. Although this did not mean that South Africa would assist in the enforcement of sanctions, its security personnel would be withdrawn. As much as anything it was a psychological blow to Smith, who believed that it was part of a campaign 'to pressurize us into coming to an accommodation with our terrorists'. Intriguingly, Smith claims to have been told by Vorster at an earlier meeting that apartheid was 'unworkable'.[20] Vorster, of course, would have denied saying anything of the kind, even if it were true. By the mid-1970s it was clear to all who wished to see that apartheid was, indeed, unworkable.

Notes

1 S.W. Pienaar (ed.), *Glo in U Volk* (Cape Town: Tafelberg Press, 1964), pp.57 and 38 (translation).

2 *Summary of the Report of the Commission for the Socio-economic Development of the Bantu Areas within the Union of South Africa* (Tomlinson Report) (Pretoria: Government Printer, U.G. 61/55).

3 *Idem*, pp.28 and 203.

4 *Survey of Race Relations 1987/88* (Johannesburg: South African Institute of Race Relations, 1988), p.460.

5 *Report of the Commission on Native Education, 1949–51* (Pretoria: Government Printer, 1951).

6 A.N. Pelzer (ed.), *Verwoerd Speaks: Speeches 1948–1966* (Johannesburg: APB Publishers, 1966), pp.83–4.

7 Pienaar, *Glo in U Volk*, p.113.

8 *Survey of Race Relations 1976* (Johannesburg: South African Institute of Race Relations, 1977), p.321.

9 *Idem*, pp.335 and 353.

10 Pienaar, *Glo in U Volk*, p.127.

11 Pelzer, *Verwoerd Speaks*, p.183.

12 *Idem*, p.40.

13 Dirk and Johanna de Villiers, *Paul Sauer* (Cape Town: Tafelberg Press, 1977), pp.135–6.

14 Pelzer, *Verwoerd Speaks*, p.516.

15 Albie Sachs, *Justice in South Africa* (London: Heinemann, 1973), p.12.

16 Max Coleman (ed.), *A Crime against Humanity: Analysing the Repression of the Apartheid State* (Cape Town: David Philip, 1998), pp.48–52.

17 Dirk Richard, *Moedswillig die Uwe* (Johannesburg: Perskor, 1985), pp.134–5.

18 *Survey of Race Relations 1975* (Johannesburg: South African Institute of Race Relations, 1976), p.182.

19 Mohamed Adhikari, *Not White Enough, Not Black Enough* (Cape Town: Double Storey Books, 2006), p.12.

20 Ian Smith, *Bitter Harvest: The Great Betrayal* (Johannesburg: Jonathan Ball, 2000), pp.170, 166.

CHAPTER 2

The decline of apartheid

The most serious crisis confronting Vorster's government began on 16 June 1976, when a small detachment of police, feeling menaced by an approaching march of up to 6,000 Soweto Africans, opened fire, having failed to disperse the crowd thanks to defective teargas canisters and the inaudibility of police commands. Two demonstrators (the official figure) were shot dead by the police in the initial confrontation; and by the end of the day, at least 15 fatalities had been recorded.

The uprising continued and sympathy demonstrations took place in many parts of the country, often resulting in deaths. According to the official commission of inquiry, the Cillié Commission, there were 575 fatalities countrywide between 16 June 1976 and 28 February 1977. Many observers, however, maintain that the figure, based upon police estimates, was a deliberate undercount, and that the actual figure was nearly double 575.

What had happened was by far the most serious clash between the state and protesters yet. It was a critical turning point in the resurrection of black opposition (see pages 89–92).

The proximate cause of the uprising was the implementation of a long-standing goal of apartheid, namely the equal status of Afrikaans and English in African schools in the 'white' areas. In 1974, the Department of Bantu Education insisted, all schools under its control would be required to use English and Afrikaans on an equal basis from Standard Five onwards: from 1975 Social Studies and Mathematics were to be taught through the medium of Afrikaans, Science and Practical Subjects in English, Religious Education, Music and Physical Education in an African language. Permission to deviate from this directive had to be given by the Department.

The new language dispensation provoked outrage among Africans, including the moderate African Teachers' Association. Opinion among African pupils themselves was overwhelmingly in favour of English as the medium of instruction. School boards in Soweto, representing parents, were bluntly informed by the Department that the question of medium was no concern of theirs, being a professional matter. Although provision was made for the granting of exemptions to the new language regulation if schools could not cope because they lacked enough teachers who were able to teach in Afrikaans, in practice very few exemptions were granted.

Throughout much of the first half of 1976 warnings about simmering anger and impending conflict were sounded by authoritative bodies and individuals. But the Department and Treurnicht, its Deputy Minister, acted with bland indifference and, almost incomprehensibly, total ignorance of what was happening on the ground. The security police, no less, who prided themselves on their vigilance, were equally unaware of the rising tension and the possibility of another Sharpeville. Equally inept were officials of the Witwatersrand Bantu Administration Board, who were charged with the administration of Soweto.

Vorster appeared to be stunned by what had happened. He had not been personally implicated in the extraordinary series of bungles that had led to the uprising, but as head of the government he had to accept responsibility – and direct responsibility for the appointment of a known *verkrampte* like Treurnicht to so sensitive a post. Apart from a brief state-ment declaring that the country was not confronted with a revolutionary situation, Vorster remained silent for nearly ten weeks after the initial con-frontation on 16 June. Government appeared paralysed. He told a meeting of the *Broederbond* in November 1976 that the recent events 'had convinced him anew that there is no way to handle race relations but the way of separate development'. If Ian Smith's claim that Vorster had told him that apartheid was 'unworkable' was true, Vorster perhaps now found himself trapped in a *cul de sac*. A Party man to the core, he would have recognized that any major reversal of policy would have split Afrikaner nationalism from top to bottom. So, the major pillars of policy would remain, subject only to minor, pragmatic adjustments.

Kragdadigheid (the uninhibited use of force) remained Vorster's prin-cipal weapon, unsheathed in October 1977 (not coincidentally one month before a general election) when 18 organizations mostly Black Consciou-ness in orientation but also the liberal Christian Institute, were banned. An appalling episode had occurred in the preceding month when Steve Biko, the pre-eminent Black Consciousness leader, was killed in horrifying circumstances while in police custody. The horror was compounded by the comment made by Jimmy Kruger, the Minister of Justice, a crude, uncouth person, that Biko's death left him cold. Remarkably, his offer to resign, in the wake of the storm that his crass remark had evoked, was turned down by Vorster.

The election held on 30 November 1977 had been called 18 months before being legally required. Partly, he was taking advantage of the electorally ever-popular display of *kragdadigheid*, and partly, it was a way of hitting back at foreign governments and international organizations who were allegedly meddling in South Africa's internal affairs. The NP took the opportunity of the campaign to float a new (and bizarre) constitutional plan for three parliaments, white, Coloured and Indian, each of which was to legislate on matters relating to its exclusive affairs. Matters of common concern would be dealt with by a council of cabinets, which, ideally, would take decisions by consensus. (It was the embryo of a constitutional plan that would be imposed in 1983 as the Tricameral Parliament.)

Much of the NP's campaign was directed against President Jimmy Carter of the United States, whose criticism of human rights violations in South Africa and elsewhere had angered the South African government. It was also a sure-fire electoral gimmick that contributed to the NP's huge victory, which gave them 82 per cent of the seats in the House of Assembly – the highest proportion recorded in South Africa's electoral history. The HNP sustained a heavy defeat, all but two of their 58 candidates losing their deposits.

It is possible, though by no means certain, that Vorster's calling an early election was not for any of the reasons cited above; rather, it was a move to give himself greater legitimacy before being engulfed in scandal. Rumours were swirling, even at the time of the campaign, that serious irregularities had occurred in the Department of Information, and that these also involved the responsible Minister, Dr C.P. Mulder, leader of the NP in the Transvaal and a rising star in the Party hierarchy, who was widely touted as Vorster's likely successor as Prime Minister. What came to be known as 'Infogate' arose out of the Department's attempts to burnish South Africa's tarnished image abroad, and to counter the hostile local English press by funding a pro-government English-language newspaper, *The Citizen*. It subsequently transpired that large amounts had been irregularly spent on secret projects. Not only did the project produce scant returns, but investigations showed that accounting procedures had been widely flouted. It also transpired that illicit funding had been provided, through a private intermediary, to fund the start-up of *The Citizen*.

Infogate, as the scandal became known, was a consequence of Vorster's lack of tight control over his ministers and their departments, although it is clear that he knew enough, including about the funding of *The Citizen*, to find himself implicated in the scandal. He had been persuaded not to resign in August 1977, when his proffered reason was exhaustion. Now, in September 1978, he did resign, no doubt conscious of his involvement being exposed.

Mulder had been the frontrunner in the succession race, but well-founded rumours about his complicity in Infogate damaged his candidacy, causing a critical block of Orange Free State MPs to switch their support from him to P.W. Botha, the Minister of Defence and leader of the Cape NP. Botha won the contest by 98 votes to 74, thereafter becoming Prime Minister.

Vorster's era had ended in the calamity of the Soweto Uprising and the disgrace of Infogate. His 12-year premiership had been the locust years of apartheid, though it would take a while yet for the system to be abolished.

An indirect consequence of the Soweto Uprising and Infogate was to widen divisions and heighten uncertainty in the NP and its support base. *Verligtes*, who mostly refrained from public expression of disquiet during the Uprising, saw it as a further indication that apartheid was failing. There was, however, intensive discussion in the inner circles of Afrikanerdom. Many recognized that while the Uprising had been triggered by the language issue, it had very quickly broadened into an attack on the entire apartheid system. Moreover, it was difficult for more reflective people to reconcile their own government's attempt to force Afrikaans down the throats of Africans with Afrikaners' rejection of British attempts after 1902 to force English down *their* throats. Many *verligtes* were also shamed by Treurnicht's astonishing ineptitude, though open criticism of his role was only voiced in 1982, when he left the NP and established the ultra-rightwing Conservative Party. Jimmy Kruger's remark about Biko's death compounded the shame. Kruger, then in retirement, subsequently joined the CP.

Volksleiers (leaders of the people) and others who occupied positions of authority had always enjoyed high esteem, indeed virtual deification in the case of Verwoerd, among Afrikaner nationalists. For many Infogate was a source of disillusionment: Vorster and some of his ministers had been shown up as ordinary, fallible people, some with feet of clay. It marked a significant shift in attitudes to leadership that had formerly been deeply entrenched in the political subculture of Afrikaner nationalism.

As noted above, Afrikaners were better educated, more diversified, and many were more inclined to criticism of apartheid and the monstrous machinery that enforced it. A new generation of writers refused to be cowed by the sanctions that community pressures could exert – and a few had their books banned as a consequence. No single book did more to prick consciences than Elsa Joubert's *Die Swerfjare van Poppie Nongena* (1978), which was the story of an African woman's battle to survive with her family in the face of apartheid's inflexible bureaucracy. It became one of the best-selling Afrikaans novels yet published.

Until the end of his premiership Vorster parroted the conventional platitudes about the need for apartheid. He remained implacably opposed to any thought of black representation in parliament, and, like Verwoerd, he insisted that the (rising) number of Africans in the 'white' areas did not matter so long as inequality and separation were maintained. It is virtually impossible to provide accurate figures for this number; but according to the 1980 census statistics, which were probably an under-enumeration, over 17 million Africans were in the 'white' areas of whom nearly 6.5 million were urban and 10.5 million were rural. They outnumbered whites by nearly four to one. Almost certainly the figures are an underestimate, and the actual number of urban Africans was probably nearer 8 million. Demography was inexorably eroding whatever (limited) credibility apartheid might once have had.

In spite of the policy that proclaimed urban Africans to be 'temporary sojourners', incremental changes slowly began to undermine it, although the basic principle that Africans could enjoy political rights only in their homelands was vigorously maintained. Homeland representatives in the urban areas were meant to provide a quasi-diplomatic link.

An earlier attempt to provide a form of local representation for urban Africans was enacted in 1961, creating partly elected Urban Bantu Councils. Although provision was made for vesting some powers in them, they remained largely advisory – and, consequently, cut little ice with most Africans. They were disparagingly referred to as 'Useless Boys Clubs'. There was another reason for their lack of legitimacy: the widespread suspicion that they represented an attempt to inveigle Africans into self-enforcement of a hated system.

From 1971 the control of urban African affairs had been removed from (white) local authorities and placed in the hands of government-appointed Administration Boards (later termed Development Boards). It was part of the process of centralization, as well as eliminating the influence of anti-government local authorities. The Boards were harsh, bureaucratic and inflexible. Even the Commission of Inquiry into the Soweto Uprising felt obliged to conclude that 'dissatisfaction with administration boards was so widespread that many Black residents were thereby easily motivated to go into revolt' (para 12.4.1). The Commission also found that the absence of any say in government, uncertainty regarding citizenship coupled with a wish to be permanent residents and citizens of South Africa, the refusal to allow ownership of land, and pervasive discrimination were all underlying factors that 'created a spirit of dissatisfaction and resistance' (paras 13.2 and 13.3).

Apart from the hasty dropping of the enforced language rule that had sparked the Soweto Uprising, the government attempted other reforms: in 1977 it replaced the Urban Bantu Councils, which had been failures, with Community Councils. These were to be elected by South African citizens (i.e. excluding 'citizens' of the TBVC states) and vested with a number of executive functions relevant to local issues. They could be required to administer the allocation of housing, approve rentals and prevent illegal occupation or squatting. All of these were controversial tasks, especially those relating to rentals, suggesting that the government was trying to fob them off onto African bodies, thereby placing itself at one remove from the people who would be directly affected.

It did not work out like that: although the Councils appeared to attract more votes, they remained essentially powerless and thus regarded by urban residents as agents of a hated system, as well as being prone to abusing their positions for corrupt purposes. In 1982 yet another effort was made to establish legitimate African local authorities; but it was another failure, moreover one that sparked an outbreak of spirited resistance in September 1984 (see page 106).

Incremental changes in housing policy also suggested an unacknowledged coming to terms with the reality that there were some permanently urbanized Africans. In 1975 it was decided that qualified (in terms of influx control laws) African men could buy houses or lease land for 30 years, with the possibility of an extension for up to another 30 years; the scheme was subsequently extended to women and their dependants. In 1978, provision was made for 99-year leasehold rights to surveyed areas in African townships. Neither of these schemes, however, applied to the west of the Eiselen Line, which demarcated much of the Western Cape as a Coloured labour preference area.

The changes marked a partial rescinding of earlier policy that provision of housing would be drastically reduced in favour of hostels for single, male migrants. So, too, the decision not to build any more secondary schools in urban areas was relaxed.

Other processes were undermining apartheid. The boom years of the 1960s, when the economy grew at over 5 per cent p.a., had the consequence of diminishing the pool of skilled labour (almost exclusively white) to its limit. One result was that 'job reservation' became a virtual dead letter. It was said to have protected only 1 in 500 white workers. A Commission of

Inquiry into Labour Legislation, chaired by Professor N.E. Wiehahn, was appointed in 1977; it found that 'job reservation' was 'no longer tenable' in view of developments affecting African workers: their educational levels were improving, more training facilities for Africans were being provided, they were experiencing upward occupational mobility in sectors not covered by job reservation determinations. Moreover, said the Commission, it was very difficult to police the legislation, which was said to be honoured more in the breach than in the observance. (Part 1, paras 3.129.3 and 3.129.4) The finding was accepted by the government. White mineworkers constituted the last redoubt of opposition to the abolition of job colour bars in the industry. Despite a chronic shortage of semi-skilled and skilled workers, and demands from mining employers for abolition of the colour bar, the redoubt managed to hold on to its privileges until 1987.

The Wiehahn Commission's major recommendation, whose acceptance by the government was to have momentous consequences, was that African trade unions should be recognized. According to the Commission, the threat posed by recognizing African trade unions was less than that posed by continuing with non-recognition. In a key paragraph it said:

The increasing opportunities for Black [African] workers to advance into job categories previously occupied by non-Blacks will soon give rise to the anomalous situation where Black workers working side-by-side with non-Black workers in the same skilled occupations find themselves excluded from the statutory trade union system purely on the ground of their colour. This has strong moral implications. Increased vertical labour mobility by job advancement through education and training particularly of the Black labour force, will place the statutory trade union system under extreme stress if the exclusion of the Black worker from the system is perpetuated. (Part 1, para. 3.35.4)

In advocating the recognition of African unions the Commission was leery of their potential political role, and recommended that the existing prohibition on employer and union affiliation to or financing of political parties be retained and possibly reinforced. In a subsequent report it observed that where 'ideologically motivated organisations' sought to achieve political results through industrial action 'no amount of compulsion in industrial law will succeed in preventing such abuses' (Part 5, para. 4.34.14). Perhaps the Commission was tacitly and obliquely suggesting that in the absence of a political settlement African trade unions would use their economic muscle for political ends. Since there were no effective political channels available to Africans this was a virtual inevitability, as turned out to be the case.

The process of recognizing African unions was initiated by the appointment of the Wiehahn Commission during Vorster's premiership, but its reports were submitted and acted upon only after P.W. Botha had become Prime Minister. Botha knew nothing about industrial relations and perhaps believed that the recognition and registration of African unions would be a means of controlling them and also of bringing some order to what might otherwise be chaos in the field of industrial relations. If so, he was mistaken.

P.W. Botha, Vorster's successor, had been elected to the premiership if not by accident, then as a consequence of Mulder's political demise. Botha, a political organizer for the NP prior to his becoming an MP in 1948, rose steadily up the Party hierarchy: Deputy Minister of the Interior, 1958–61, a full cabinet post charged with various ministerial portfolios between 1961 and 1966, and becoming Minister of Defence in 1966, a portfolio he retained for two years after becoming Prime Minister in September 1978. He had also become leader of the NP in the Cape in 1966.

Botha came into the prime ministership with the reputation of a hawk. As Defence Minister he had formed strong bonds with a number of generals, some of whose promotions he had sponsored. Notable among these was Magnus Malan, who had been appointed chief of the defence force in 1976. In 1980 Botha made him Minister of Defence.

As a minister, Botha had not displayed any reformist inclinations. Indeed, as Minister of Community Development and of Coloured Affairs he had had primary responsibility for the enforcement of one of apartheid's cruellest laws, the Group Areas Act. Botha was known to be a ruthlessly efficient manager, possessing a volcanic temper, said to be capable of reducing some of his ministers to tears.

As Minister of Defence Botha had overseen the birth of the doctrine of the 'total onslaught', a paranoid, Manichean view of a world in which the West was threatened by a total strategy led by an aggressive communism. It required a total strategy in response. He told an audience in November 1978 that the Third World War had begun, but it was a different kind of war:

It is a war that involves not just armed force, but one in which it was attempted to gain control of people's spirits, people's thoughts, people's convictions. When people's souls and spirits had been captured, it softens you up, renders you powerless and then the military onslaught is so much easier.[1]

In more specific terms, the White Paper on Defence, published in 1977, spelled out what the total onslaught was attempting to achieve in Southern Africa:

a The expansion of Marxism by fomenting revolution in Southern Africa.

b The overthrow of the white regimes in Southern Africa so that the militant Africa bloc can realize its aspirations with regard to the destruction of so-called colonialism and racialism and the establishment of Pan-Africanism . . .

c The striving after an indirect strategy in order to unleash revolutionary warfare in Southern Africa and, by means of isolation, to force the [Republic of South Africa] to change its domestic policy in favour of Pan-Africanism.

This was crude stuff, reflecting its authors' (including, no doubt, Botha himself) insular view of the world. It was paranoid, but as a cynic observed, even if you are paranoid, it does not mean that someone is not out to get you. Without suggesting that the total onslaught doctrine was perspicacious or that the total strategy was an appropriate response, it should be borne in mind that the Cold War was still in progress and that the Soviets did not hesitate to fish in troubled waters; that in 1975 both newly liberated Angola and Mozambique had installed Marxist-Leninist regimes; that the ANC was symbiotically linked with the South African Communist Party (SACP), and received much of its support, including training of guerrillas, from the Soviet Union.

Neither Botha nor his colleagues could understand why the West did not openly embrace South Africa as a staunch ally in the fight against communism. Neither he nor they could appreciate that democratic govern-ments elsewhere regarded South Africa's institutionalized racism and its negation of the rule of law as an abomination that created fertile soil for the supposed attractions of Marxism-Leninism. Moreover, the use of the Suppression of Communism Act to restrict activist individuals, communist and non-communist alike, provided a further cachet for communism, elevating it to the status of apartheid's doughtiest opponent. This could only enhance the popularity of the SACP, many of whose members were prominent in the underground struggle.

The total strategy provided a rationale for a far more comprehensive revamping of the security system. Critical to this process was the State Security Council, which had been established in Vorster's time, but had not played a significant role. Botha wanted a more active national secur-ity management system, with a wider embrace of state departments and tentacles that penetrated far and wide into society. The State Security Council stood at the apex of this system, and in a short time it became the most powerful body in government, eclipsing in many respects the cabinet itself. Supposedly the Council was advisory, but with Botha in the chair, surrounded by high-level 'securocrats', as the senior personnel from the various security agencies were known, its recommendations were hard for cabinet to reject. Another important component of the securocratic system was the National Intelligence Service, headed by Niel Barnard, a young former professor of political science. Its function was principally the analysis of raw data, though Barnard would later play a critical role in initiating contact between the South African government and the ANC.

The total response strategy outlined above, and its institutional and practical expression, indicated that Botha would not hesitate to use the heavy hand of repression to eradicate the multifarious manifestations of the total onslaught. Indeed, this would be so. There was, however, another side to Botha: the reformer. To the surprise of many, he delivered what sounded like a strongly reformist speech at Upington in August 1979. This was the 'adapt or die' (though he did not use exactly these words) speech, in which he insisted that the interests of Africans and Coloureds not be neglected: 'We can take good neighbourliness in this country to its full consequences only if we do justice to every population group. . . . Your politics must not consist of hate, but of love . . .'. He added that policy had to be adapted to meet changed circumstances.[2]

Botha was critical of some of his predecessors: were some of the petty apartheid rules necessary, he had asked D.F. Malan? And South Africa was paying the price for ignoring the recommendations of the Tomlinson Commission. Vorster, he said, had squandered an opportunity to carry out constructive aspects of NP policy: he had a large majority and plenty of money, but not enough had been done. He was also highly critical of the sloppy and ineffective administration in Vorster's time.[3]

Botha's aim was to modernize apartheid, but without jeopardizing 'the right of self-determination of the white nation'. In other words, white control was not negotiable. In the first eight years of his leadership Botha actually pulled down some of the main pillars of the apartheid system: legislation to recognize African trade unions was enacted in 1979; the Mixed Marriages Act and the section of the Immorality Act criminalizing sex across the colour line were repealed; and in 1986 influx control was abolished.

The centrepiece of Botha's administration was a 'reform' of a dubious nature: the Tricameral Constitution that was enacted in 1983. It provided for a powerful executive State President, a parliament consisting of three chambers, the House of Assembly (for whites), the House of Representatives (for Coloureds), and the House of Delegates (for Indians). In principle, legislation relating to 'own' affairs, i.e. relating specifically to the affairs of a particular group, could be enacted by the particular chamber, while 'general' affairs covered matters relating to all population groups. General affairs, including legislation, required the assent of all three chambers. The control and administration of African affairs was vested in the State President. A complex mechanism was created for handling conflicts among the chambers, such as the refusal by one or more chambers to pass a general affairs bill or the passing of different versions to the President's Council, which was structured so as to ensure that a majority of its members were white (and mostly, in practice, NP members). The Council was empowered to make a decision on which version of a bill could be enacted into law.

It was a bizarre constitution, but one that was to have momentous consequences. The exclusion of Africans provoked a storm of protest – and sparked the formation of the United Democratic Front, the biggest black opposition movement in the country's history (see pages 103ff). It also split the NP and, with it, Afrikaner nationalism.

Treurnicht had been appointed to the cabinet in 1979, despite his disastrous handling of the education crisis in 1976. He had consistently sniped at Botha over relatively minor issues – such as a 'mixed' school rugby tournament – but the showdown came with the new constitution. In February 1982, Treurnicht had objected to a comment in an NP propaganda publication which had said, referring to the Tricameral Constitution, that it was only logical that there could not be more than one government in a country. Treurnicht responded to the publication's editor, declaring that 'mixed' government was a wholly unacceptable idea.

What happened next was high political drama: Treurnicht was adamant, and Botha would not tolerate an affront to his authority. Tension mounted in the NP, approached breaking point. The NP caucus met on 24 February 1982, and was immediately plunged into an acrimonious debate about Botha's notion of 'healthy power-sharing', which, according to Treurnicht, smacked of the power-sharing proposed by the liberal Progressive Federal Party. Botha did not want to go down in history as the leader who split the NP again; and Treurnicht, no doubt, hoped that his powerful position as leader of the NP in the Transvaal would put him in a strong position to succeed Botha, when he retired – or was ejected from the leadership.

Matters got out of hand: when Fanie Botha, the Minister of Manpower and the second most senior cabinet member, proposed a motion of unqualified support for the Prime Minister and his right to interpret policy, which after more heated debate was put to the vote. The motion was carried by 100 votes to 22, 18 of the latter being Transvaal MPs. One cabinet member, Ferdi Hartzenberg, supported Treurnicht.

Treurnicht, however, was not yet finished: he hoped to mobilize the powerful Transvaal NP's Head Council in his favour by calling a meeting for 27 February. His opponents, led by F.W. de Klerk and two other senior ministers planned a counter-offensive, one part of which was to spring a surprise on Treurnicht and his supporters by having Botha turn up at the meeting. It was a risky strategy since he was not a member of the Head Council, and if a majority of its members voted to refuse him entry it would have been a damaging blow. In the event, a flabbergasted Treurnicht could hardly deny entry to the NP's *hoofleier* ('leader-in-chief') so Botha was invited and delivered what his admiring biographers describe as 'the best performance of his career'.[4]

De Klerk had drawn up an ostensibly conciliatory motion, inviting Treurnicht and company to repent of their ways and return to the fold. But there was a proviso: were they to reject the motion he and his supporters would be stripped of all their positions and expelled from the Party. After five hours of debate, the motion was put and carried by 172 votes to 36. Treurnicht had been trounced – but he was not yet destroyed. De Klerk, on the other hand, won plaudits for his skilful tactical sense, and shortly after he was unanimously elected Transvaal leader, the second most powerful position in the NP. Treurnicht's supporters founded the Conservative Party (CP) a few weeks later.

The split had positive and negative effects on the NP and the wider Afrikaner nationalist movement. With the exodus of a significant number of *verkramptes* Botha was now freer to embark on such reforms as he contemplated. Moreover, the inflexibility and dogmatism of the Conservatives held up a mirror to Nationalists, showing them what their party had been like not all that long before: the element of repulsion and dissociation would be a spur to *verligtes*.

On the other hand, the split traumatized Afrikanerdom far more than the earlier HNP split. Its repercussions were experienced throughout the community, in the churches, bureaucracy, defence and police forces and the *Afrikaner Broederbond*. Moreover, the formation of the CP had unleashed a ferocious war of ethnic outbidding, the CP proclaiming itself to be the true custodian of Afrikaner values. There was no way of knowing what growth potential the CP possessed, but there was a disquieting indication that could be extrapolated from the rise in the HNP's share of the vote in the election of April 1981 in which it won over 14 per cent of the overall vote, compared with 3.3 per cent in 1977. It still did not win a seat, but in contests where the HNP was pitted against the NP it increased its share of the vote from 8 per cent in 1977 to 29 per cent.[5]

Another factor that compounded the NP's worries was that, whereas the HNP's style was that of crude, rough streetfighters, the CP was far more sophisticated and better packaged. Treurnicht himself was the epitome of the suave, smooth and well-spoken clergyman that he had once been. A number of gloomy observers claimed that it was 'inevitable' that the CP would eventually win power, since the dynamic of white politics invariably favoured more racist politicians and parties.

A number of ultra-rightwing organizations had sprouted in the 1970s, a process that continued into the 1980s. They varied considerably in size and style, from the large, neo-Nazi, paramilitary *Afrikaner-Weerstandsbeweging* (Afrikaner Resistance Movement) to small groups, some consisting of intellectuals and others, like the *Wit Wolwe* (White Wolves) of activists, often with murderous proclivities. It was unclear to what extent institutions such as the police, army and bureaucracy were strongholds of the ultra-right but, again, a number of observers were pessimistic. Their pessimism, however, did not reckon with two countervailing tendencies: one was the inability of the ultra-right to join forces in a unified opposition. The HNP, for example, had confidently expected Treurnicht to join them in 1969, and they never forgave him for refusing to. The bad blood continued, thwarting any possibility of an electoral pact between the HNP and the CP.

Second, the *embourgeoisement* of many Afrikaners had been consolidated: a thrusting entrepreneurial class, professionals, and a steady stream of graduates had not only diversified the Afrikaner community, but also sharpened their critical faculties. Growing numbers could not only see that apartheid was doomed to failure, but found that what was done in the name of the policy brought shame on Afrikanerdom. It is important not to overstate the extent of liberalization among Afrikaners – or, for that matter, among the English-speakers, or to suppose that all *verligtes* were ready to tear down apartheid.

The first national trial of strength between the NP and the CP/HNP axis occurred on 2 November 1983 when white voters were asked in a referendum whether they favoured implementation of the Tricameral Constitution, which had been passed by parliament. 'Yes' supporters argued that the constitution sought to accommodate South Africa's pluralism by providing for group representation. Many in the English community, including most of its prominent businesspeople, acknowledged that while the constitution was deeply flawed it was 'a step in the right direction', and as far as the NP could go.

The 'No' voters comprised an odd mixture of the liberal PFP, led by F. van Zyl Slabbert and the assorted components of the ultra-rightwing. For the PFP the constitution was a disastrous mistake: not only did it constitutionalize apartheid but it would be profoundly polarizing – and ultimately destabilizing. Unfortunately for Slabbert, an estimated 50 per cent of PFP supporters bucked the Party line and voted 'Yes', or abstained from voting. The result of the referendum was a huge victory, by nearly 66 per cent to over 33 per cent, for the 'Yes' vote. Even the most moderate African leaders, including most homeland chief ministers, were dismayed at what they considered to be a slap in the face. Low percentage polls were recorded in the elections for the Coloured and Indian Houses, respectively 18.1 per cent and 16.2 per cent if measured against the number of eligible rather than registered voters.

The Tricameral Constitution came into effect in September 1984. P.W. Botha was unanimously elected as State President, and thereafter appointed Allan Hendrickse, leader of the (Coloured) Labour Party, and Amichand Rajbansi, leader of the (Indian) National People's Party, to the cabinet, although neither was given a portfolio.

In significant respects the new constitution was the turning point in what proved to be the decisive decade in the downfall of apartheid. Apart from triggering the formation of the UDF and the split in the NP, it brought home to many whites, including Nationalists, that the hard realities of apartheid's palpable failure had to be confronted. The exclusion of Africans from the purview of the constitution forced the issue of African political rights to the top of the agenda. The question 'And what about the black [African] people?' was the title of an NP pamphlet released a few months after the inauguration of the new constitution. It was a timely question.

In the early 1980s official policy remained that Africans could enjoy political rights only in relation to their respective homelands. An attempt to give urban Africans greater say in local affairs was made in 1982 with the Black Local Authorities Act, which purported to create local government similar to that for whites. It made little impact: voter turnout in those townships where elections were held was generally lower than the previous elections for Community Councils in 1977: Soweto managed only a 10.7 per cent poll.

Botha had tried his best to make the homelands credible as putatively independent states, but the policy unravelled before his eyes. Consolidation, even to the limited extent envisaged, proved impossible, and the entire costly project was pronounced dead by the government's own consolidation committee. Equally dismaying for the NP was their conclusion that the homelands (independent or otherwise) could ultimately accommodate no more than 40 per cent of the African population – and even that was an optimistic assumption. The homelands and 'independent' states were, moreover, hardly credible examples of a successful programme of 'decolonization'. For the most, they were palpable economic failures, bottomless pits into which the South African taxpayer poured money. Those that were independent, the TBVC states, were corrupt and authoritarian, prone to *coups*.

To compound these problems, several homelands categorically refused to take independence. The most notable was KwaZulu, whose chief minister, Mangosuthu Buthelezi, had been an outspoken critic of apartheid since the 1960s. Since the Zulu were the biggest African ethno-linguistic group, accounting for 22 per cent of the total population by 1990, opting for independence and its concomitant loss of citizenship would have lent credibility to apartheid, at least in the minds of its supporters. Buthelezi's rejection of independence, on the other hand, was a significant blow to apartheid's grand plan.

While Botha had no intention of abandoning apartheid's fundamental principle, namely maintaining white control over the 'white' areas, he allowed incremental changes that further eroded 'traditional' apartheid dogmas – but without in the least slackening his iron grip on security. The most important of these changes was abandonment of the absurd view that urban Africans were 'temporary sojourners'. Botha told parliament in January 1985 that government now accepted that large numbers of Africans lived permanently in 'white' South Africa. It had also been concluded that these people could not be politically accommodated through homeland government structures. It had therefore been decided, he continued, to regard them in constitutional terms as entities that were to be developed to give them the power to control their own affairs 'up to the highest level'. The proviso was that no population group would be placed in a position to dominate others.[6] Nor, he made clear, was there any thought of adding a fourth (African) chamber to the existing parliament.

A year later Botha informed parliament that his government accepted a common citizenship for all South Africans: 'The peoples of the Republic of South Africa constitute one nation. But our nation is a nation of minorities.'[7]

Perhaps the most significant change of all was the abolition of influx control in 1986. It followed on from a study of urbanization by a committee of the President's Council, published in 1985. It found that attempts to counteract the rapid urbanization of the African population had largely been defeated by the economic boom of the 1960s. Urbanization had continued unabated at a rate of about 3.9 per cent per annum. As against an increase of 37.6 per cent in the total African population from 1960 to 1970, the increase in the urban African population was 42 per cent. Much of the increase was due to the natural increase of already urbanized people.[8]

Various efforts had been made to tinker with influx control, such as prosecuting the employers of Africans who were illegally in urban areas, and linking the right of urban residence to housing and employment. The strategy had also been to drive a wedge between urban 'insiders' (those with section 10 rights) and 'outsiders'. None had succeeded, and as economic conditions in the homelands deteriorated even further the townward stream of migrants looking for employment continued.

With a chronic shortage of housing, estimated (conservatively) to be 200,000 units in 1985, it was inevitable that squatter or informal settlements would spring up around the major urban centres. By the mid-1980s over 2 million people lived in these settlements. Some were illegal migrants, others were 'qualified' urban residents who, unable to acquire houses and wishing to live with their families, built shacks for themselves. Technically, squatting was illegal and the authorities made numerous attempts to remove squatters, destroying their shacks in the process. This continued until a domestic and international outcry against inhumane forced removals (sometimes during freezing winter conditions) forced a suspension.

By the early 1980s it was apparent that influx control was no longer effective, despite numerous arrests and convictions – 163,862 arrests occurred in 1984 alone. It was also apparent that the system could not be enforced other than by abhorrent 'dragnet' methods, including raids on homes, in buses, and at places of employment. It was hardly surprising that Africans were enraged at the affront to their dignity. It was no less surprising that many rural people, facing desperate conditions in the homelands or 'white' rural areas, simply moved to towns where the chance of finding some employment outweighed the risk of prosecution or conviction. As many as 40 per cent of the urban African population were technically 'illegal' in a number of cities and towns.

The abolition of influx control was the last of Botha's significant reforms. From 1986 until August 1989, when he was forced to resign, South Africa drifted rudderless, beset by massive internal unrest, mounting international pressure, a serious border war in Namibia/Angola, and the ANC's guerrilla attacks. The government sought in vain a formula that could square African participation in the highest levels of government with Botha's insistence that statutorily recognized groups be the building blocks of any future constitution.

The Commonwealth Eminent Persons Group (EPG) (1985–6) did its best to broker a settlement between the government and the ANC, and produced a sensible template for possible negotiations; but its efforts were blown out of the water when, in May 1986, the South African Defence Force launched devastating raids on Harare, Gaborone and Lusaka, ostensibly against *Umkhonto we Sizwe* safe houses.[9] At least some members of the cabinet were supportive of the EPG initiative, but it is clear that the securocrats, and Botha himself were determined not to tolerate this 'foreign meddling'.

Security had become the paramount issue. It is also apparent that the 'total onslaught' dogma had made an impact on white public opinion. R.F. 'Pik' Botha, Foreign Minister in the cabinet, and one of the ministers who supported the EPG initiative, has described the mood of the times: 'From the middle 1970s onwards there was only one cry from most whites: Eliminate the terrorists. After bomb and landmine explosions in which civilians were killed and maimed, the countrywide reaction was: eradicate the rubbish'.[10] As noted, Botha had revitalized the State Security Council (SSC), and made it the focus of securocrat power. From 1979, an elaborate National Security Management System was created, consisting of Joint Management Centres (JMCs) in each of 12 designated regions, sub-JMCs in each of the 60 sub-regions, and a Mini-JMC in approximately 450 mini-regions. The purpose of the system was to act as an early warning mechanism, to cut through the bureaucratic red tape that often hamstrung the delivery of services and facilities by civilian authorities, and to engage in WHAM – winning hearts and minds. Information, requests and reports flowed directly up the hierarchy, finally reaching the SSC. The entire system was dominated by the military, with a limited extent of civilian representation.[11]

The system had only a limited effect. Apart from offending civilian authorities at all levels, its WHAM campaigns were, if anything, counter-productive. The efficacy of its early warning function was doubtful, seeing that the temper and durability of opposition across much of the country caused Botha to declare successive states of emergency: in 36 magisterial districts in July 1985, and nationally in June 1986. Even more draconian powers than those in already existing security legislation were given to the state, including powers of detention, restrictions on the media, prohibitions on gatherings, including at funerals, and provision for countering school boycotts, which had become widespread.

By the mid-1980s it was apparent that the apartheid system was finding it necessary to deploy increasing amounts of coercion. It was not in danger of being overthrown, but the tumult and the campaign to make the country 'ungovernable' was making effective control difficult. It was not a sign of effective government and stability when troops had to be deployed to back the police up in many unrest situations. Detentions under the emergency regulations increased rapidly, numbering an unofficially estimated 38,000 between June 1985 and June 1988. Approximately a further 10,000 were detained over approximately the same period. Over 70 per cent of both categories were released without being charged.

A further manifestation of the iron first occurred in February 1988 when the UDF was served with a restriction order, preventing it from 'executing or continuing any actions'. An organizational shell was permitted to continue. It was the culmination of a process in which most of the top leadership and many grassroots activists had been detained and thereafter either prosecuted or restricted.

Draconian security measures, widespread insecurity among whites and a rising tide of ultra-rightwing racism created fertile soil for another phenomenon: 'dirty tricks' targeting opponents of the government. They had been known before but in the turbulent 1980s and with little or no effective oversight they flourished. Torture, by no means unknown before, became routine for detainees – and the torturers could act with impunity in the likely knowledge that no court would either convict them of assault (and in some cases, murder) or reject evidence literally beaten out of detainees. A few security police, 21 out of 288 charged, were, in fact, convicted of various (unspecified) criminal offences between 1981 and 1989.[12]

The number of assassinations, usually of high-profile activists, rose in the 1980s. The Truth and Reconciliation Commission quoted an applicant for amnesty:

In some cases it was necessary to eliminate activists by killing them. This was the only way in which effective action could be taken against activists in a war situation . . . to charge someone through the normal court structure and go through the whole process was cumbersome and occasionally inadequate and impossible.

He added that assassination was generally directed at high-profile activists 'whose detention in terms of security legislation would give momentum to the liberation struggle. The security police and the country could not afford a Nelson Mandela again.'[13] According to the Human Rights Committee, an anti-apartheid NGO, 150 activists were killed, 54 of them outside the country, between 1974 and 1989.[14] (The figure does not include persons executed in ANC camps.)

By the 1980s the government faced the problem of what to do with Nelson Mandela, by then the world's most famous political prisoner. For

ordinary prisoners life imprisonment meant as little as 15 years with remission for good behaviour. For political prisoners, including those sentenced
to life imprisonment, there was no question of remission. So far as one
could surmise life imprisonment meant exactly that. Mandela, however,
was different: he was an iconic figure domestically, and the focus of considerable international hostility to apartheid. But he was elderly, and the
government was concerned about what might happen were he to die in
prison. Being a tough and principled character Mandela had refused several
offers of release that were tied to conditions that he found unacceptable.
Botha realized that Mandela could not be released other than into a process
that must involve negotiation with the ANC. Botha was not prepared to
do this – unless the ANC forswore violence and severed its links with the
South African Communist Party.

Despite the public demonization of the ANC, another process was under
way under conditions of strict confidentiality and, as far as Botha was
concerned, deniability. Stealthy emissaries from government were making
contact with the ANC in exile, and with Mandela in prison. These included
Willie Esterhuyse and Sampie Terreblanche, Stellenbosch University professors, Niel Barnard, head of the National Intelligence Service, and Richard
Rosenthal, a human rights lawyer who had volunteered his services as an
intermediary. A breakthrough had occurred when, in 1986, Mandela was
taken from prison to meet Kobie Coetsee, the Minister of Justice. It was a
cordial meeting, lasting three hours. Mandela wrote:

I was greatly encouraged. I sensed the government was anxious to overcome the
impasse in the country, that they were now convinced they had to depart from
their old positions. In ghostly outline, I saw the beginnings of a compromise.[15]

Mandela, who believed that a negotiated accommodation was the only
way forward, was out on a limb, ahead of many of his ANC colleagues.
Botha, too, would have paid a heavy price in terms of support lost to the
CP had knowledge of the stealthy emissaries and ministerial meetings with
Mandela leaked. Most white opinion, shaped by decades of propaganda,
much of it emanating from the South African Broadcasting Corporation,
was still far from accepting that negotiation offered the only hope of a
peaceful settlement.

Another influential body, however, recognized that there was no
alternative to negotiation: this was the Afrikaner *Broederbond*. It was not the
power behind the throne, as its critics alleged, but it did represent much of
the Afrikaner elite, including senior politicians. It had decided in July 1985
that contact should be made with the ANC, and during 1986 the chairman,

Professor Pieter de Lange, met Thabo Mbeki, the diplomatic face of the ANC in exile, in New York. In November 1986 the *Broederbond* produced a document that committed it unambiguously to a negotiated settlement. It accepted that there could be no guarantees, but:

We have to think in terms of probabilities, calculated risks. The biggest risk we could take was to avoid risks altogether. If Afrikaners could not reach a negotiated settlement, it was inevitable that they would face structures forced on them without having had any say in the matter.[16]

An overwhelming majority of members accepted the document.

Botha became more beleaguered in his final three years in office. After a disastrous speech in 1985 – the so-called Rubicon speech – the currency halved in value and the sanctions noose tightened. When foreign banks called in their loans and a debt standstill was imposed the country's plight worsened. Unable to import capital, savings had to be exported to reduce debt, which limited growth to 2 per cent per annum, which was below the population growth rate. The Governor of the Reserve Bank told Robin Renwick, the British Ambassador, that the security chiefs had claimed that all that was required to solve South Africa's problems was to imprison a few thousand more agitators. The Governor, Gerhard de Kock, was incredulous.[17]

Botha suffered a severe stroke in January 1989 and was incapacitated for several months. Shortly after returning to office in April he announced that the office of State President and that of leader of the NP were to be separated, and that the caucus should proceed to elect a new Party leader. In the election F.W. de Klerk beat the Minister of Finance, Barend du Plessis by eight votes. That du Plessis, a *verligte*, had run so strongly was an indication that many in the caucus wanted reform to press ahead. In his acceptance speech de Klerk spoke of the need to take bold initiatives.

For his part Botha had made a fatal mistake: he had undoubtedly wanted to continue to determine policy, but his decision to vacate the Party leadership meant that he had cut himself off from his power-base. It was an error that suggested an impairment of judgement caused by the stroke. What followed were a tense few months of diarchy during which Botha continually sought to undermine de Klerk's authority.

The issue came to a head at a cabinet meeting on 14 August 1989. The proximate cause was Botha's insistence that de Klerk and Pik Botha (the Minister of Foreign Affairs) had violated protocols by accepting an invitation to visit President Kaunda of Zambia. Botha claimed that he had not been informed beforehand. De Klerk interpreted Botha's behaviour as yet another manifestation of his attempt to undermine him. The cabinet meeting was a tense affair, with minister after minister suggesting that Botha was not well enough to continue in office, but also wishing to avoid humiliating him. After some characteristically angry responses, Botha calmed down and accepted that he would have to resign.[18] He was embittered and subsequently allowed his NP membership to lapse.

De Klerk, a trained lawyer, came into the leadership with a somewhat ambiguous reputation, some, including NP MPs, believing him to be on the conservative wing of the Party. This was a misreading: he had not taken sides in the internal debates between *verligtes* and conservatives, preferring to be regarded as a centrist. In many debates, however, he had challenged Treurnicht, whom he disliked, and invariably bested him. Crucially, de Klerk had a capacity to read the writing on the wall, and he knew not only that apartheid had failed, but that talking to the real leaders of the African people was inevitable. He was, however, unaware of the contacts with Mandela and the stealthy emissaries' dealings with ANC people abroad.

De Klerk was not part of Botha's inner circle; nor was he in the loop established by the securocrats. In his capacity as Transvaal leader of the NP he was a member of the State Security Council, but he deplored the extent to which it had eclipsed the cabinet. He recounts an incident at a meeting of cabinet members on the Namibia/Angola border (circa 1985) when 'Plan B' was mooted in the event all constitutional options failed: it involved suspending the existing constitution and ruling by decree. The proposal was heavily punted by elements in the security establishment, but de Klerk and other senior ministers vehemently opposed the idea. De Klerk writes: 'The idea was never raised again, but from that time . . . I was clearly identified by the security establishment as a dove, and therefore as a person who could not be trusted with their inner secrets'.[19]

Problems with elements in the security establishment would dog de Klerk's presidency. Not long after assuming office he addressed gatherings of the top echelons of both the army and the police, insisting that they refrain from any political involvement and apply the law impartially. Obedience to the civilian authority had been strongly entrenched in the security services, but the principle had not been tested since the political and security forces' leadership shared similar views. By 1990 things had changed and, with strong CP support in both police and army, renegade elements would do their best to thwart de Klerk's efforts to transform the country.

The strength of the CP had been shown in the (white) election held on 6 September 1989. It won 39 seats (out of 166), with over 30 per cent of the votes cast. The CP had not made much progress since the 1987 election in which it won 27 per cent of the vote, but, disquietingly for the

NP, it won 40 per cent of the votes in the Transvaal and 46 per cent in the Orange Free State, which suggested that up to 50 per cent of Afrikaners had supported it. Moreover, for the first time since the 1961 election, the NP won fewer than 50 per cent of all the votes cast. It underlined what had been apparent for much of the decade, namely that Afrikaner nationalism was irrevocably split.

De Klerk campaigned vigorously in the election campaign on a reform platform of six goals: normalizing the political process; removing racial discrimination; negotiating a new constitution; promoting economic growth; maintaining law and order; and building bridges to other communities. De Klerk expressed satisfaction with the result and declared that he now had a mandate for reform; but there had been no mention during the campaign of exactly how far-reaching his reforms, notably the unbanning of the ANC, would go.

Two factors assisted de Klerk: first, the vexed issue of Namibia had been settled, demonstrating that even apparently intractable conflicts could be resolved by negotiation; second, the collapse of the Berlin Wall in November signified the end of communist rule in much of Eastern Europe, eliminating a source of the anti-communist paranoia that had provided the rationale for much of past repression.

The road ahead was strewn with obstacles. Botha had pulled down major pillars of apartheid and de Klerk would finish the job. To carry a majority of whites with him would require a superhuman effort.

Notes

1 Ivor Wilkins and Hans Strydom, *The Super-Afrikaners: Inside the Afrikaner Broederbond* (Johannesburg: Jonathan Ball, 1978), p.214.

2 J.J.J. Scholtz (ed.), *Vegter en Hervormer* (Cape Town: Tafelberg Press, 1988), p.33 (translation).

3 *Idem*, pp.16–7 (translation).

4 Dirk and Johanna de Villiers, *PW* (Cape Town: Tafelberg Press, 1984), p.125.

5 *Idem*, p.194 (translation).

6 Scholtz, *Vegter en Hervormer*, pp.27–8.

7 *Idem*, p.53 (translation).

8 *Report of the Committee for Constitutional Affairs of the President's Council on an Urbanisation Strategy for the Republic of South Africa*: PC 3/1985 (Cape Town: Government Printer), p.34.

9 The Commonwealth Group of Eminent Persons, *Mission to South Africa: The Commonwealth Report* (London: Penguin Books, 1986).

10 *Rapport* (Johannesburg), 22 June 2008 (translation).

11 Annette Seegers, *The Military in the Making of Modern South Africa* (London: I.B. Taurus, 1996), pp.163–5.

12 *Race Relations Survey 1989–90* (Johannesburg: South African Institute of Race Relations, 1990), p.195.

13 *Report of the Truth and Reconciliation Commission* (Cape Town, 1998), Vol. 2, p.221.

14 Coleman, *Crime against Humanity*, pp.247–51.

15 Nelson Mandela, *Long Walk to Freedom: The Autobiography of Nelson Mandela, (Boston, MA: Little, Brown, 1994)* p.519.

16 Afrikanerbond, *Bearer of an Ideal 1918–1997* (Johannesburg, 1997), para.7.2.4.

17 Robin Renwick, *Unconventional Diplomacy in Southern Africa* (London: Macmillan, 1997), pp.117–18.

18 For an account of the cabinet meeting see Daan Prinsloo, *Stem uit die Wildernis: 'n biografie oor oud-pres. PW Botha* (Mossel Bay: Vaandel Publishers, 1997), pp.390–419.

19 F.W. de Klerk, *The Last Trek – A New Beginning: The Autobiography* (London: Macmillan, 1998), p.116.

CHAPTER 3

The decline and resurrection of black opposition

For many Africans the NP's victory in 1948 seemed irrelevant: both the victors and the losers were committed to segregation: as Albert Lutuli, soon to become ANC leader, said, '[i]t did not seem of much importance whether the whites gave us more Smuts or switched to Malan'.[1] Sadly, they would soon learn that it *did* make a difference. Apartheid was an altogether more comprehensive and ruthless system of enforcing racial inequality.

From 1948 to 1960 was a tough time for all black opponents of apartheid. As the narrative will show, no black organization was strong enough to resist the tidal wave of discriminatory and other repressive measures that the government imposed. Hard though it tried, the ANC could do little more than protest. It was a reactive response since the overbearing control exerted by government made seizing the initiative virtually impossible.

During the war years the ANC had undergone significant changes. Under the leadership of Dr A. B. Xuma its internal organization and financial situation had been tightened up, though in both respects it remained weak. As in many colonial situations, the exigencies of war had created new conditions, both material and psychological. The pass laws, for example, had been suspended for several years with a resulting spurt of urbanization; and the absence of many white males on active service had created gaps that were filled by blacks.

The ANC had been heartened by the signing of the Atlantic Charter, which seemed to hold out the promise of a new world order based upon respect for human rights and 'the right of all peoples to choose the form of government under which they will live'. Moreover, the war had been fought against the most appalling form of racism yet seen, and one of its consequences was a strengthening of hostility to racism worldwide.

The ANC's response to the Atlantic Charter was to draft its own application of the Charter's precepts, entitled *Africans' Claims in South Africa*, which was adopted in December 1943. It spelled out in detail the impact of inequality on the lives of Africans, and demanded the extension of the rights listed in the Charter. The demands included the abolition of all discriminatory legislation and the extension of full citizenship rights, including the franchise, to all adults. The comprehensiveness and firmness of *Africans' Claims* broke new ground for the ANC. It was its first unambiguous demand for universal adult suffrage.

For most of its history the ANC had been a dignified, sober and cautious body that avoided confrontational stances. That, too, was changing. The formation in 1943–4 of the ANC Youth League (ANCYL) was the forerunner of a concerted effort by young professionals to shake the ANC out of what they regarded as its torpor. The Youth League's founder members included names that became famous in subsequent years: Oliver Tambo, Nelson Mandela, Walter Sisulu, A.P. Mda and Anton Lembede. Lembede was the brightest star in an impressive firmament.

Coming from humble rural origins, Lembede achieved a master's degree in philosophy and also trained as a lawyer. Collectively, the YL would act as a ginger group within the ANC, succeeding even in becoming the tail that wagged the dog. Lembede was an articulate exponent of a strand of ANC thought that ran counter to the dominant inclusivist tendency of the ANC mainstream. Lembede's themes emphasized a specifically African nationalism based around the uniqueness of a particular African personality and set of cultural values. Only African nationalism, encompassing all Africans, could achieve freedom.

Lembede, foreshadowing later arguments associated with the Black Consciousness movement, argued that white rule had had a severe effect on African psyches, apart from its material impact. In ways that resembled Afrikaner nationalist analyses of the effect of conquest and British overlordship on Afrikaners, Lembede wrote of the inferiority complex and the wish to emulate whites that characterized many Africans. Lembede died in 1947 at a young age. There is no knowing what his trajectory in the ANC might have been had he lived, but he surely would have been a major figure.

The 'Africanism' of the YL expressed itself in various ways, the most notable of which was a fierce anti-communism, directed against the emerging alliance with the Communist Party (and with individual communists after the Party was banned in 1950), and opposition to cooperation with non-Africans. The YL was also militant, more militant than the cautious Xuma approved. He was accordingly voted out of office, to be replaced by another medical doctor, James Moroka, who, the YL (wrongly) hoped, would be more receptive to their urgent demands for greater militancy.

This was achieved in December 1949 when the ANC's annual conference adopted the Programme of Action, the key clause of which expressed the ANC's resolve to work for:

a *The abolition of all differential political institutions the boycotting of which we accept and to undertake a campaign to educate our people on this issue and, in addition, to employ the following weapons: immediate and active boycott, strike, civil disobedience, non-co-operation and such other means as may bring about the accomplishment and realization of our aspirations.*

b *Preparations and making of plans for a national stoppage of work for one day as mark of protest against the reactionary policy of the Government.²*

This was a milestone in the history of the ANC. It heralded the end of deputations, delegations and participation in powerless advisory bodies. By adopting methods pioneered in South Africa by no less than Mahatma Gandhi himself in his South African days – and followed up by the Natal and Transvaal Indian Congresses – the ANC was close to stepping across the line of legality, albeit with strictly nonviolent methods.

The one-day stayaway on 26 June 1950, mentioned in (b) of the Programme, was patchily supported. It had been preceded by a day of demonstrations on 1 May, which ended in disaster, when police opened fire on demonstrators in and around Johannesburg, resulting in 18 fatalities. Ironically, both the police and the Africanists blamed communists for organizing the protests. The involvement of whites and Indians in what the Africanists regarded as purely ANC issues would fester throughout the 1950s.

An ambitious campaign to protest against unjust laws by refusing to obey them was launched on 26 June 1952. It had been conceived by the ANC and the Indian Congress – again, to the dismay of the Africanists, many of whom harboured sharp anti-Indian prejudices. The major thrust of the Defiance Campaign was for volunteers deliberately to ignore the 'Europeans Only' signs found on every official building and on trains and buses. Other targets included curfew and pass regulations. Volunteers had been given training: they were not to resist arrest – indeed, they were to court it; and once arrested, they were not to seek bail or to pay a fine. The hope of the organizers was that the campaign would gradually extend from the cities, eventually involving countrywide mass action, including industrial action.

The government regarded the challenge to its authority in a serious light. It was the first major campaign that deliberately transgressed the law. Some 8,500 volunteers eventually participated, mostly from the Eastern Cape, which had long been an ANC stronghold. By November 1952, however, the Campaign was fizzling out, amidst riots in Port Elizabeth, East London, Kimberley and Johannesburg. Thirty-four people, including six whites, were killed in the violence.

Why did the violence occur when the resisters had shown remarkable discipline and restraint? Lutuli, who was intimately involved in the organization of the campaign, says of the violence:

We watched these developments with horror. This sense of horror is not lessened by our understanding of how these outbursts of violence may come about. The policies pursued by the whites make this sort of thing inevitable. Every so often the yoke becomes unendurable, something explodes, and for a while blind resentment takes control. The conditions which lead to these tragedies are carefully kept in existence by the majority of white South Africans. They react with horror at the outcome of their lust for white domination. But they will do nothing to remove the root cause.[3]

It is difficult to fault Lutuli's analysis. Many Africans were undoubtedly cowed by the might of the state, but underneath the apparent submissiveness was anger that, if sufficiently provoked, could cause the abandonment of restraint. This would be especially so in crowd situations in times of heightened political tension, such as during the Defiance Campaign. Many of those who represented the state's power were police, often young Afrikaners who shared the prevailing prejudices of the white community. They were obliged to enforce the oppressive laws that upheld white rule. In later years black police were increasingly employed in black areas. They provoked even greater resentment because they were deemed to be collaborators with a hated system.

The Defiance Campaign brought mixed results for the ANC and its allies. It raised the ANC's national profile and led to an increase of its paid-up membership from less than 10,000 to some 100,000, though this figure was not sustained. The Campaign, moreover, was widely reported in the foreign and domestic press, putting South Africa's racial policies under the spotlight.

On the other hand, the Campaign played into the hands of the NP, helping it to win an increased majority in the 1953 election. The Party took the opportunity to enact tough legislation in an attempt to curb future campaigns of civil disobedience; and when a court acquitted the accused who had illegally entered a 'Europeans Only' waiting room on grounds that the separate facilities for 'Non-Europeans' were not equal, a law, the Reservation of Separate Amenities Act, 1953, was passed, providing that separate amenities did not have to be equal. This became a common response when sympathetic judges found loopholes in the law: block the loophole by legislative means.

In addition, the government was making more extensive use of the arbitrary powers it had assumed under the Suppression of Communism Act of 1950. Apart from proscribing the Communist Party, the Act empowered the Minister of Justice to restrict or ban persons deemed to be communists or furthering the aims of communism, 'communism' being defined so widely as to encompass a wide range of activities aimed at pressing for political, economic or social change. 'Banned' individuals were generally prevented from attending gatherings, belonging to particular organizations, and con-fined to a particular area. Over time, the range of restrictions was substantially widened. Banning orders had initially been imposed particularly on trade union officials, but from 1952 they were used against ANC and other leaders in the Congress Alliance. By 1956 over 70 individuals (including 54 Africans) had been banned.[4]

Significant changes took place in the ANC. Moroka had been deposed from the leadership, to be replaced by Lutuli. Moroka had effectively sold the pass when prosecuted for his involvement in the Defiance Campaign. Lutuli was made of sterner stuff, choosing to continue his ANC activities, even if it meant his being removed from his chieftainship of a small community (or 'tribe') at Groutville, north of Durban. After his dismissal as chief, Lutuli made a statement that became famous in the annals of the ANC. It included a striking (and oft-cited) paragraph:

In so far as gaining citizenship rights and opportunities for the unfettered development of the African people, who will deny that thirty years of my life have been spent knocking in vain, patiently, moderately and modestly at a closed and barred door?[5]

Lutuli's presidency was severely handicapped by repeated banning orders that confined him to Groutville for much of the time. He was honoured in December 1961 with the award of the Nobel Peace Prize.

The ANC could claim limited success in the Defiance Campaign, and then only as a consciousness-raising exercise. Subsequent efforts at protest in the early 1950s failed to halt the spate of discriminatory legislation. It could not stop the Western Areas Removal Scheme, whereby small freehold areas, such as Sophiatown (near Johannesburg), were disestablished and their inhabitants removed to Soweto; even more cataclysmic in its efforts on African schoolchildren was the Bantu Education Act of 1953, against which the ANC launched a boycott, and even an attempt to set up unofficial rival schools. But it was a hopeless task. The apartheid juggernaut was too strong.

The spurt in membership of the ANC tailed off after 1953. Despite the efforts of its leadership, which was being crippled by laws, the ANC remained a weak organization, chronically short of funds, lacking paid organizers and a press. Its latent support in most of the bigger urban centres was considerable, but it was difficult to mobilize this into active support. Being an activist carried obvious dangers, including loss of employment, banning, banishment from an urban area, and other forms of harassment.

In his presidential address to the Cape ANC in August 1953, Z.K. Matthews, a professor at Fort Hare University College and the senior African academic in the country, appealed for the convening of 'a congress of the people' to draw up a Freedom Charter for the democratic South Africa of the future. The proposal captured the imagination of the ANC and its allies and eventually bore fruit at the Congress of the People, held at Kliptown (near Johannesburg) on 25 and 26 June 1955.

Much of the previous year had gone into organizing the Congress. In principle, the aim was to distil popular grievances into a charter that reflected popular goals. Collecting the grievances was a marathon effort: supposedly, thousands of grievances, written on scraps of paper or transcribed by volunteers, were collected, whereafter the drafting of the Freedom Charter began. How many slips of paper there were, how many individuals responded, and what their proposals for redress were, is not known because the trunk in which they were stored went missing. The actual drafting was entrusted to Rusty Bernstein, a former member of the Communist Party. He was at pains to insist that he had not imposed his own views on the draft.[6]

Nearly 3,000 people, mostly African but also some Indians, Coloureds and whites, attended the actual Congress, where the clauses of the Charter were read out, debated and approved. Late in the afternoon of the second day, the Congress was effectively broken by the police, though not before the Charter as a whole had been approved. It later became apparent that the police action was part of the build-up to a major trial of key members of all of the organizations that formed the Congress Alliance.

The importance of the Freedom Charter, which was subsequently accepted by the ANC as its formal policy, is the near-canonical status that it achieved among ANC-aligned groups, especially in the 1980s. It was a poetically written document, drafted to ensure as wide as possible acceptance among the diverse components of the Congress Alliance. The preamble contained the clause 'that South Africa belongs to all who live in it, black and white and that no government can justly claim authority unless it is based on the will of all the people'. 'The people' were diverse: another clause was headed 'All national groups shall have equal rights', and provided that there would be equal status of all such groups in public institutions, courts and schools, and all people would have equal rights to use their own language and develop their own cultures.

The economic clauses provided that 'The People shall share in the country's wealth.' This involved some measure of nationalization: 'The mineral wealth beneath the soil, the banks and monopoly industry shall be transferred to the ownership of the people as a whole.' Land, moreover, was to be 'redivided amongst those who work it, to banish famine and land hunger'.

The remaining clauses of the Charter presented orthodox liberal goals, including equality before the law, equal human rights, and several that accorded with the principles of a welfare state.

The terms of the Charter attracted immediate criticism from the Africanists within the ANC, who had already objected to the role that non-African communists had played in the run-up to the Congress of the People. They now took umbrage to the use of the term 'national groups', which was an implicit repudiation of the Africanist demand 'Africa for the Africans'. It drove a further wedge between them and the mainstream ANC.

The Liberal Party, founded in 1953, and led by Alan Paton, was torn between its desire to identify with African demands and its apprehension that the Congress of the People had been manipulated by communists. The Party's initial enthusiasm faded, as the organizers ignored its suggestions for making the Congress more representative. Many members of the Party were staunchly anti-communist, and their view that there was a danger of being sucked into a communist-inspired 'united front' was widespread.[7] Probably, communists and their fellow-travellers were not greatly distressed by the Liberals' non-participation, regarding them as rivals in the quest for ideological supremacy.

The economic clauses, cited above, sparked considerable controversy – and the avid attention of the security police was clear evidence that the Charter was a blueprint for a Marxist-Leninist state. Nationalization of key industries and what could have been interpreted as a proposal to collectivize agriculture were avowedly socialist issues, although Mandela insisted, to the ire of some of the hardline communists, that the nationalization clauses were intended to achieve no more than a basis on which a black bourgeoisie could develop. Again, whatever interpretation was placed on these clauses, it was not the blueprint that the security police and, subsequently, the prosecution in the Treason Trial would allege.

The state's response to the Freedom Charter and the preceding activities of the Congress Alliance was not long in coming. In December 1956 156 members of the component organizations of the Alliance were arrested and charged with treason. The accused included 105 Africans, 23 whites, 21 Indians and 7 Coloureds. The African accused included Albert Lutuli, Z.K. Matthews and Nelson Mandela. All were released on bail.

The trial, including the preparatory examination, dragged on until 1961, with the number of accused steadily being reduced until, eventually, only 28 remained. All were acquitted in a unanimous decision by the three judges, who found that the state had failed to prove the charge that the accused sought to overthrow the state by violent means; moreover, it had not proved that the Freedom Charter was the blueprint for a Marxist-Leninist system.

If the government had hoped that this would be a show trial that demonstrated the perfidy of the ANC and its allies, it had not only been disappointed but embarrassed as well. Despite the presence of handpicked judges, the outcome showed that judicial propriety, in the form of respect for the facts, still prevailed. In the following decades the objectivity of even conservative judges, who were deliberately chosen to preside over political trials, would largely decline. The accused, moreover, had been defended by some of the best advocates in the country. In most future major political trials, too, high-calibre defence would be provided, which could, if only to a limited extent, mitigate the declining quality of an increasingly politicized judiciary. Mandela's comment on the verdict was grimly prescient: 'The lesson [the state] took away was not that we had legitimate grievances but that they needed to be far more ruthless.'[8]

The protracted Treason Trial had seriously disrupted the lives of the accused and their families – and no compensation was paid by the state. The only positive spin-off was that the common ordeal and constant interaction had consolidated the Congress Alliance. Some of the accused commented that the Trial had provided a continuous meeting of the Alliance leadership – at state expense. The Alliance had taken shape in the aftermath of the Defiance Campaign, though its roots lay in earlier cooperation between the ANC, the Communist Party, and the South African Indian Congress. With the banning of the Communist Party in 1950, a number of white ex-members formed the Congress of Democrats in 1952. In addition, the South African Coloured People's Organization and the South African Congress of Trade Unions (formed in 1955) became members of the Alliance. The Communist Party itself regrouped underground in 1953, now calling itself the South African Communist Party (SACP).

The formation of the Alliance brought some advantages to the ANC: it could claim to be more broadly based, even though its allies were far smaller. Even more important, though, was the additional organizational and strategic muscle that the ANC acquired. Its alliance with the SACP was to be crucial after 1960 (when the ANC was banned) since the SACP acted as a conduit with the ANC's major source of foreign assistance, the Soviet Union.

Critics objected that the racial compartmentalization of the Alliance mirrored the official categorization of the population. In particular, the Africanist wing of the ANC vehemently opposed cooperation with non-Africans, especially white and Indian communists. Their fear was that white and Indian involvement would inevitably lead to non-Africans acquiring dominant influence over the ANC, reinforcing Africans' sense of inferiority. The NP government, moreover, could exploit anti-communist hysteria by pointing to the ANC's formal link with the radical Congress of Democrats, many, though not all, of its small membership retaining Marxist sympathies. It should be pointed out that the ANC at this time did not allow membership of non-Africans, but it had long permitted dual membership with African members of the Communist Party.

Africanist discontent festered throughout the 1950s: there were objections to the multiracial organization of both the Defiance Campaign and the Congress of the People. Beginning in 1953 the Africanists published their own broadsheet, which enjoyed wide circulation, especially in Johannesburg. Mandela, Tambo and Sisulu had modified their earlier Africanist views. Working with non-African communists had mellowed Mandela's erstwhile hostility. The Youth League had lost much of its previous influence by the early 1950s, and many leaders had joined the ANC mainstream, accepting the traditional inclusivist traditions. Others, however, continued to uphold the Africanist tradition.

The rising star among the Africanists was Robert Mangaliso Sobukwe, a graduate of Fort Hare, where he had been a leading figure in the Youth League. After some years as a teacher, Sobukwe, now aged 30, was appointed in 1954 as a 'language assistant' in the Department of African Languages at the University of the Witwatersrand, Johannesburg. Although he did not immediately assume a leading public role among the Africanists, who were centred around Orlando (part of Soweto), recognition of his qualities soon pushed him to the fore.

Sobukwe's biographer and friend, Benjamin Pogrund, provides a crisp account of thinking among the Africanists:

Multiracialism was a dirty word to them; they saw it as the means whereby minority whites, and Asians, crept into the liberation struggle and took over control. At a level of principle, they saw it as reinforcing racial thinking, because, even while it posited the coming together of racial groups, it did so on the basis of the existence of different racial groups, thus perpetuating the notion of racial separateness.[9]

Sobukwe personally, as Pogrund and other white friends attested, was not anti-white, but the slogan 'Africa for Africans' that was adopted by the Africanists and the breakaway Pan-Africanist Congress (PAC) lent itself to, and inflamed, anti-white thinking among rank-and-file followers. Few of those on the receiving end of raw racism could appreciate the sophisticated definition, used by Sobukwe, that 'African' included anyone who owed his or her primary loyalty to Africa and was prepared to live under African majority rule.

The breakaway of the Africanists occurred at a tempestuous conference of the Transvaal ANC in November 1958, and led directly to the formation of the PAC in April 1959, with Sobukwe as its president. The proceedings were characterized by an exuberant emotionalism and wildly over-optimistic claims about the PAC's prospects. Indeed, claims were to be made that white supremacy would be toppled by 1963.

The PAC's first initiative was the Status Campaign, demanding courteous treatment for Africans and rejecting the demeaning use of racist terms. It was hoped that Africans' self-respect might be increased, a goal central to Sobukwe's analysis of the 'slave mentality' that burdened the African masses. The second initiative was a far more ambitious campaign against the pass laws to be launched on 21 March 1960. It was to have fateful consequences.

In terms of the call, issued by Sobukwe, men in every city, town and village would leave their passes at home, move to a police station and surrender themselves for arrest: there would be no bail, no defence, and no fine. The campaign was to be strictly nonviolent, and if crowds were asked to disperse they were to do so. Sobukwe even wrote to the Commissioner of Police, urging him to instruct his men to refrain from actions that might lead to violence.

In planning this protest, the PAC had stolen a march on the ANC, which was planning to stage its own countrywide anti-pass campaign, beginning on 31 March and culminating on 26 June with a mass burning of passes. The

ANC had invited the PAC to join the protest, but was turned down. Mandela testily accused the PAC of opportunism that was 'motivated more by a desire to eclipse the ANC than to defeat the enemy'.[10]

By early 1960 there was a mood of expectation among both black and white: the British Prime Minister, Harold Macmillan, had delivered his 'Wind of Change' speech to the South African parliament on 3 February, in which he served notice on the government that aspects of its policy were unacceptable to Britain. The speech was delivered shortly after Verwoerd's announcement that a referendum would be held among white voters to decide on a republic.

As far as Africans were concerned, it must have been evident from what the ANC and the PAC were saying that some kind of showdown with the government was in the offing. Apart from the proposed anti-pass demonstrations, rural protests against the imposition of Bantu Authorities and the enforcement of land betterment schemes were occurring in several Bantustans. In Cato Manor, Durban, nine policemen (four whites and five Africans) were slain by an enraged crowd of Africans on 24 January, in the course of a search for illicit liquor. It was an event that undoubtedly contributed to the jumpiness of the police at Sharpeville on 21 March.

Sharpeville, a township near Vereeniging (some 35 miles south of Johannesburg), was in an area that had been well organized by the PAC, so that the response to the PAC's call was good. Some time after 1 p.m. a crowd, estimated to be between 5,000 and 7,000 (police estimates put the figure at 20,000), gathered around the perimeter fence of the Sharpeville police station. A scuffle at the gate ensued during which one of the police fell over, and the crowd pushed forward. No order to open fire was given, but some of the apprehensive young policemen opened fire: in a short time 67 people were dead or dying, some 70 per cent having been shot in the back. A milestone in South Africa's modern history had been reached.

More disturbances occurred in Cape Town on 21 March, but the main drama took place on 30 March when a column of Africans, estimated to be 30,000-strong, marched from the outlying townships to the centre of the city to demand the release of their leaders who had been arrested in terms of a state of emergency declared on the same day. They were led by a young student, Philip Kgosana, who spoke to the local Divisional Commissioner of Police, requesting a meeting with the Minister of Justice. The officer agreed to convey the request to the minister and requested Kgosana to persuade the crowd to disperse – which he did. When Kgosana returned later in the day for his anticipated meeting he was promptly arrested – and never got to see the minister, who, in any case, would have been utterly unsympathetic.

The ANC, horrified by the shootings, had called for a national day of mourning, including a stayaway from work, on 28 March. This was supported by the PAC. The stayaway was widely supported largely by Africans in Cape Town, Johannesburg and Port Elizabeth.

By mid-April, the state of emergency, during which some 20,000 persons had been detained, had largely succeeded in clamping down on protest. The pass laws, which had triggered the original protest, were suspended on 26 March, causing many to hope that they could never be reimposed; but it was a vain hope: by 10 April they were being enforced once again.

The costs of Sharpeville and other clashes was high: over 80 people had been killed and hundreds injured. Legislation to ban both the ANC and the PAC was rushed through parliament in April with the support of the official opposition. It marked the end of an era, and the beginning of a new one that would involve the use of violence.

For Sobukwe, who had done his best to ensure that there would be no violence, the events were also a personal tragedy. He was convicted of incitement and sentenced to three years' imprisonment. At the end of his sentence he became the victim of new legislation that enabled the state to keep individuals convicted of political offences in indefinite custody. In a perverse way it was a mark of the government's respect for Sobukwe's qualities as an opponent of apartheid. Under the terms of the 'Sobukwe clause', as the new legislation was dubbed, he was incarcerated in a house on Robben Island, where he remained for six years. On release in 1969 he was allowed to rejoin his family in Kimberley, but only under severe restrictions that included 12-hour house arrest. He opened a law practice in 1975, but died of cancer in February 1978 at the young age of 54. None of his successors could match Sobukwe's stature and commanding authority, which is part of the reason why the PAC in exile was perennially rent by squabbling factions.

Sharpeville was undoubtedly a serious blow to the confidence and self-esteem of the NP, which was further rocked by the unsuccessful attempt on Verwoerd's life on 9 April by a mentally disturbed white farmer. The South African government was subject to universal condemnation for its racial policy, and activists were beginning to advocate sanctions, while some in South Africa were pondering whether the time had not come to adopt violent means of opposition.

There had been murmurings in the ANC since the collapse of the Defiance Campaign about the necessity of reconsidering nonviolence. The failure of protests, demonstrations and stayaways for the remainder of the 1950s appeared to confirm these misgivings. If nonviolence was habitually met with the state's violence it seemed logical to suppose that violence would be the only effective weapon.

After its banning, the ANC slowly regrouped underground. Tambo had been ordered into exile by his colleagues – and managed to escape from South Africa shortly after Sharpeville; and Lutuli was confined to the relatively isolated village of Groutville and was hardly capable of playing a leading role in clandestine counsels of the Alliance. The *de facto* leadership of the ANC fell increasingly on Mandela's shoulders.

The decision to engage in limited forms of violence was taken at a secret meeting of the ANC's National Executive Committee in July 1961. Mandela offers a vivid account:

At the meeting I argued that the state had given us no alternative to violence. I said it was wrong and immoral to subject our people to armed attacks by the state without offering them some kind of alternative. I mentioned again that people on their own had taken up arms. Violence would begin whether we initiated it nor not. Would it not be better to guide this violence ourselves, according to principles where we saved lives by attacking symbols of oppression, and not people? If we did not take the lead now . . . we would soon be latecomers and followers to a movement we did not control.[11]

Mandela had correctly anticipated that Lutuli, who was present, would oppose such an argument, being deeply steeped in the ANC's tradition of nonviolence. But, wrote Mandela, 'we worked on him the whole night', and eventually he acquiesced in the conclusion that a military campaign was inevitable, saying 'If anyone thinks I'm a pacifist, let him try to take my chickens, and he will know how wrong he is!'[12]

Agreement was reached that what was to become *Umkhonto we Sizwe* – the Spear of the Nation (known simply as MK) – would be a separate and independent organ, linked to the ANC and under the overall control of the ANC, but fundamentally autonomous. It was hoped that this organizational stratagem would shield ordinary ANC members and the Alliance partners that were not banned from being compromised by association with MK and, hence, liable to prosecution. The policy of the ANC could still be presented as nonviolent.

During the Rivonia trial (see below) in April 1964, Mandela provided a detailed exposition of MK's aims and its proposed methods: it had opted for sabotage, avoiding, at least for the time being, guerrilla warfare, terrorism or open revolution. Sabotage of government and other symbolic structures would not involve loss of life and would minimize racial bitterness. He quoted from MK's Manifesto, which was before the court as an exhibit:

We of Umkhonto We Sizwe have always sought to achieve liberation without bloodshed and civil clash [sic]. We hope, even at this late hour, that our first actions will awaken everyone to a realization of the disastrous situation to which the Nationalist policy is leading. We hope that it will bring the Government and its supporters to their senses before it is too late, so that both the Government and its policies can be changed before matters reach the desperate stage of civil war.

He proceeded to argue that South Africa was heavily dependent on foreign trade and capital: destruction of power plants and interference with rail and telephone communications would not only scare away foreign capital but also be a heavy drain on the economy 'thus compelling the voters of the country to reconsider their position'.[13]

Initially MK had a membership of some 250 persons – of all races, though mostly Africans. In this respect it was unlike the ANC, which did not admit non-Africans to membership until 1969. Many of the non-African recruits to MK were also members of the SACP, several of whose white members had had Second World War experience with the South African army.

In the first 18 months from MK's first attacks in mid-December 1961 some 200 cases of sabotage were recorded, mostly on a small scale, but occurring in most of the major cities and some smaller towns. Most of these attacks adhered to MK guidelines, but some did not, suggesting a lack of discipline among some units.[14]

The founders of MK were over-optimistic – or naïve – in their hopes that their efforts would make white opinion more amenable to redressing black grievances. On the contrary, as the draconian legislation to counter saboteurs showed, MK's very existence hardened white opinion. A second misreading of the state's capacity to hit back was an underestimation of the diligence and ruthlessness of the security police. The fact that they were armed with new powers by the security legislation, able with apparent ease to recruit informers or 'turn' detainees, and capable of mounting sustained surveillance of known activists, made them a formidable enemy. None but the toughest of detainees could withstand the torture that was increasingly used to break them.

Rusty Bernstein, a leading figure in the SACP and one of the accused in the Rivonia trial (see below), wrote:

Torture of detainees in order to extract information became routine; reports told of victims reduced to the state of zombies by prolonged sleep deprivation during which they had talked involuntarily and without consciousness, like sleep-walkers. Some of the best of our comrades had cracked under torture. No one could be certain what places or information remained secret, what had been involuntarily given away. We had not been prepared for institutionalized torture.

Our codes of conduct were based on our mutual determination to take the consequences of silence regardless of the penalties. They had served us well for years – but they could not survive the new combination of sleep deprivation and physical torture. Information was leaking out – but no one knew what.[15]

Opposition activists would have to face similar dangers until the eventual fall of apartheid. Informers were an additional hazard: they were able to penetrate to the very core of both legal and illegal organizations, as well as reach those in exile.

Disaster struck some of those in MK's high command on the afternoon of 11 July 1963. They had gathered to discuss an ambitious plan, Operation Mayibuye, whose central thrust was a proposal to ratchet up the relatively modest sabotage campaign by embarking on guerrilla operations. The venue was Lilliesleaf, located in the (then) semi-rural area of Rivonia, north of Johannesburg. It was a small, secluded farm that had been acquired by the SACP as a safe house, but was also used by the MK high command. When the police broke in they found Walter Sisulu, Govan Mbeki, Ahmed Kathrada, Raymond Mhlaba, Rusty Bernstein (who was not an MK member, but was on the central committee of the SACP), and a young barrister, Bob Hepple. Another MK member, Dennis Goldberg, was arrested elsewhere on the property. Mbeki had tried, unsuccessfully, to burn the copy of the plan in a stove.

For the police, it was a treasure trove of highly incriminating documents, virtually certain to lead to conviction and, possibly, the imposition of the death penalty. How exactly the police had rumbled the supposedly safe house is not known. Bernstein suggests that security had become lax: 'in the top MK echelons, there was a growing gung-ho spirit of recklessness'.[16] Possibly a detainee who had visited Lilliesleaf previously, had talked; or possibly a neighbour had seen regular comings and goings of blacks and reported this to the police as 'suspicious'.

Two key members of the high command had not been at Lilliesleaf when the police raided: Mandela was in jail, serving a five-year sentence for incitement, deriving from the call for a three-day strike in May 1961, and also for leaving the country without a passport. Mandela had described himself as the 'prime mover' in the establishment of MK. Another prime mover was Joe Slovo of the SACP, who was fortunate enough to have avoided arrest by being sent out of the country shortly before the fateful raid on Lilliesleaf. He would remain in exile, leading a sometimes dangerous existence, until 1990.

The Rivonia trial was a landmark event in the struggle for black rights.[17] It began on 9 October 1963 and concluded with sentencing on 11 June 1964.

The trial was yet another manifestation of the difficulty, indeed impossibility, of justice being done in an unequal society, in which the laws were enacted by the dominators to frustrate the demands of the dominated. In his previous trial in 1962, Mandela had made the point firmly, saying that:

... a judiciary controlled entirely by Whites and enforcing laws enacted by a White Parliament in which we have no representation, laws which in most cases are passed in the face of unanimous opposition from Africans, cannot be regarded as an impartial tribunal in a political trial where an African stands as an accused.[18]

The court, as in many other cases, was unmoved.

Presiding over the Rivonia trial was Quartus de Wet, Judge-President of the Transvaal Provincial Division of the Supreme Court. He had been appointed to the bench prior to the NP's taking office in 1948, and while he was not a political appointee of the kind that became frequent in following decades, he shared the racial stereotypes of blacks that were common among whites. For the most part he enforced the proprieties that were expected in court, on occasion rebuking Percy Yutar, the prosecutor, whose behaviour was often disgraceful, behaving more like a propagandist for apartheid than an officer of a court.

The accused were defended by an outstanding team of lawyers. Since most of the accused had little option but to acknowledge guilt concerning their involvement in MK, the critical issue was whether the death penalty would be imposed. The judge had at least accepted that the prosecution had failed to prove that Operation Mayibuye's proposal for a broader campaign of violence had been accepted. Nevertheless, the remaining charges were sufficiently serious, in terms of the existing draconian security legislation, to make the death penalty a distinct possibility.

Judge de Wet, however, decided that since the state had not charged the accused with treason, for which the death sentence was mandatory, he could show 'leniency' by imposing life imprisonment on all those convicted, Bernstein having been acquitted. De Wet could not resist an insulting comment in the course of passing judgment:

I am by no means convinced that the motives of the accused were as altruistic as they wish the court to believe. People who organize a revolution usually take over the government, and personal ambition can't be excluded as a motive.[19]

There had not been a shred of evidence to suggest that 'personal ambition' had animated any of the accused. Indeed, what is remarkable about Mandela's speech from the dock before sentence was handed down was his selfless commitment and bravery in his quest for freedom.

In passing it is worth noting the contrast in the treatment of political prisoners between those convicted under apartheid and those Afrikaner militants convicted of anti-government activities in the early 1940s when South Africa was at war. The latter, members of the *Stormjaers*, a component of the paramilitary *Ossewa-Brandwag*, committed far more sabotage than MK had by 1963, and had laid plans for other subversive actions. Over 50 were charged with treason in 1942, but the state's case fell apart when a key witness disappeared, only to be found much later, a broken man.[20] It required little imagination to understand what had happened to him. None of the *Stormjaers* and others (including an Afrikaner Nazi spy) who were convicted of serious offences was executed; and shortly after the NP came to power in 1948 all were released, the Minister of Justice saying that this was an attempt to end the 'rancour of unpleasantness' of the war years. Attempts by defence lawyers in the apartheid era to remind judges that there was some limited precedent for regarding political motivation as a mitigating factor met with scant success.

The Rivonia trial smashed MK, which took more than a decade to regroup with any degree of effectiveness. It also spread dismay and gloom among supporters of the Congress Alliance. The security police were acting with ruthlessness and ferocity in hunting down and prosecuting persons accused of furthering the aims of banned organizations or violating other security laws. In 1963 alone, according to official figures, 2,169 persons had been arrested, of whom 922 were convicted, 421 were acquitted and 104 were awaiting trial. In March 1964 official figures showed that since December 1961, when large-scale sabotage had begun, 62 persons had been convicted of murder, 258 of sabotage and 1,466 of other crimes of a subversive nature. Another 562 persons who would have been charged had fled the country.[21]

After its banning, the PAC had spawned its own violent unit, Poqo. Unlike MK, Poqo was a terrorist organization in the sense that it engaged in indiscriminate attacks on whites and some black alleged collaborators. It arose among angry and alienated young African migrants in the Western Cape, where influx control was enforced with particular harshness. It did not appear to have any coherent strategy apart from indiscriminate killing. Nor did it seem to operate under any effective direction or control by the PAC, whose interim leader, Potlako Leballo, was in exile in Basutoland (now Lesotho). Leballo, whose personality and style of leadership was entirely different from Sobukwe's, was given to wild and exaggerated claims, for instance, that Poqo had 150,000 members and that the PAC would take control of South Africa by 1963. It was also a security slip by him that enabled the security police to round up hundreds of Poqo members. By mid-1964, according to official figures, 1,162 Poqo members had been convicted, including 78 of murder and 269 of sabotage.[22] Poqo's back had been broken, and it petered out over the next few years. Sobukwe was probably horrified by Poqo's tactics, which also contributed in no small measure to his continued incarceration.

By the mid-1960s the government was satisfied that it had rooted out subversion. It could now concentrate on development of the homelands or Bantustans, as they were unofficially termed. The aim was a transparent one: to divert Africans' political aspirations away from representation in the central government to emerging political structures in the homelands. Chiefs were to be the fulcrum of homeland development in accordance with the government's view that these were the natural leaders of the African people. Since the early 1950s an elaborate structure of Bantu Authorities had been established, many chiefs having been won over to acceptance of the system because it offered them greater powers.

One such chief who had eagerly cooperated with the authorities was Kaiser D. Matanzima, paramount chief of the Emigrant Thembu people of Transkei. He was the nephew of Nelson Mandela, although Mandela was considerably younger, and the two men had enjoyed a warm relationship, especially when both were students at Fort Hare.

Another route was followed by Mangosuthu Buthelezi, a young Zulu chief, who played a cat-and-mouse game with the authorities by refusing to accept Bantu Authorities on grounds that the members of his clan, the Buthelezi, had rejected the system. Rejection angered the government, which made several attempts, all unsuccessful, to remove him from the chieftainship, even, it was rumoured, by means of assassination.[23] Although a strong Zulu traditionalist, Buthelezi was also well educated, and regarded himself as an ANC supporter, aligned with that strand of the ANC symbolized by Lutuli, whom Buthelezi regarded as his mentor.

The first stage of Transkei's 'independence' (granted in 1976) began in November 1963 with elections to a Legislative Assembly consisting of 45 elected members and 64 chiefs. The result showed that a clear majority of voters favoured the opposition to Matanzima, but that a majority of the chiefs (encouraged by a little arm-twisting by officials) supported Matanzima's election by the Legislative Assembly to the position of chief minister.

Only three other Bantustans followed Transkei's example of accepting independence: Bophuthatswana (1977), Venda (1979) and Ciskei (1981). None could be described as a credible democracy enjoying legitimacy among their ethnically based electorates. Moreover, relatively few of their citizens based in 'white' South Africa turned out to vote.

Two Bantustan leaders, Enos Mabuza of KaNgwane and Buthelezi of KwaZulu, flatly refused to take independence. Mabuza even aligned himself with the ANC. KwaZulu was a different matter because in population terms it was the biggest of the Bantustans, with its citizenry (resident and non-resident) accounting for some 25 per cent of the total African population. Buthelezi's refusal was a blow to the government, creating a big hole in its aspirations to have at least a majority of (white and non-African) citizens in the 'white' areas, with Africans being required to accept citizenship of their respective Bantustans and therefore ineligible for political rights in the 'white' areas. It was a fantasy, and Buthelezi's obduracy underlined its absurdity.

By the late 1960s Buthelezi had at least contributed to breaking the vacuum in black political resistance and carved a niche for himself as a significant national player. His ability to use his position as chief minister of KwaZulu gave him a degree of invulnerability to state repression which he used to launch attacks on apartheid. His relationships with successive white leaders and their ministers were invariably frosty.

Inevitably, though, Buthelezi's strategy of working within official structures provoked controversy: should one collaborate with the intention of subverting those structures from within or boycott them? In some respects it was a mirror image of debates among Afrikaners who recognized that apartheid had failed: did you continue to work inside the structures of Afrikaner nationalism trying to effect change, or did you break and join the opposition? Mandela, while expressing his abhorrence of Bantustans, nevertheless argued that they should be used to give a platform to ANC policies. During the 1980s when relations between Buthelezi's party, Inkatha, and the ANC had soured, the issue became one largely of academic interest (see below page 98).

Another major force arose in the late 1960s that also contributed to breaking the vacuum of black politics. This was the phenomenon of Black Consciousness (BC), pre-eminently associated with the name of Steve Biko. The central thrust of BC was its aim to liberate black minds from the psychological shackles of white domination. As Biko put it, 'the most potent weapon in the hands of the oppressor is the mind of the oppressed'.[24] It was not a new insight; many similar ideas had been propagated by Lembede and Sobukwe, as well as foreign writers like Fanon.

The argument was that blacks, dominated and regimented by whites, were continually subjected to laser-like messages sent out by white authorities and individuals that proclaimed their inferiority. For example, every 'Whites Only' sign sent out such a message, as did the rude white official who insulted African men by calling them 'boys'. Blacks, cowed by the weight of oppression, internalized the messages, which reinforced their submissiveness. BC's first step, according to Biko, was

. . . to make the black man come to himself; to pump back life into his empty shell; to infuse him with pride and dignity, to remind him of his complicity in the crime of allowing himself to be misused and therefore letting evil reign supreme in the country of his birth.[25]

'Black' in BC's vocabulary referred less to skin colour than to the common status of population groups that were discriminated against. The term 'non-white' was rejected, since being the negative of a supposedly superior group was demeaning. But, unlike the PAC and the ANCYL of the 1940s, 'black' included Coloured and Indian people as well, who, despite their often racist attitudes to Africans, were nevertheless victims of oppression. 'Non-white' was reserved as a term of abuse for blacks who collaborated with 'the system'.

The significance of BC is that it led to a significant remobilization of blacks after the bleak 1960s. There was a direct causal link between its emergence and the Soweto Uprising of 1976.

Its first organizational vehicle, the South African Students' Organization (SASO), formed in 1969, resulted from dissatisfaction with multiracial, though white-led, student organizations, the National Union of South African Students and the University Christian Movement. Racially mixed bodies became taboo for BC adherents, the reasoning being that whites, by virtue of their superior education and resources, would inevitably gravitate to leadership positions. Some of BC's sharpest barbs were reserved for white liberals and radicals, who were deemed to be generally arrogant and patronizing. It was, in any event, impossible for whites, however well disposed, to identify totally with the black cause since they could not experience the crushing burden of racial oppression and could always retreat into the comfort zone of racial privilege. White liberals, then, should forget about assisting blacks and con-centrate on fighting injustice in white society.

In Biko's view, black solidarity was to be built up until it could engage its white counterpart on an equal basis: whites would eventually have to accept the inevitable and negotiate. He explained this by means of an Hegelian synthesis:

The thesis is in fact a strong white racism and therefore, the antithesis to this must, ipso-facto, be a strong solidarity amongst blacks on whom this white racism seeks to prey. Out of these two situations we can therefore hope to reach some kind of balance – a true humanity where power politics will have no place.[26]

If this was anticipating a future deadlock between the contending forces it was an accurate prediction of what was already in the making; but the thought that power politics would have no place was misplaced, unless it meant that neither side would be able to dominate the other.

The BC theorists rejected the analysis of the South African conflict as one essentially of class, which the ANC, under the influence of the SACP, accepted. There could be no class solidarity between black and white workers since the latter were the most ardent defenders of the racial order. Moreover, for purposes of mobilization, the appeal to race or 'blackness' was more likely to have resonance among the masses than any alternative which removed (or diluted) race from the equation. But inflaming racial passions was a dangerous strategy. The more sophisticated and intellectually acute leaders of the BC movement might abjure a black counter-racism, but would the rank and file? Just as many followers of the PAC did not share Sobukwe's subtle understanding of the word 'African', so the black youth – or many of them – would interpret the BC message as anti-white, which in the South Africa of apartheid was hardly a cause for surprise.

The preceding overview has begged the critical question of why BC emerged when it did, and why it grew like a veld fire.[27] It had picked up and incorporated themes enunciated by earlier movements, but what was the driving force of the late 1960s and 1970s?

Partly it was a generational phenomenon: the drivers of BC were virtually all young people in their 20s, many of them students at the 'bush colleges,' the derogatory term for the ethnic university colleges set up after 1959, but also at the University of Natal's segregated medical school in Durban. Biko and several other leading figures studied there, although Biko's activism had caused neglect of his studies that led to his exclusion. These institutions were the ideal hot-house environments for debate and for the growth of furious rejection of their subordinate status. This was especially true of the 'bush colleges', where harsh restrictions were enforced and most of the teaching staff as well as the rectors were dedicated Afrikaner nationalists. What was crucial was the rapid growth of student numbers.

The age cohort of those in their early 20s had spent their entire life under apartheid: they had grown up in harsh, impoverished circumstances, and seen for themselves how their fathers could be humiliated by policemen or other officials, and their mothers subjected to the additional burden of carrying passes. Then there had been Sharpeville, followed by the banning of the ANC and PAC, mass arrests and the Rivonia trial, all of which would have been discussed in families, schools, and, perhaps especially, by young black students. Despite the African tradition of respect for the elders, many in the younger cohort began to question why the older generation had been reduced to craven submissiveness.

Local circumstances were a powerful goad, but so was the international context: decolonization was proceeding apace in Africa, South Africa's abhorrent system was increasingly the focus of international condemnation, and, of course, in the late 1960s student protest had erupted in many countries. In the United States, the civil rights movement had taken off: Eldridge Cleaver, the Black Panthers, the notion of Black Power, and the writings of luminaries such as Fanon, Aime Cesaire and others were widely absorbed (despite censorship).

In short, South Africa had become a flammable environment for the genesis of a new round of black protest. Biko and his colleagues provided the spark. Neither the ANC or the PAC had anything to do with the rise and spread of BC. The ANC was worried at the prospect that a formidable rival could develop, one, moreover, whose philosophy was regarded, especially by Marxists, as crude (because it rejected class analysis) and was liable to degenerate into anti-white racism. Biko, who came from a PAC-oriented family, was determined that the BC movement would not align itself with either organization, insisting that both the ANC and the PAC were important movements in the history of black people, and that Mandela and Sobukwe were the 'true leaders' of the people. He personally wanted the ANC, PAC and the BC movement to unite as one liberation movement.[28]

At the ANC's National Executive Committee, held in Lusaka in June 1985, Tambo praised the BC movement's contribution to the liberation struggle, while criticizing the limitations of its view that the struggle was racial. He added that by 1976 the ANC had decided that it was time to meet Biko, who, he said, acknowledged that he and his colleagues now recognized the ANC as the leader of the revolution and that the Black People's Convention (a confederal political organization established in 1971–2) should function within the context of the ANC's strategy. Tambo further disclosed that attempts to meet Biko in 1976 and 1977 had failed.[29]

The Black People's Convention, initiated by SASO, was intended primarily as an umbrella organization for a variety of groups whose memberships were generally older than SASO members. In January 1972 an ad hoc committee, chaired by Drake Koka, a trade unionist, released a statement saying that there had been for far too long 'a political vacuum in the black community'. The new organization, formally launched in July 1972, included among its aims: the liberation and emancipation of blacks from psychological and physical oppression; the reorientation of theology in order to make religion relevant to the aspirations of black people; the formulation and application of the principles of BC and Black Communalism and an education policy designed by blacks for blacks. The Black People's Convention was to operate openly as an overt people's movement that aimed at a target of 1 million members in three years.[30]

The influence of BC extended into various fields, including churches, drama, poetry, community development, health projects and, to a limited extent, trade unions. SASO, in particular, initiated a programme for leadership development in collaboration with the Black People's Convention. This led to the formation of a network of youth organizations across the country.

SASO's influence in conscientizing students was clearly seen in the wave of campus protests and boycotts in mid-1972. They had been triggered by a speech delivered by O.R. Tiro on 29 April 1972 at a graduation ceremony held at the University of the North. Tiro, who was chairman of the SASO branch on campus, attacked the system of Bantu education and apartheid in general – and was promptly expelled by the university authorities. Boycotts and other protests followed at other black universities and higher educational institutions, followed in turn by expulsions. SASO's statement, on 14 May 1972, called for a boycott of these universities and other institutions that would force them to close down. It declared 'that this can be escalated into a major confrontation with the authorities'.[31]

In an analysis of the crisis Ben Khoapa, Director of Black Community Programmes (an offshoot of the BC movement), wrote:

Black students are increasingly resisting efforts to get them to co-operate in their own educational genocide. No longer can they be contained by white rhetoric; nor can they be seduced into rejecting the interests of their own people. They have learnt what a large number of black people are beginning to learn from our young people that the revolution is not over and it is not just beginning, it's continually with us. The struggle is the educational struggle . . .[32]

Khoapa's comment about the 'educational struggle' was a significant indication of where major conflicts would be contested. Apart from the pass laws, education was the most galling issue for blacks, uniting the younger generation with many of their elders in rejection of a patently unequal and oppressive system.

The crisis of mid-1972 was the first time in which SASO had bared its teeth on a national scale. Moreover, its call for boycotts had stirred Indian and Coloured students into cooperating with their African counterparts. Boycotts were staged at the (Indian) University of Durban-Westville and the (Coloured) University of the Western Cape.

In line with the BC slogan 'Black Man, you're on your own,' a principal focus of the BC movement was development of communities and individuals. These programmes sought to promote self-reliance and the avoidance of dependency and exploitation of 'victim status'. Mamphela Ramphele, a key SASO activist and close associate of Biko, has written a tough-minded analysis of these programmes:

The dual onslaught of political impotence, induced by state repression, and economic dependency, resulting from poverty and welfarism, wrought havoc on the self-image of Black South Africans, who lost self-confidence as a people. Some even began to believe that they deserved the oppression they suffered because of innate inferiority.[33]

The case studies she describes enjoyed varying success, although the comprehensive banning of all BC-related organizations in 1977 prevented any hope of the progammes reaching maturation by instilling sustainable self-reliance in the communities involved. The model used in the experiments, however, was certainly on the right tracks, even if the young SASO idealists underestimated the difficulties they would encounter.

In one respect, however, success was substantially achieved: the leadership training programme for youth organizations. It had particular relevance for members of the South African Students' Movement, effectively an offshoot of SASO for high school pupils. According to Ramphele, youth who had undergone these programmes spearheaded the Soweto Uprising in 1976. She adds that BC managed to succeed in empowering individuals at all levels, a success that had a multiplier effect on the wider black community.[34]

It is, of course, difficult to estimate the extent of the multiplier effect, or how far the BC veld fire actually burned. Few rural communities, urban migrants who lived in hostels together with fellow rural migrants, and those of an older generation with loyalties to the older movements would have readily responded to the blandishments of the BC messages. Nevertheless, sufficient numbers were influenced to form a critical mass.

The government's initial reaction to the BC phenomenon was ambiguous: on the one hand, it applauded the breakaway of blacks from the National Union of South African Students, which it regarded as a dangerous organization; and it also welcomed the BC philosophy as a vindication of its policy that Africans should 'develop along their own lines'. BC had strongly rejected the idea of 'integration' in so far as this implied acceptance of 'white' norms and cultural standards. These initial reactions showed how little BC's aspirations had been understood. On the other hand, there was wariness, a suspicion that those aspects of BC which it welcomed might conceal a powerful new threat.

The crisis on black university campuses in 1972 confirmed these suspicions. Reaction was swift: early in 1973 virtually the entire top echelon of SASO was banned, including Biko. Other bannings followed in the course of the year, most of them connected to SASO and other BC organizations. It was a crippling blow. Harassment, including surveillance, detention and prosecutions were now continuous. Black universities imposed increasingly severe restrictions on student political activity, including banning SASO branches. Hobbled though it was, SASO managed to struggle on. Trials became a way of enabling the accused and defence witnesses to publicize BC.[35]

Events in southern Africa gave the BC movement hope: the coup in Portugal in 1974, followed by the gaining of independence by Angola and Mozambique, were especially significant, showing to some what sustained guerrilla wars might achieve. Rallies to celebrate the independence of Mozambique were banned, including a notably defiant attempted gathering in Durban.

The tide of youthful anger was running strongly by the early 1970s. There were discussions in BC organizations about BC's relationship with the ANC and PAC. A trickle of people had fled the country to join one or other of the exile organizations and return as trained guerrillas. Another hopeful sign was the outbreak of strikes by African workers in the Durban area in 1973. The strikes were not inspired by BC, which had not made much impact on black workers, but they were the harbinger of a major new source of black leverage: an independent union movement (see pages 100ff).

In Soweto, anger was rising at the attempt by the Department of Bantu Education to require that certain subjects in senior grades be taught through the medium of Afrikaans (see pages 41–2). By early 1976 it was apparent that Soweto was hotting up for a crisis. This was happening at a time of increasing economic hardship that provided a background for the mounting frustration. The boom years of the previous decade had disappeared, and unemployment was increasing. For youngsters approaching the end of their school years the prospects of finding employment were beginning to look bleaker.

With a population of approximately 1 million, Soweto represented the biggest concentration of urban Africans in the country. Some data collected around the time of the Uprising give an indication of the wretched circumstances in which many of its inhabitants lived:

- A Markinor survey found that the number of Sowetans economically worse off in 1975 than they were in 1973 had risen from 10 per cent to 41 per cent.[36]

- A survey by the Johannesburg Chamber of Commerce found that a revision of the budget for a family of five had shown a cost of living increase of 75.4 per cent since 1970.[37]

- Up to 14 people, often of different families, lived in tiny one- or two-roomed houses.[38]

- Only one in three Soweto houses had electricity, meaning that 700,000 people were without it.[39]

- There was a backlog of approximately 800 classrooms (or the equivalent of some 30 schools) in Soweto, aggravated by a chronic shortage of artisans to build schools and houses.[40]

This was a shameful record for a satellite town of the richest city in Africa. The Johannesburg City Council, however, could do little to remedy the situation, apart from issuing dire warnings – such as that by J.J. Oberholzer, chairman of the Council's Management Committee, that the number of people without housing was approaching 100,000: 'Unless the Government moves fast to relieve these shocking conditions there will be a vicious backlash from homeless urban Blacks.'[41] A survey by the *Sunday Times* (Johannesburg) showed that of 514 persons interviewed, 281 put home ownership as the most important factor that would improve the quality of their lives; only 38 failed to place home ownership on their list of priorities.[42]

The language issue gathered momentum in the early months of 1976. It was apparent that most school boards (consisting of Africans) rejected the new system, as did virtually all principals and teachers. A number of teachers had affirmed that they could teach in Afrikaans, but did so only because they feared that by being truthful and denying their ability to do so would jeopardize their chances of promotion. Even the Urban Bantu Council (widely known by Sowetans as the 'Useless Boys Club') had warned that enforcing the use of Afrikaans could result in another Sharpeville. Neither the warnings nor the applications for exemption from the language requirement made any impression on the government.

Beginning in March and leading up to the eve of the fateful day, 16 June 1976, there had been several episodes indicating pupil dissatisfaction, including strikes, stonings and, in one case, an attack on a teacher of Afrikaans (an African woman). Tensions were running high.

Virtually under the noses of the security police and other officials, a few pupils were planning a protest demonstration. The ringleader was Tsietsi Mashinini, one of 13 children born to a working-class Soweto family. An excellent pupil and a good debater, he was a senior pupil at Morris Isaacson

High. He was also said to show natural qualities in leadership. He joined the BC youth movement, the South African Students' Movement (SASM), and became president of the branch formed at his school. The biographer of the Mashinini family, Lynda Schuster, writes that he was drawn to the cultural activities offered under SASM's aegis because 'the emphasis on black pride and self-reliance fitted well with [his] loathing of whites'.[43]

The SASM recognized that the language issue was one that could mobilize the pupils of Soweto: it was not only a gross manifestation of racism but also one that could threaten their ability to pass examinations. Mashinini and another SASM leader, Seth Mazibuko, sounded out pupils at Morris Isaacson and several other schools to assess whether the mood favoured a township-wide boycott. Schuster records that about half the high schools and junior secondaries favoured a boycott, while the other half were fearful of retributions from the security police. At a meeting on 13 June the issue was debated – after six alleged informers had been ejected.[44] It was remarkable that even by this late stage the security police appeared to have had no inkling of what was about to happen: a massive demonstration against the imposition of Afrikaans.

An action committee was formed, schools were informed, and the business of making placards got under way. Pupils would march from their various schools, converging in Orlando West (part of Soweto), proceeding thereafter to the Orlando Stadium, where a meeting would be held. The organizers were insistent that there was to be no violence and no provocation of the police.

Even the subsequent Commission of Inquiry, headed by the conservative Judge P.M. Cillié, found no evidence that the demonstrating pupils were disorderly or defiant: 'Many walked and sang or chatted and did not make themselves guilty of bad behaviour.' There were instances of pupils being dragooned into joining the march and some cases of cars being stoned and set alight, and an attack on a school inspector.

The confrontation took place in Vilakazi Street in front of the Orlando West High School and involved a 48-strong detachment of police (40 Africans and 8 whites). Since none of the participants in the march was prepared to give evidence, the Commission was reliant on police witnesses, press reports and journalists: 'There was conflicting evidence on practically every incident and aspect of the events.' Eventually, Cillié accepted the police version of events, although some witnesses insisted that the crowd, estimated at 10,000, was peaceful and orderly until the police fired. What is beyond doubt is that the police were poorly equipped and that the officer in command lacked a loud-speaker. Certainly, the small detachment felt threatened, and as the Commission found, several members opened fire in desperation without any order having been given. The Commission also found the police to be largely responsible as their lack of knowledge of what had been planned had left them inadequately-prepared.

The Commission found that the pupils' opposition to the language policy was facilitated by the officials' inflexible enforcement and underestimation of the opposition. Ultimate responsibility for the tragedy, however, lay with the cabinet, and particularly with Deputy Minister Andries Treurnicht, whose ostrich-like attitude caused him to ignore repeated warnings from well-informed observers.

Thirteen people were killed on 16 June, and many more injured. According to reports, most had been shot in the back. The violence continued on succeeding days, and protestors began to torch official buildings and other symbols of white authority. There was also looting of shops, especially liquor stores. Chinese-owned shops appear to have been singled out as targets. It was not long before disturbances spread to other towns, not only those on the Witwatersrand and elsewhere in the Transvaal, but elsewhere in the country, notably in the Western Cape, where Coloured students and pupils came out in solidarity with the Soweto protestors, and Port Elizabeth in the Eastern Cape. As far as fatalities were concerned, Natal and the Orange Free State were relatively unaffected. According to the Commission's estimate, 575 persons had died before the Uprising petered out in February 1977.[45] This figure was based largely on figures supplied by the police, but many observers, notably Sowetans themselves, believed the death toll to have been much higher, perhaps as many as 1,000. It is impossible to say whether the official or unofficial figure is correct.

According to official figures released in June 1976, 2,430 people had been detained since June 1976, of whom 817 had been tried and convicted, and nearly 500 others were either awaiting trial or were still being investigated. A large proportion of those detained were high school pupils.[46]

In a limited sense, the Soweto pupils achieved their goal: the Afrikaans-medium requirement was hastily dropped. But from very early on, the protestors' demands widened to encompass a complete rejection of apartheid. No doubt, for some of the ringleaders the language issue had been a peg on which to hang their opposition to the system.

There was no evidence to suggest that either the ANC or the PAC had had a hand in stirring the protest, although individual members of both organizations assisted in various ways once it had gathered momentum. At least 4,000 (and possibly many more) youngsters fled the country in the course of the Uprising, and most gravitated to ANC camps elsewhere in Africa.

The ANC had more resources and was better able to cope with the influx than the faction-ridden PAC. A significant number of the young exiles were itching to get their hands on guns and return to fight in South Africa.

A number, having been convicted, went to prison. Mandela and his colleagues on Robben Island were elated that the spirit of mass protest had been revitalized, but they were also taken aback by the ferocity of their new fellow-prisoners. Mandela writes:

> These young men were a different breed of prisoners from those we had seen before. They were brave, hostile and aggressive; they would not take orders, and shouted 'Amandla! [Strength!]' at every opportunity. Their instinct was to confront rather than cooperate . . . In these young men we saw the angry revolutionary spirit of the times.[47]

The government had been stunned by the Soweto Uprising. This was reflected in Vorster's long silence after the initial confrontation, which was perhaps attributable to the internal tensions in the NP: some *verligtes* considered the imposition of Afrikaans and, more generally, the way in which the Uprising had been handled, to have been disastrous; the *verkramptes*, on the other hand, favoured both imposing Afrikaans and heavy-handed repression. The Uprising had been serious and costly in terms of fatalities, but it had not threatened the state. Indeed, over the entire period of the Uprising not one policeman was killed in the course of the clashes. Several black policemen, however, were attacked, indicating a growing trend that 'collaborators' were to be regarded as legitimate targets.

The crackdown on BC organizations in October 1977, preceded by the murder of Biko, and detentions of individuals, left BC in disarray. None of the organizations had built contingency plans into their operations, even though they must have anticipated such a crackdown, especially with an election coming. But even if the organizations had been decimated the angry mood among a large segment of the population remained. BC was principally a 'state of mind,' as its exponents claimed, and this did not change. South Africa would not be the same again.

Notes

1 Albert Luthuli, *Let My People Go* (London: Collins, 1962), p.107. (Note: A revised orthography of Zulu names renders the author's name as Lutuli.)

2 Thomas Karis and Gwendolen Carter (eds), *From Protest to Challenge: A Documentary History of African Politics in South Africa 1882–1964* (Stanford, CA: Hoover Institution Press, 1977), vol. 2, p.338.

3 Luthuli, *Let My People Go*, p.126.

4 *A Survey of Race Relations in South Africa 1955/6* (Johannesburg: South African Institute of Race Relations, 1956), p.40.

5 Luthuli, *Let My People Go*, p.235.

6 Rusty Bernstein, *Memory against Forgetting: Memoirs from a Life in South African Politics 1938–1964* (London: Viking, 1999), pp.154–5.

7 Randolph Vigne, *Liberals against Apartheid: A History of the Liberal Party 1953–1968* (London: Macmillan, 1997), pp.42–8.

8 Mandela, *Long Walk to Freedom*, p.248.

9 Benjamin Pogrund, *Sobukwe and Apartheid* (Johannesburg: Jonathan Ball, 1990), p.100.

10 Mandela, *Long Walk to Freedom*, p.224.

11 *Idem*, p.260.

12 *Idem*.

13 Karis and Carter, *From Protest to Challenge*, vol. 3, pp.778–9.

14 Tom Lodge, *Black Politics in South Africa since 1945* (Johannesburg: Ravan Press, 1983), p.235.

15 Rusty Bernstein, *Memory against Forgetting*, p.99.

16 *Idem*, p.249.

17 Joel Joffe, *The Rivonia Story* (Bellville: Mayibuye Books, 1995) is the most comprehensive account.

18 Karis and Carter, *From Protest to Challenge*, vol. 3, p.727.

19 Joffe, *The Rivonia Story*, p.212.

20 George Cloete Visser, *OB – Traitors or Patriots?* (Johannesburg: Macmillan South Africa, 1976), p.127.

21 *A Survey of Race Relations in South Africa 1964* (Johannesburg: South African Institute of Race Relations, 1965), p.83.

22 *Idem*, p.84.

23 Ben Temkin, *Buthelezi: A Biography* (London: Frank Cass, 2003), p.126.

24 Millard W. Arnold (ed.), *Steve Biko: No Fears Expressed* (Braamfontein: Skotaville Press, 1987), p.21.

25 *Idem*, p.19.

26 *Idem*, pp.45–6.

27 See Lodge, *Black Politics in South Africa* for a detailed account.

28 Arnold, *Steve Biko*, pp.97–8.

29 Adelaide Tambo (ed.), *Preparing for Power: Oliver Tambo Speaks* (London: Heinemann, 1987), p.126.

30 SASO, unpublished pamphlet.

31 SASO, *Alice Declaration: Statement by SASO on the Boycott of Black Universities, May 14, 1972.*

32 *Black Review 1972* (Durban: Black Community Programmes, 1973), p.22.

33 Mamphela Ramphele in N. Barney Pityana, Mamphela Ramphele, Malusi Mpulwana and Lindy Wilson (eds), *Bounds of Possibility: The Legacy of Steve Biko and Black Consciousness* (Cape Town: David Philip, 1991), p.156.

34 *Idem*, pp.164 and 173.

35 Pityana in Pityana *et al., Bounds of Possibility*, pp.201–2.

36 *Argus* (Cape Town) 18 April 1975.

37 Chamber of Commerce, Johannesburg, *Statement*, 23 July 1976.

38 *Rand Daily Mail* (Johannesburg), 15 April 1975.

39 *Sunday Express* (Johannesburg), 27 July 1975.

40 *Rand Daily Mail*, 3 March 1976.

41 *Idem*, 12 April 1975.

42 *Sunday Times* (Johannesburg), 22 April 1975.

43 Lynda Schuster, *A Burning Hunger: One Family's Struggle against Apartheid* (London: Jonathan Cape, 2004), p.56.

44 *Idem*, p.61.

45 *Verslag van die Kommissie van Ondersoek oor die Oproer in Soweto en Elders van 16 Junie 1976 tot 28 Februarie 1977* (Cillié Commission) (Pretoria: Government Printer RP106/1979), vol. 1, paras 107–8, 126, 127.

46 *Survey of Race Relations in South Africa 1977* (Johannesburg: South African Institute of Race Relations, 1978), p.144.

47 Mandela, *Long Walk to Freedom*, p.471.

CHAPTER 4

Endgame

Intensifying civil wars in Rhodesia and South West Africa, coming after the independence of Angola and Mozambique added fuel to the smouldering flames that lay beneath the apparent quiescence. Sharpeville had been followed by more than a decade of quiescence, but this would not be repeated after the Soweto Uprising. The Uprising had breathed new life into the ANC, whose years of exile had been barren and bleak. Apart from renewing the international community's hostility to apartheid and increasing South Africa's isolation, new blood was joining the ANC, both in exile and, not long thereafter, inside the country in the form of trained MK guerrillas.

As noted above, the majority of those who fled South Africa after the Uprising had linked up with the ANC, rather than the PAC. Why the ANC should have been the preferred option has never been satisfactorily explained, especially since the BC movement's views were closer to the PAC's. The conventional explanation, that the ANC-in-exile was better organized and possessed greater resources than the disorganized, faction-ridden PAC and, hence, more able to accommodate the influx, is a major part of the answer. Apart from military training, desired by many, the ANC was also a conduit for scholarships for further education, mostly in Britain and the Soviet Union. (Informal evidence suggests that applicants' political preferences were vetted prior to being considered for assistance.) There is little doubt, though, that the ANC's premier role in the history of opposition and the prestige of its leadership swayed many preferences.

Given the eagerness of many of the young refugees to return to South Africa as guerrillas, the ANC could offer far more than the PAC, whose contribution to the armed struggle hitherto had been non-existent. The ANC's armed struggle had also been in the doldrums for some time: no MK activity had taken place inside South Africa since before the Rivonia trial, although it had been involved in the Wankie Campaigns in Rhodesia in 1967–8, which, although unsuccessful, had produced a core of trained, battle-hardened veterans. Tambo spoke frankly about the ANC's weakness in the mid-1970s:

Organizationally, in political and military terms, we were too weak to take advantage of the situation created by the [Soweto] uprising. We had very few active ANC units inside the country. We had no military presence to speak of. The communication links between ourselves outside the country and the masses of our people were still too slow and weak to meet the situation as was posed by the Soweto uprising.[1]

Despite MK's lack of success, the fact was that it had tried, and was continuing to do so. With the number of MK recruits being augmented by some 3,000 there seemed every reason to believe that it would become a more effective striking force – certainly more effective than the PAC's armed wing seemed likely ever to be. Moreover, friendly governments in Angola and Mozambique, and at least the possibility of safe houses in Swaziland, Botswana and Lesotho, offered safer routes in and out of South Africa.

By the late 1970s, the ANC's priority had moved to the 'armed struggle', subsequently becoming the 'people's war'. In 1978 an MK delegation, led by Tambo, visited Vietnam and discussed guerrilla warfare with the legendary General Giap. The conclusion that was drawn was that armed struggle had to be based on, and grow out of, mass political support. A three-year plan was adopted, in which mobilization of both urban and rural areas would be undertaken. This would be the underpinning of the 'people's war'.

MK activity picked up substantially after 1977: police statistics show a steady increase of attacks, averaging twenty to thirty per annum, and then rising sharply to approximately 140 in 1985, and thereafter increasing dramatically to nearly 300 in 1988.[2] For the most part, the damage caused to life and property was relatively small, apart from some daring attacks, such as those on SASOL (the oil-from-coal plant), Koeberg (a nuclear energy plant) and the headquarters of the South African Defence Force (SADF) in Pretoria.

The impact was more psychological: whites became jumpier, especially after the distinction between 'hard' and 'soft' (civilian) targets was blurred in the mid-1980s; but the attacks could not be credited with making the mass of whites more amenable to the idea of negotiating with the ANC. For Africans, the impact was different: 'armed propaganda' demonstrated that the ANC was active. A poll conducted in the Pretoria-Witwatersrand-Vereeniging triangle showed that support for the ANC had risen from 27 per cent to 42 per cent between 1977 and 1981.[3] Other polls suggested that significant percentages of urban Africans either applauded attacks or would be prepared to offer refuge to MK operatives on the run.

There was a cost to armed struggle. The big question was whether it made sense to take on the enemy where he was strongest, namely in the area of security. With limited rural areas of strategic importance, South Africa's terrain, unlike that of Vietnam, did not lend itself to guerrilla warfare. Perforce the main theatre of conflict was the urban areas. The ANC's answer to this was that armed struggle was one of four prongs, the others being mass mobilization of the people, the flexing of economic muscle by the organized working class, and international isolation complemented by economic sanctions, sporting and cultural boycotts and the like. Together, the four prongs would generate synergy that, in time, would enable the ANC to seize power.

Even by the mid-1980s, seizure of power, stridently advocated by many MK soldiers, seemed a romantic notion, even if it were conceded that damage was being done to the white power structure. Tambo acknowledged that 'it would be a terrible mistake to rely on armed struggle alone'.[4] It had to be complemented by political action.

A difficulty for MK was the vigilance and aggressiveness of the security forces. Informers were everywhere, and the SADF did not hesitate to launch aerial attacks on ANC bases, offices and supposed safe houses, often with considerable loss of life. A *New York Times* journalist asked the head of the security police about his informers in the ANC: 'I have them all way to Moscow', he replied. The journalist, Joseph Lelyveld, repeated this boast to Tambo, who acknowledged that it was true: 'He was right! He was right! . . . They've been giving us a rough time, making us work very hard. At one time there was a group of ten, [MK soldiers] and only one of them was genuine'.[5]

Guerrillas who were captured could expect to be interrogated and tortured to extract every ounce of information. If prosecuted and convicted they might well be sentenced to death. Or, they might be 'turned', that is, forced to become an Askari, serving in the hit squads operated by clandestine units of the security forces, or sent back to the ANC as a double agent.[6] It is not surprising that levels of paranoia in MK camps in Angola and elsewhere were high, or that alleged *impimpis* (informers) were dealt extremely rough justice, often by 'necklacing' (being trussed in a burning tyre) in the African townships in South Africa, or summary execution in the MK camps.

By the early 1980s the ANC had eclipsed all its rivals in terms of popular support; but Mangosuthu Buthelezi, chief minister of KwaZulu and leader of the Inkatha movement remained a thorn in its flesh. Inkatha, originally conceived as a Zulu cultural movement, had been revived by Buthelezi in 1977, with the intention of creating a mass base. Buthelezi, a former member of the ANC Youth League, had regarded himself as a supporter of the strand of the ANC personified by Luthuli, whom he thought of as his mentor. During the bleak 1960s and early 1970s Buthelezi used his semi-protected position as a Bantustan leader to criticize apartheid, and he played a significant role in filling the political vacuum of the times.

The ANC was implacably opposed to Bantustans, but nevertheless sought to encourage the formation of mass organizations where none existed. According to Tambo's account, Buthelezi had assumed his position in KwaZulu after consultation with the ANC, which now encouraged him to participate, but:

Unfortunately, we failed to mobilize our own people to take on the task of resurrecting Inkatha as the kind of organization that we wanted, owing to the understandable antipathy of many of our comrades towards what they considered as working within the Bantustan system. The task of reconstituting Inkatha therefore fell on Gatsha Buthelezi himself who then built Inkatha as a personal power base far removed from the kind of organization we had visualized, as an instrument for the mobilization of our people in the countryside into an active and conscious force for revolutionary change.[7]

There could be no doubting Buthelezi's opposition to apartheid, notwithstanding the allegations of his being a 'collaborator', expressed particularly by the BC movement and many in the ANC itself. Buthelezi had opted to work 'inside the system' as a strategy for eroding apartheid from within. Indeed, his refusal to accept 'independence' for the Zulu – the largest African ethnic group in South Africa – was one of the main reasons for apartheid's ultimate failure. (He was never given credit for this, despite the acknowledgement by several Nationalists that this had indeed been so.)

The relationship between the ANC and Inkatha was discussed at length at a meeting in London between delegations from the two organizations in October 1979. The ANC insisted that it had been arranged at Inkatha's initiative and agreed to only after extensive consideration by the ANC's national executive committee, some of whose members evidently argued that meeting Buthelezi would bestow a legitimacy on him that was inimical to the ANC's interests. Like Mandela, with whom Buthelezi had had a long and cordial relationship, Tambo was an old associate, dating back to the days of the Youth League.

Far from resolving the differences between the ANC and Inkatha, the meeting widened the divisions. Buthelezi put a number of questions to the

ANC, each soliciting recognition and approval of the legitimacy of Inkatha's role and strategy with the broad liberation movement, notably: 'Will the ANC leadership in exile publicly acknowledge the fact that Inkatha is a vital force in the struggle?' The ANC declined to do so – and was infuriated when information about the supposedly confidential proceedings was leaked to the press, allegedly by Inkatha sources, though this was denied by Inkatha.

The issues separating the two organizations were fundamental: Inkatha rejected the armed struggle, declaring itself in favour of nonviolent opposition; it rejected sanctions on grounds that they would do little more than further impoverish an already poverty-stricken population; and it favoured private enterprise over the ANC's increasing tendency to support an (as yet) ill-defined form of socialism.

The ANC regarded Inkatha less as a partner than as a potential rival, one, moreover, that was based on Zulu ethnicity. Since its inception the ANC had set itself against 'tribalism', fearing that ethnic conflict among Africans would frustrate African unity and play into the apartheid government's hands. Many ANC members were scornful of traditionalism, in particular the institution of chieftainship, which was the scaffolding of Inkatha's power-base in the rural areas of the KwaZulu Bantustan. Buthelezi, who usually denied being a Zulu ethnic nationalist (though not convincingly), managed to combine the sophistication of a well-educated modern politician with respect for traditional culture.

The parting of the ways after the abortive London meeting inaugurated more than a decade of intense conflict between Inkatha and the United Democratic Front, which was founded in 1983, and soon became a kind of internal surrogate for the ANC. The ANC took to making vitriolic attacks on Buthelezi through its publications and also on its broadcasting service, Radio Freedom. In the early 1980s it became clear that the ANC exile community in Lusaka (Zambia) regarded Buthelezi as a menace who was regularly branded as a 'stooge', a 'dog', (a deadly insult among the Zulu), and a 'snake' whose head should be crushed. Even his claims to be the traditional prime minister to the Zulu king were disputed in a book-length hatchet job.[8] Patti Waldmeir, a (London) *Financial Times* correspondent based in Lusaka, reported that ANC officials made no secret of their wish to kill him.[9]

It was hardly surprising that Buthelezi took umbrage at the torrent of insults. Nor was it surprising when the UDF began to recruit support in Natal that Buthelezi regarded it as an interloper muscling in on 'his' political heartland. A deadly conflict ensued – and spread to parts of the Transvaal where large numbers of Zulu migrant labourers worked, often living in barrack-like hostels. In the decade after 1985 nearly 12,000 people were killed in the Natal violence, making it by far the biggest component of the death toll in political violence in all the years of apartheid.[10]

The violence would continue up to, and beyond, the founding election in 1994, even threatening on occasion to derail the intense constitutional negotiations of the early 1990s (see pages 130–32). Who was to blame? Ultimately, of course, the denial of effective voting rights to blacks under apartheid meant that political competition could not be peacefully channelled through the ballot box. Nor could it be denied that on occasion the security forces either assisted Inkatha *impis* (raiding groups) or turned a blind eye to their depredations; but to attribute all of the violence to such assistance, as ANC-inclined observers were wont to do, is a gross exaggeration. The conflict derived ultimately from political competition, in which the respective antagonists were largely traditionalists with a rural orientation, and urbanites who had, in greater or lesser measure, turned their backs on the traditional rural lifestyle. The tragedy was that violence was allowed to gather momentum, and become seemingly unstoppable. Indeed, the more apparent it became that apartheid was eroding and significant change was in the offing, the more intense the violence became.

Could the violence have been avoided, as well as the 'micro-ethnic cleansing' (forced removals from settlements of supporters of the 'wrong' side) that accompanied it? The stubborn, intransigent people on either side saw the conflict in zero-sum terms, which made an accommodation difficult, if not impossible. Buthelezi was not the kind of person to allow himself to become a meek, pliant surrogate of the ANC. Jacob Zuma, himself a Zulu, then a senior ANC official and now current State President, acknowledged that the ANC had made mistakes in the way it had handled a proud man like Buthelezi. Speaking of the post-1990 period, he said to Waldmeir: 'It was important for Buthelezi to feel welcomed, embraced, and part of the process. . . . [If Mandela had done so at the beginning of the process] you could have had absolutely the end of the problem, that is my feeling'.[11] This was even truer in 1979, before the hostility degenerated into local civil war.

Some years later Buthelezi said:

Had we joined forces in 1979, the terrible destitution of the people would not have been aggravated by the violently destroyed and disrupted communities. There would not be the legacy of bitterness and hatred that there now is. There would not be a whole generation of young people who have known only a decade of the hideous black-on-black violence and killing for political purposes.[12]

In the early 1970s, a new force began to make itself felt: the muscle of African labour, flexed through trade unions. Unions for Africans were not illegal but they were not officially recognized and could therefore not participate in the statutory industrial bargaining machinery. Trade union officials, especially those belonging to the South African Congress of Trade Unions, a member of the Congress Alliance, were especially hard hit by bannings. Strikes by African workers, moreover, were illegal, and commonly resulted in police intervention, usually at the behest of employers, dismissal of strikers and their replacement by what were insultingly called 'interchangeable units of labour'.

Given the overwhelming dependence of the economy on black labour, it is perhaps surprising that black workers did not exercise their potential leverage sooner to wring concessions out of employers and, ultimately, the state. There had, after all, been a nascent class consciousness, enveloped in a sense of racial oppression, even before the advent of apartheid. The power of the state and of employers who enjoyed its protection, however, was sufficient to thwart the capacity of workers to mobilize on a national scale. Moreover, since virtually all African workers were unable to rise above 'the level of certain forms of labour' (Verwoerd's phrase), strikers were relatively easily replaced, commonly by the simple expedient of lifting the influx control barriers to permit the hiring of new recruits.

By the early 1970s the 'interchangeability' of labour was beginning to change: increasingly Africans were benefiting from the possibility of a limited degree of upward occupational mobility as the pool of skilled white workers began to dry up, and job reservation steadily became a dead letter, either through exemptions or because employers were ignoring the law.

The trigger for an era of labour militancy was a wave of strikes in and around the Durban area in 1973 when over 60,000 Africans in 150 companies went on strike or engaged in work stoppages. This heralded the emergence of independent African unions, and also the elevation of possible trade union rights for Africans to a high priority on the national agenda. It was apparent that the existing machinery for the resolution of workers' grievances, works and liaison committees in individual enterprises, fell far short of full trade union rights. A number of more enlightened employers, notably Harry Oppenheimer, chairman of the giant Anglo American Corporation, argued that where independent unions were representative of particular workforces, employers should regard them as legitimate negotiating partners. Multinational companies, especially American ones who were beginning to feel the heat of the growing sanctions and divestment lobby, agreed.

Initially, the government rejected the idea of African unions, but a newly appointed Minister of Labour, Fanie Botha, took the initiative by having the State President appoint the Wiehahn Commission in 1977 (see page 47).

The government acted upon the Commission's recommendations, and legislation was enacted by 1979 to recognize independent unions and to include them in the industrial conciliation system that operated for non-African unions. An estimated 9 out of 10 African industrial workers could now belong to registered trade unions.

Together with foreign pressure, fears that industrial relations would become a battleground, involving uncontrolled independent unions, had no doubt persuaded the government to accept Wiehahn's recommendations. The assumption was that registration would bring the unions under greater control. Unions, for example, could not legally have links with, or provide funds for, political parties; and their books would be subject to auditing. Hopes that the unions would steer clear of politics proved illusory, perhaps inevitably so: a majority of African trade union members would probably have supported either the ANC or the PAC, both of which were banned. In the absence of effective structures for the expression of political demands, unions were likely to become proxies for these purposes.

By no means all independent unions initially accepted the principle of registration or the view that they should act as political proxies. So-called 'workerist' unions maintained that it was premature to consider involvement in popular struggles before they had established themselves as powerful and effective organizations firmly rooted in the shop floor. 'Populist' unions, on the other hand, maintained that workers were also members of communities and could not divorce themselves from wider political issues. As the struggle intensified in the 1980s, the division became less relevant, workerists recognizing that they could not avoid some measure of political involvement, while also insisting that organization on the shop floor and the accountability of union officials and shop stewards were of critical importance.

After some years of negotiation, several of the bigger union groupings merged in 1985 to form the Congress of South African Trade Unions (COSATU); others, who were Black Consciousness in outlook, rejected COSATU's non-racial stance and formed the National Council of Trade Unions (NACTU) in 1987. Although NACTU formally committed itself to the liberation struggle it eschewed political linkages. Its Africanist/BC roots, however, manifested themselves in its founding principle that the movement should be under African working-class control.

Both of these union federations were large: by 1987 membership of COSATU-affiliated unions was over 700,000; NACTU-affiliated unions claimed a membership of nearly 500,000 (though later figures are substantially lower). The differences between COSATU and NACTU reflected the longstanding division in African politics between the ANC and the PAC, but they did not entirely preclude some measure of cooperation. COSATU, however, moved closer to the ANC, twice sending delegations to the ANC headquarters in Lusaka and signing on to the Freedom Charter in 1987 – which was opposed by a workerist faction. COSATU also collaborated closely with the United Democratic Front (see below), which was also strongly supportive of the ANC.

The leverage of the unions is reflected principally in their capacity to obtain higher wages for their numbers and withhold labour: between 1980 and 1988 the number of strikes, including work stoppages, but excluding stayaways for political reasons, rose from 207 in 1980 to 1,148 in 1987, declining to 1,025 in 1988. In August 1987, a major trial of strength took place between the National Union of Mineworkers and mines belonging to companies affiliated to the Chamber of Mines. The strike closed down one-third of gold and coal mines for three weeks. Both sides claimed victory, but Cyril Ramaphosa, the general secretary of the NUM, offered a face-saving comment, pronouncing the outcome to be 'neither a defeat for the union nor a victory for the chamber [of Mines]'.[13] Ramaphosa, a young law graduate who had come up through the ranks of the BC movement, was earning his spurs as a shrewd strategist and an effective negotiator – and would be the ANC's chief negotiator in the constitutional negotiations of the 1990s.

Membership of a trade union was clearly advantageous: members' wages increased significantly more than those of non union members. But the non-economic effects were also significant: membership gave workers greater security and heightened their sense of personal efficacy. Highly politicized unions like those belonging to COSATU kept their members informed of developments, thereby increasing their political consciousness and amenability to mobilization.

The flexing of labour's muscle in the turbulent 1980s played a crucial role in the dismantling of apartheid. Combined with the mass mobilization of millions across the country, it gave the apartheid government little choice but to negotiate. The alternative was the continuation of siege-like conditions, a weakening economy, strangulation by sanctions, and an increase in violence to the point that could be described as civil war. In the mid-1980s many were convinced that this bleak outlook would be realized.

The principal instrument of mass mobilization in the 1980s was the United Democratic Front, formed after a mass rally in Mitchell's Plain (Cape Town) in August 1983.[14] The trigger for its formation was the impending implementation of the Tricameral Constitution and legislation dealing with urban Africans (the so-called 'Koornhof Bills'). It was intended to be a broad front, consisting of affiliated associations of various kinds, spanning a cross-section of class and ideological perspectives, united by common opposition to apartheid in general, and the forthcoming constitution as an egregious manifestation of apartheid. Although Mandela was to describe both COSATU and the UDF as 'in some measure' surrogates for the ANC in the 1980s, there is no evidence to suggest that either organization was founded on the initiative of the ANC. Both, however, were exactly the kinds of movement that the ANC wished to see occupying legal, domestic space inside the country: mobilized labour and mobilized masses would be powerful opponents of the apartheid government.

The UDF, obviously, could not initially declare itself to be in alliance with the ANC, which would invite prosecution and banning, but its choice of presidents and patrons made clear where its political affinities lay: Archie Gumede (also chairman of the Release Mandela Committee), Albertina Sisulu and Oscar Mpetha were all stalwart ANC supporters; and nearly all of the patrons, who included Nelson Mandela, Govan Mbeki and Walter Sisulu, were leading lights in the ANC. Later in the decade support for the ANC grew more overt, especially after the UDF adopted the Freedom Charter in 1987.

By the later 1980s, over 600 organizations were affiliated to the UDF, giving an overall membership of some 2 million. Membership was not accorded to individuals. The affiliated organizations covered a wide variety of interests: youth groups, student bodies, religious bodies, women's groups, community organizations (mostly known as 'civics'), sports clubs and others. Youth predominated, making up as much as 40 per cent of the overall membership. Most of the membership was black, but it was a fundamental principle of the UDF that it was to be non-racial. Relatively few predominantly white organizations affiliated, however, and these were mostly student bodies.

Of the assorted affiliates the 'civic' was the most novel, as well as being the most powerful force galvanizing communities into the release of considerable social energy. The prototype of a civic was the Port Elizabeth Black Civic Organization (PEBCO), founded in 1979, and led by Thozamile Botha. Its aim was to articulate the grievances of the black community, which the official Community Council was failing to do. PEBCO took up local issues such as rents, water accounts, poor roads and lack of infrastructure. PEBCO provided a model that was to be emulated in hundreds of towns and villages. During a trial in 1985 for treason of 16 senior leaders of the UDF, Popo Molefe, the general secretary, offered a comprehensive definition of a civic:

*I understand a civic association to be a broad, community-based organization
that concerns itself immediately with . . . the bread and butter issues, the
problems experienced by the residents relating to housing, services at that level,
facilities, problems related to education, high rentals, how these are determined
and so on . . . [V]ery often, because of the interconnection between what happens
at a local level and what happens nationally, they tended to be influenced or
called to respond to the issues that arise as a result of the national policy of
the government.*

*The civic association is a broad organization that is supposed to cater to the
interest of a broad community, and within that community you have people
with different backgrounds and different interests, and committed to different
ideological positions . . .*[15]

The differing ideological positions referred to by Molefe were writ large in
the UDF as a whole, but for the most part varying shades of socialism were
espoused, especially by students and trade unionists who made up a large
component of the overall membership.[16] The UDF preached a democratic
alternative to apartheid, but many of its affiliates were critical of 'liberal'
or 'bourgeois' democracy, proclaiming instead a form of participatory or
populist democracy that would be 'people-driven'.

Given the nature of the UDF as a front consisting of autonomous
affiliates, it was inevitable that it would lack overall ideological coherence.
Indeed, a number of senior leaders insisted that the UDF's very nature pre-
cluded a common ideology. Molefe told the court in 1985 that the UDF was
unified around broad principles that rejected apartheid while remaining

*a loose conglomeration of organizations, each one of them retaining its own
ideological position, its own constitution, its own separate membership . . .
striving for liberation. But it does not regard itself as a liberation movement . . .
A liberation movement would entail much more than that. It may require one
ideological position, [a] far-ranging programme of action, and tight discipline.*[17]

Essentially, the UDF was about 'the politics of refusal,' a description
offered by the Revd Allan Boesak, a young theologian who had been a key
figure in the founding. The major target initially was a 'million signature'
campaign, rejecting the Tricameral Constitution and seeking to persuade
Coloured and Indian people not to vote for their respective Houses in the
elections that were held in August 1984. The number of signatures collected
fell far short of a million, thanks in part to sustained harassment by the
police, but the campaign certainly contributed to the low percentage polls
in both elections.

The situation in the country changed dramatically on 3 September 1984 when confrontation between residents of Sebokeng, a township 35 miles south of Johannesburg, and the police broke out. The violence spread to other parts of the Transvaal, resulting in 129 deaths by the end of the year. School boycotts, local community insurrections and protest demonstrations, including at funerals, became part of an ongoing insurrection.

The initial confrontation had centred on township issues: illegitimate (African) Community Councils, corrupt Councillors, increased rentals at a time of rising unemployment, and the perennial issue of poor schools. The exclusion of Africans from the new constitution also heightened a sense of marginalization. The UDF's role in the insurrection was less one of orchestrating protests (though local affiliates were certainly involved in doing so) than linking the concerns of individual communities together in a countrywide context. This acted as a powerful spur to mobilization.

Contrary to many expectations, the government had not banned the UDF, despite lurid accusations of alleged connections to the ANC, SACP and other suspect organizations. It did, however, keep key UDF officials and prominent local organizers under close surveillance and subjected many to continual harassment. It did not actually ban it outright in 1988 when regulations prohibiting the UDF from 'executing or continuing actions' were promulgated. The failure to ban the UDF was possibly due to a reluctance to incur further international hostility at a time when economic sanctions were being tightened. Initially, moreover, the government may have considered that banning the UDF shortly after its founding may have diminished the new constitution's credibility even further.

In July 1985, however, the government did crack down, imposing a state of emergency on 36 districts, mostly in the Eastern Cape and the industrial areas of the Transvaal. This was extended to the greater Cape Town area and some nearby inland towns in October. The affected districts, unsurprisingly, were the centres of UDF affiliates' activities. The terms of the state of emergency gave wide powers to the police and the army (over 30,000 troops had been deployed in townships during 1985) to detain individuals as well as other draconian controls, including restrictions on the media's ability to report clashes between township residents and the security forces.

The state of emergency, according to the authorities, had curbed 'violence and lawlessness' sufficiently to be able to be lifted, but if there was a lull it was only temporary, and on 12 June 1986 a second state of emergency was declared, this time covering the entire country. This would not be entirely lifted until 1991.

The toll on the UDF and other black organizations was considerable. By the end of 1985 at least 136 UDF activists had been detained, including 45 of the 80 members of national regional executives: they were either in detention, awaiting trial or had been assassinated. In May, 16 UDF leaders were accused of furthering the aims of a 'revolutionary alliance', principally the ANC and SACP; and in June 22 persons, including senior UDF office-bearers, Patrick Lekota and Popo Molefe, were charged with high treason.[18] (All accused in both trials were eventually acquitted.) Fatalities in political violence during 1985 and 1986 exceeded 2,000.

The UDF insisted on its commitment to nonviolence, but it was unable to prevent members of some of its more radical affiliates from breaching the principle. Community Councillors, black policemen and alleged *impimpis* (informers) were regarded as legitimate targets for killing, in 406 cases, according to police statistics, by the hideous method of 'necklacing' – trussing the victim in a tyre and igniting it with petrol; another 395 victims died as a result of burning (details are not provided).[19] It is impossible to verify these figures, although it is true that necklacing was widely used, even if not approved by either the ANC or the UDF (who were, however, slow to condemn it unequivocally).

In many cases, fatalities occurred when police opened fire on demonstrators. Nonviolent methods of crowd control, including riot shields to ward off stones, were primitive and, although used on occasion, did little to limit the number of deaths. There is also evidence to suggest that police presence at gatherings, including funerals, was a provocation; and conversely, when the police kept a low profile or stayed away, violence was often avoided.

Most of the fatalities in the turbulent 1980s occurred in what the authorities called 'black-on-black' violence: violence against collaborators, violence between activists and vigilantes – often migrants who took umbrage at the lack of respect for their elders shown by young activists – and violence between rival political organizations. The worst rivalry was between Inkatha and UDF activists in Natal and in Transvaal towns where Zulu migrants resided in hostels adjacent to townships. There were also violent clashes between UDF activists and members of the smaller BC organization, the Azanian People's Organization, which claimed a number of lives.

Some of the so-called 'black-on-black' violence could be attributed to efforts by the security forces to drive wedges between rival organizations, but this cannot account for all of it: it boiled down to fights for turf. Ultimately, of course, this could be blamed on a system that denied Africans the right to channel their rivalries through the ballot box.

The mid-1980s took a heavy toll on the UDF and its structures, but it nevertheless soldiered on. Its very nature as a highly decentralized structure with autonomous affiliates made it impossible to function as a unified, coordinated body, but, ironically, afforded it a measure of protection since lower-level leaders, usually at community level, emerged to replace those who had been detained or killed.

During 1985 the ANC's Kabwe conference praised the UDF as 'a mass instrument of democratic change'. Tambo announced that the time had come to make apartheid unworkable and the country 'ungovernable'. He added: 'We must take the struggle into white areas.' The UDF had had some contact with the ANC since its inception, and indirectly through underground ANC members who were also members of UDF affiliates. At a meeting in Stockholm early in 1986 ANC and UDF delegates held extensive discussions, with the ANC urging the UDF to formulate a new Programme of Action.[20] The meeting and other contacts breathed new life into the UDF's spirit of resistance.

From this emerged the strategic plan of 'people's power'. As noted above, (African) Community Councils had been a particular target of protest, and in many areas being a Councillor had become a hazardous occupation. By May 1986, according to the government, 41 out of 192 Community Councils and other local bodies had ceased to have a quorum. It was also stated that some 20 per cent of the total of 1,277 councillors countrywide had been armed with guns for self-defence.[21] Reports of collapsing Councils and resignations of apprehensive Councillors continue to pour in. An administrative vacuum was forming, even though contingency plans were made to continue the administrative functions of collapsed Councils. But with rent boycotts in many townships, inadequate revenue bases were worsened.

The UDF, which had consistently demanded single, non-racial municipalities, saw people's power as an opportunity to assume some of the functions no longer performed by Councils. 'Civics' undertook garbage removal, street cleaning and other chores. It was a brave effort, but it could not be sustained over a long time.

Distrust of the judicial system led to the institution of 'people's courts'. Lodge writes: 'More than any other feature of the insurrectionary movement, people's justice testified to the movement's ideological complexity and to the extent to which it was shaped from below by popular culture'.[22] The informal courts dealt with a wide variety of offences, civil issues, domestic quarrels, drunkenness, and incorporated traditional notions of justice into their procedures. Unfortunately, as with attempts to establish informal courts or private law-enforcement groups, it was difficult to prevent some from becoming 'kangaroo courts' that punished alleged offenders with extreme brutality.

The vacuum with the most damaging long-term consequences was in education: school boycotts had been widespread since 1984, and the education of African youngsters was being seriously disrupted. In 1986 it was estimated that approximately 250,000 African pupils in 260 schools were affected by boycotts and disturbances. By the end of the year no education was taking place in 73 schools.[23] The pupils had legitimate grievances – and had had them for a long time. Poor-quality education in an authoritarian context was the norm. 'Liberation before Education' was the widely used slogan of the times. Ken Hartshorne, a former education official, showed that in the period 1980–89 just over one million African pupils took the matriculation or senior certificate examinations: of these nearly 50 per cent failed, and though many would repeat the examinations, about 400,000 would leave school without a certificate:

The majority joined the ranks of the unemployed in spite of their having completed secondary schooling, became disillusioned about the value of education, suffered from a sense of failure, became alienated from their communities and turned to violence and the disruption of the society which had rejected them.

Percipiently, Hartshorne added that 'in the longer term [they could] be the most dangerous challenge to the political life of a new, representative government'.[24]

Many of these marginalized youngsters became '*comtsotsis*', young gangsters who tagged along with the more disciplined youthful members of UDF affiliates. *Comtsotsis* were responsible for much of the crime and violence that occurred during confrontations and consumer boycotts that proved to be effective in parts of the country, notably in the Eastern Cape.

Concerns about the amount of schooling that was being missed caused anxiety to parents. At a conference organized by the Soweto Parents' Crisis Committee in December 1985 an attempt was made to urge children to return to school. Similar crisis committees were formed in other parts of the country. The UDF echoed the call, as did the ANC, which asked the children to regard school as 'trenches' in the struggle. Arising out of these activities the National Education Crisis Committee was formed, and held a conference in Durban in March 1986. Calls for a return to school, however, were complemented by demands for the introduction of 'people's education', a facet of people's power, that would involve new curricula and the accountability of schools to the communities they served.

In his keynote address to the conference, Zwelakhe Sisulu, a scion of famous ANC stalwarts, Walter and Albertina Sisulu, spoke with passion of people's power and what it had achieved thus far, but warned that while the shackles of direct government control had been broken (which was hardly true), there was a power vacuum because the people had not yet managed 'to control and direct the situation'. It was a subtle point: 'ungovernability' had certainly inflicted damaging blows, notably on Community Councils and the legitimacy of the state. The campaign could go so far and no further: it could seriously impede the effectiveness of government in black areas and accelerate economic decline; but a knockout blow that captured the state proved impossible. In short, the conflict was deadlocked.

The ANC in exile watched events and was encouraged by what it saw. Even though a number of underground ANC activists were involved in the UDF, and it was clear that the UDF regarded itself as an internal ally, the ANC could hardly take credit for initiating the movement or for sustaining it. But it could take credit for inspiring hundreds of thousands of activists. MK could hardly claim military success – if this were measured by significant dents made in the state's security capability, but it could claim to have an important psychological effect. Every guerrilla attack served as a reminder of the ANC's presence.

Many in the ANC in exile, and particularly MK soldiers, spoke the language of revolution and the ultimate seizure of power. In 1979 the Politico-Military Strategic Commission had reported to the ANC's national executive committee (after the visit to Vietnam) in vigorous terms:

The strategic objective of our struggle is the seizure of power by the people as the first step in the struggle for the victory of our national democratic revolution. Seizure of power by the people means and presupposes the all-round defeat of the fascist regime by the revolutionary forces . . . It means the dismantling by the popular power of all the political, economic, cultural and other formations of racist rule and also necessitates the smashing of the state machinery of fascism and racism and the construction of a new one committed to the defence and advancement of the people's cause.[25]

This was heady, even romantic, stuff, no doubt inspired by the stirring successes of the North Vietnamese against a far stronger foe. But the jungles of Vietnam were not the township wastelands of South Africa, and the problems of infiltrating guerrillas across the borders, even if porous, were great.

It was the impossibility of successfully waging a guerrilla or 'people's war' against the might of the security machine that prompted Mandela to conclude that the struggle could best be pushed forward by negotiations:

We had been fighting against white minority rule for three-quarters of a century.
We had been engaged in the armed struggle for more than two decades. Many
people on both sides had already died. The enemy was strong and resolute.
Yet even with all their bombers and tanks, they must have sensed they were on
the wrong side of history. We had right on our side, but not yet might. It was
clear to me that a military victory was a distant if not impossible dream. It
simply did not make sense for both sides to lose thousands if not millions of
lives in a conflict that was unnecessary. They must have known this as well.
It was time to talk.[26]

Whether 'they', particularly in the form of P.W. Botha and the hawks around
him, knew this is open to doubt. It is certainly true that many in the Afrikaner
nationalist establishment, leading writers, intellectuals and businesspeople
recognized that major reforms were necessary. Few, however, were prepared
to accept majority rule as the inevitable outcome of negotiations.

Mandela had interpreted a visit by the Minister of Justice, Kobie Coetsee,
when he was in hospital as 'an olive branch'. Coetsee's visit was followed
by others. In particular, Niel Barnard, director general of the National
Intelligence Service, held talks with Mandela on approximately 40 occasions
prior to Mandela's release in February 1990. In addition, leading Afrikaner
intellectuals held meetings with ANC people in England and elsewhere.[27]
Officially, any contact with the ANC – a 'terrorist'/'communist' organization
– was denounced by the government, even while its own stealthy emissaries
were sounding out ANC officials, notably Thabo Mbeki, about the possibilities
of a settlement. There were two sticking points: the ANC's refusal to
abandon the armed struggle, and its refusal to sever the close ties with the
SACP. The mid-1980s and after was still the time of the Cold War, and with
Cuban troops and Soviet advisors assisting the Angolan government's forces in
the border war, anti-communist fears remained strong among the securocrats
and many white voters.

By calling for negotiations (though flatly rejecting offers of conditional
release) Mandela had gone out on a limb that would fuel rumours that
he was 'selling out'. He was doing no such thing, making it clear that he was
answerable to the ANC's leadership and was therefore unable to commit it
to the course that he favoured. The strong commitment of MK soldiers and
other ANC activists to the 'seizure of power' made it difficult for the idea of
a negotiated settlement to gain acceptance. Many of the militants, no doubt,
saw violence in Fanonesque terms as a therapeutic catharsis. Besides, few knew
of the secret dealings between senior ANC officials and government emissaries,
just as very few whites outside the inner circle were aware of them.

There were good grounds for the ANC to doubt whether the feelers were really the prelude to a negotiating situation: had not the government, having seemed to play along with the Eminent Persons Group, then blown it out of the water, after the ANC had continuously agreed to meet it? And was it not true that the government's favoured 'negotiating' partners were the more pliable moderates who, while not uncritical of apartheid, were prepared to cooperate with government-created institutions? The suspicion that government-initiated negotiations might be a trap into which an unwary ANC would be led lingered even into the early 1990s, when it had been unbanned. Moreover, there was little in the government's overt behaviour to suggest that it was anywhere near readiness to negotiate. The 1980s were turbulent years, and successive states of emergency, mass detentions, and numerous fatalities (including several assassinations) were hardly propitious conditions for starting what was bound to be a delicate and difficult process.

Yet, as Mandela had indicated, it was exactly those conditions that made it imperative to reach out in search of an honourable peace. Mandela could not have known it, but the man who would simultaneously be his rival and partner, F.W. de Klerk, was thinking along similar lines, but, incredibly enough, was kept unaware that people in government were talking to the ANC.

Despite its emphasis on the armed struggle and the seizure of power, wiser counsels in the ANC had kept the door slightly ajar for the possibility of negotiations. In his political report to the ANC's national executive committee in 1985, Tambo said that the government was using the question of negotiations 'to divide our movement, demobilize the masses of our people by holding out the false promise that we can win our liberation other than through its overthrow'. But, he added, the ANC could not be seen to be rejecting a negotiated settlement: no revolutionary could be against such a settlement in principle.[28]

By the late 1980s, it appeared to some in the ANC that there was a glimmer of hope that a negotiating situation could be in the offing. The ANC was aware that in critical respects the government was up against the ropes, even if it was not in danger of being overthrown. Despite what Tambo called its 'dismal' record of negotiations, the ANC did not want to be caught off guard if a potentially genuine negotiating situation were to arise. He pointed to what had happened to the Zimbabwean nationalist parties who had been unprepared for the Lancaster House negotiations that preceded Zimbabwe's independence in 1980: a constitution had effectively been forced on them, on a 'take-it-or-leave-it' basis. It was also the case that the Frontline States, South Africa's regional neighbours, had paid a heavy price for their proximity, and they favoured a peaceful accommodation. It was prudent, in the circumstances, to enter negotiations, should they arise, with prepared bargaining positions.

Under Tambo's watchful eye, a drafting team set about producing what would become the Harare Declaration, issued by the Organization of African Unity in August 1989.[29] It was to prove a seminal document. Its core clause read:

We believe that a conjuncture of circumstances exists which, if there is a demonstrable readiness on the part of the Pretoria regime to engage in negotiations genuinely and seriously, could create the possibility to end apartheid through negotiations. Such an eventuality would be an expression of the long-standing preference of the majority of the people of South Africa to arrive at a political settlement.

The Declaration went on to list the principles on which a new constitutional order should be based:

- South Africa should become a united, democratic and non-racial state, based upon common and equal citizenship;
- universal suffrage on a common voters' roll;
- a multiparty system, though not permitting parties that were committed to furthering racism;
- guaranteed human rights protected under a Bill of Rights;
- equality before the law and independent judiciary;
- an economic order that would promote and advance the well-being of South Africa.

It was important to create the necessary climate for negotiations. At the very least the South African government should:

- release unconditionally all political prisoners and detainees;
- lift all bans and restrictions on proscribed organizations and persons;
- remove troops from the townships;
- lift the state of emergency and repeal all legislation designed to circumscribe political activity;
- cease all political trials and executions;
- create the conditions in which free political discussion could take place.

The actual process of negotiations should be preceded by discussions between the liberation movement and the government to achieve the suspension of hostilities by means of a mutually binding cease-fire. Negotiations could thereafter proceed to discuss and agree upon the principles on which a new constitution should be based, and the necessary mechanism for drafting it.

The Declaration proposed the formation of an interim government to supervise the process of drawing up and adopting the constitution. The interim government would also govern the country, as well as effecting the transition to a democratic order, including the holding of elections. After the adoption of the new constitution, 'all armed hostilities will be deemed to have formally terminated'.

The Declaration was a carefully considered, coherent document, but, understandably, it was confined to broad principles and proposals, and, hence, short on details – in which many devils would lurk.

On 5 July 1989, Mandela was taken to meet P.W. Botha. In the context of the times it was perhaps surprising that the world's most famous political prisoner should be taken to have tea with the leader of one of the world's most reviled regimes. Mandela himself had requested the meeting some months before; but the stroke Botha had suffered had delayed it. What Botha's motive was in assenting to the meeting is unknown, but there were suggestions that he had done so to spite de Klerk, now leader of the NP. Mandela was tense prior to the meeting, resolving that if Botha were to unleash his volcanic temper he would inform him that he found such behaviour unacceptable. Botha, however, disarmed him: 'He was unfailingly courteous, deferential and friendly.'[30]

Mandela had prepared carefully for the meeting, drafting notes that repeated his fears of large-scale slaughter if the conflict were to continue unchecked, and set out the ANC's beliefs, including a defence of its alliance with the SACP. He proposed a meeting between the government and the ANC, at which crucial political issues would have to be addressed: the apparent irreconcilability of the ANC's demand for majority rule and a unitary state and the insistence of whites on structural guarantees that majority rule would not mean domination of the white minority by blacks. The challenge of reconciling these positions could be met only if both parties were willing to compromise.[31]

What Botha thought of Mandela's statement is not known. In fact the brief meeting did not feature substantive discussion of the conflict, except when Mandela asked him to release all political prisoners, including himself, unconditionally. But, in the one tense moment of the meeting, Botha declined.

Nothing of substance came out of the meeting, but its symbolism was significant, and Mandela realized it:

While the meeting was not a breakthrough in terms of negotiations, it was one in another sense. Mr Botha had long talked about the need to cross the Rubicon, but he never did it himself until that morning at Tuynhuys [the State President's Cape Town office].[32]

Few could have foreseen how dramatically the situation would change in southern Africa and the world over the next six months: de Klerk would replace Botha; Namibia would receive independence; and the Berlin Wall would be torn down. All three events had huge significance for South Africa.

Notes

1 Tambo, *Preparing for Power*, p.129.

2 For police data on attacks see H.D. Stadler, *The Other Side of the Story* (Pretoria: Contact Publishers, 1997).

3 Howard Barrell, *MK: The ANC's Armed Struggle* (London: Penguin Books, 1990), p.46.

4 Tambo, *Preparing for Power*, p.172.

5 Joseph Lelyveld, *Mind Your Shadow: South Africa, Black and White* (London: Michael Joseph, 1985), p.331.

6 Stephen Ellis and Tsepo Sechaba, *Comrades against Apartheid: The ANC and the SACP in Exile* (London: James Currey, 1992), p.112.

7 Tambo, *Preparing for Power*, p.146.

8 Mzala (pseudonym), *Gatsha Buthelezi: Chief with a Double Agenda* (London: 2ed Books, 1988).

9 Patti Waldmeir, *Anatomy of a Miracle: The End of Apartheid and the Birth of the New South Africa* (London: Penguin Books, 1997), p.172.

10 For a comprehensive account of the Natal violence see Anthea Jeffery, *The Natal Story: 16 Years of Conflict* (Johannesburg: South African Institute of Race Relations, 1997).

11 Waldmeir, *Anatomy of a Miracle*, p.175.

12 Temkin, *Buthelezi*, p.207.

13 *Race Relations Survey 1987–8* (Johannesburg: South African Institute of Race Relations, 1988), p.681.

14 See Jeremy Seekings, *The UDF: A History of the United Democratic Front in South Africa 1983–1991* (Cape Town: David Philip, 2000).

15 Quoted in Rose Moss, *Shouting at the Crocodile: Popo Molefe, Patrick Lekota and the Freeing of South Africa* (Boston, MA: Beacon Press, 1990), pp.23–4.

16 Tom Lodge and Bill Nasson, *All, Here, and Now: Black Politics in South Africa in the 1980s* (Cape Town: David Philip, 1991), pp.132–5.

17 Quoted in Moss, *Shouting at the Crocodile*, p.43.

18 *Race Relations Survey 1985* (Johannesburg: South African Institute of Race Relations, 1986), p.41.

19 Stadler, *The Other Side of the Story*, pp.166–9.

20 Seekings, *The UDF*, pp.166–9.

21 *Race Relations Survey 1986* (Johannesburg: South African Institute of Race Relations, 1987), p.118.

22 Lodge and Nasson, *All, Here, and Now*, p.135.

23 *Race Relations Survey 1986*, p.445.

24 Ken Hartshorne, *Challenges and Crisis: Black Education 1910–1990* (Cape Town: Oxford University Press, 1992), p.80.

25 Karis and Carter, *From Protest to Challenge*, vol. 5, p.729.

26 Mandela, *Long Walk to Freedom*, p.513.

27 See Allister Sparks, *Tomorrow Is Another Country* (Johannesburg: Struik, 1994).

28 Tambo, *Preparing for Power*, p.161.

29 For the text of the Declaration see Hassen Ebrahim (ed.), *The Soul of a Nation: Constitution-making in South Africa* (Cape Town: Oxford University Press, 1998), pp.451–5.

30 Mandela, *Long Walk to Freedom*, p.539.

31 Ebrahim, *The Soul of a Nation*, p.449.

32 Mandela, *Long Walk to Freedom*, p.540.

CHAPTER 5

Negotiations and the founding election

There is a cynical adage that 'men and nations act rationally when all other options have failed'. Broadly, this was true in South Africa's case: the NP finally realized that apartheid had failed and had to be jettisoned; and the ANC recognized that they would be unable to seize power. Both had reached the conclusion that a negotiated settlement offered the only hope of avoiding a bloodbath that might reduce the country to a wasteland.

Mutual appreciation of the deadlock had not been an easy process: leaders on both sides, black and white, had faced dissent. Afrikaner nationalism had been irrevocably split since the breakaway of the Conservatives in 1982. De Klerk's NP had faced stiff opposition from them in the 1989 election. The CP won 39 seats, which was still far short of the 93 won by the NP, but over 40 per cent of Afrikaners had voted for the CP; and, for the first time since 1953, a bare majority of votes had been cast for parties other than the NP.

Apart from the CP, an array of menacing far-right organizations had sprung up, most notably the *Afrikaner Weerstandsbeweging* (Afrikaner Resistance Movement) whose demagogic leader, Eugene Terre' Blanche, was capable of stirring up crowds into a frenzy. Other smaller groups, including some that lurked in the inner recesses of the security forces, demonstrated dangerous proclivities to violence, including assassination.

Another concern was the loyalty of the army and the police, many of whose (white) members, especially in the middle and lower ranks, were sympathetic to the CP. Obedience to the civilian leadership was supposed to be a strongly entrenched principle, but it had not been tested since the policies of successive NP governments were viewed favourably by the overwhelming majority of security-force personnel. What might happen if a radical change of course resulted in a breakdown of law and order was a matter for uneasy speculation. Even before his announcement of dramatic changes on 2 February 1990 de Klerk had ruffled feathers in the security establishment by stripping away much of the institutional power that had been built up under Botha. For example, the State Security Council, which had substantially eclipsed the cabinet as the locus of power, was deprived of most of its influence, and various secret projects (whose nature remained secret) were terminated.

For the ANC, the problems were different, and not nearly as serious as those confronting de Klerk. Virtually all blacks loathed apartheid, but this did not imply the absence of political rivalries among black organizations. The ANC was confident that it enjoyed overwhelming majority support among African voters, which, indeed, had been indicated by opinion polls commissioned by the government. The PAC, the Azanian People's Organization and minuscule homeland parties posed little threat, but in KwaZulu and Natal Inkatha would be difficult to beat.

As noted, there had been considerable resistance among militant ANC supporters to the idea of negotiating with a hated enemy. But their opposition soon faded. One can readily imagine that even among angry and impatient MK soldiers, housed in spartan camps far from South Africa, the prospect of returning home and not having to face the extreme dangers of fighting a ruthless enemy trumped any principled commitment to rejecting negotiation. For many, exile had been a dispiriting and often debilitating existence, cut off from home and family.

De Klerk's announcement of the unbanning of the ANC, SACP, PAC and other proscribed organizations, the impending release of Mandela, and the intention to negotiate an inclusive, democratic constitution, had caught the ANC off guard, despite its prior preparation of a negotiating position. Several thousand exiles had to be repatriated, amnesty against prosecution had to be secured, and offices had to be acquired.

The bigger problem, however, was integrating the ANC: exiles and 'inziles' (as domestic activists were called) tended to have differing political cultures. In the circumstances of exile – and assisted by the powerful influence of the SACP – the ANC had developed its own hierarchical and often authoritarian form of 'democratic centralism'. But it remained a potentially fractious organization, (barely) held together by the diplomatic skills of Tambo.

By contrast, the UDF, from which most of the inzile members of the ANC would be drawn, was highly decentralized and practised an internal form of participatory democracy. The same was true of COSATU, which entered an alliance with the ANC: internal democracy and the accountability of officials were its hallmarks. The unbanning of the ANC and its re-establishment as a legal political movement drained the life-blood from the UDF, most notably because many of its key activists were drafted into a number of critical roles in the ANC. Effectively, it had run out of political space and, despite the regrets of many, it dissolved itself in 1991.[1]

Mandela had often described the ANC as a 'broad church', implying that it was open to all ideological persuasions. The 'church' became even broader after 1990 with the influx of new members: identifiable strands ('factions' would be too strong a word) included hardline communists, some of them unrepentant Stalinists, democratic socialists, proponents of Scandinavian-style social democracy, a few, mostly from an older generation, who could be termed 'Christian liberals', and, very significantly, those who had emerged through the ranks of the BC movement, many of whom were strongly 'Africanist' in outlook. The strands cut across the exile/inzile distinction, as well as the amorphous group of ex-political prisoners, collectively known as the 'Robben Islanders'. Differences and often sharp clashes of opinion remained, but any fissiparous inclinations were subordinated to the grand prize of winning power. Negotiations were termed a new 'sphere of struggle'.

What was of critical importance in persuading ANC doubters that negotiations were the only viable option was the international pressure to seek a settlement. In particular, the Soviets, who had been the ANC's principal source of funds, arms and training, had been pressing the ANC for some time that this was the right option.

Both leaderships had their hands full in keeping their supporters in line and supportive of their respective organizations; but what would be remarkable was that neither suffered any significant breakaways during the actual course of the negotiations, despite the palpable unhappiness of some over particular developments.

The negotiating process, of course, was not confined to the ANC and the NP, although they were the major players. Inkatha was a significant force in KwaZulu and Natal, and its on-off (mostly off) relationship with the process was a source of concern that endured until the eve of the founding election in April 1994. Likewise, the (fragmented) forces of the far right shunned the process, but were a menacing threat. The very fact that they were fragmented and could not agree on a common set of proposals diminished, but did not remove, the threat of insurrection that they potentially posed.

It is generally the case that transitions to democracy have been facilitated by growing economies. By contrast, the South African economy had steadily weakened from the mid-1970s throughout the 1980s. If not prostrate by 1990 it was limping badly. Growth rates in the 1960s had averaged nearly

6 per cent per annum, but declined in the 1970s to nearly 4 per cent, and to 1 per cent in the 1980s. Inflation averaged over 15 per cent in the 1980s. Foreign fixed investment declined sharply in the 1980s, as did investment by private local companies, which exacerbated the problem. Local business-people's confidence had weakened, resulting in what has been termed 'internal disinvestment', that included a search for less risky and more profitable opportunities abroad.[2]

There is considerable debate about the effect sanctions, including disinvestment, had in ending apartheid. De Klerk writes:

On the whole, I believe that sanctions did more to delay the process of transformation than they did to advance it. They further isolated South Africans from the enormous change agent represented by Western cultural and political influence. . . . They created a natural resistance among most white South African individuals and companies and often made them less willing to consider change. The National Party won more than one election by appealing to the resentment that many whites felt against the international community – and particularly the United States – for their role in imposing sanctions against us. Most importantly, sanctions impeded economic growth, which I believe was by far and away the most important change factor in South Africa.[3]

De Klerk is referring principally to measures like the Comprehensive Anti-Apartheid Act of 1986, passed by the American Congress in 1986 over President Reagan's veto. It is certainly true that the international sanctions campaign heightened anti-American xenophobia and pushed a number of whites into the CP camp. To the extent that sanctions per se impeded growth they would, over a long haul, have struck at some of the roots of the increasing black leverage that was a major cause of the deadlock – growing consumer power, trade union muscle and upward occupational mobility, in particular. Moreover, despite the oft-repeated claim that the majority of blacks favoured sanctions, there is evidence to suggest that they did so *provided* it did not jeopardize their jobs.

What did, however, have a considerable impact was the decision of Chase Manhattan Bank in 1985 to call in its outstanding loans to South Africa, a move that was shortly followed by a number of other international banks. Historically, the South African economy had depended for growth on the inflow of foreign capital. Apart from saddling the state with a heavy burden of interest, the inability to obtain further foreign loans, combined with the reluctance of local investors, meant that the economy faced a ceiling of 2 per cent on its potential capacity for GDP growth – which was lower than the population growth rate.

Whether the foreign banks' refusal to roll over loans was a sanction is a matter of dispute: mostly, the banks claimed that their decision was based on an estimation of risk. This was probably true in some measure, but it is also highly likely that the 'hassle factor', as American companies termed it, was also significant. Why put up with a great deal of hostility from pro-sanctions campaigners when South Africa accounted for only a small percentage of one's business? In Britain, Barclays Bank, which had been long established in South Africa, sold its interests to a local consortium principally because its younger clients were closing their accounts in protest against the South African connection.

Exactly how much sanctions contributed to, or hindered, the transition, as de Klerk avers, remains debatable. Their impact, and perhaps most of all, that of sporting sanctions, were partly psychological in heightening whites' sense of isolation. Moreover, there was always a sense that 'the goalposts would be moved' and sanctions ratcheted up, whatever reformist moves were made. Their effectiveness was never put to the test of long-term enforcement, because after de Klerk's initiative in February 1990, they were steadily withdrawn, despite the ANC's demands that they be maintained until the transition had become irreversible.

Nelson Mandela's release from his prison quarters near Cape Town on 11 February 1990 was a momentous event:

As I finally walked through those gates to enter a car on the other side, I felt – even at the age of seventy-one – that my life was beginning anew. My ten thousand days of imprisonment were at last over.[1]

The journey of some 35 miles to Cape Town's old City Hall was a triumphal procession, with people lining the road and a huge multitude assembled to hear him speak from a balcony. His speech, said to have been written by radical UDF supporters (though this has never been confirmed), was tough and uncompromising, no doubt intended to reassure ANC supporters that, contrary to rumours, he had not reneged on ANC policy. Mass action should continue; sanctions must remain; and the armed struggle would be waged until a climate conducive to negotiations had been achieved. Moreover, he reiterated the ANC's commitment to nationalizing banks, mines and monopoly industry. The negative impact of the speech was partly softened by words of praise for de Klerk, whom he described as 'a man of integrity'. De Klerk was not mollified.

The issue of violence, including the armed struggle, remained a bone of contention, with both sides accusing each other of involvement in the killings that seemed unstoppable. Botha's insistence that there could be no talk of negotiating with the ANC until it abandoned its commitment to armed struggle had been summarily rejected by the ANC: indeed, why should it throw in one of its (presumed) major bargaining chips even before negotiations had started? And was it not also true of many conflict situations that negotiations for peace began even before hostilities had ceased? Botha's inflexible stance, however, had been modified by means of a formula which proclaimed that participation in negotiation would be open to all parties who sought peace.

Mandela repeatedly accused de Klerk over the next few years of either orchestrating violence in an attempt to weaken the ANC or of not using the powers at his command to stop the violence. For his part de Klerk denied these allegations, and insisted, in turn, that the ANC itself was deeply implicated in violence and intimidation. What de Klerk did not know – and he appears to have been kept in the dark by some of his ministers – was that secret units lodged deep in the interstices of the security forces were actively engaged in efforts to scupper the transition. Horrifying information about their activities would emerge, largely due to the investigations conducted by a commission of inquiry set up by de Klerk and chaired by Judge Richard Goldstone.

In May 1990 'talks about talks' between the government and the ANC got under way. The Groote Schuur Minute committed both parties to ending the climate of violence, as well as to a peaceful negotiations process. It established a working committee to make recommendations for the release of political prisoners and the granting of immunity in respect of political offences to those inside and outside the country. The government also committed itself to review security legislation and to work towards lifting the state of emergency (which was done in June 1990, except in Natal, where conflict between Inkatha and the UDF/ANC continued to rage).

Both sides considered the meeting to have been successful. It opened the way for the next round of talks, held in Pretoria in August. Prior to the meeting the ANC sprang a surprise, by announcing its suspension of the armed struggle. Mandela had initially demurred at the proposal, put forward by Joe Slovo of the SACP, but then came around to accepting it. He resisted vehement objections from some on the ANC's NEC, saying that the purpose of the armed struggle had always been to bring the government to the negotiating table, which had now been achieved. It was necessary, he said, to show the ANC's good faith, as well as to reward de Klerk. Moreover, 'suspension' was not he same as 'termination', since a suspension could always be lifted. MK, he noted, was not active at the time[5] (although it was probably involved in the Natal violence). The Pretoria Minute, ratifying the

ANC's decision and further committing the parties to a peaceful solution, was duly agreed. The Minute expressed the hopeful view that the way was now open to proceed towards constitutional negotiations. In fact it would not be until December 1991 that the first formal attempt at constitutional negotiations, the Convention for a Democratic South Africa (CODESA), would begin.

In the meantime, violence continued unabated, souring the relationship between de Klerk and Mandela, as mutual recriminations were voiced. The truth was that it was impossible for the leaders to keep all of their respective sets of supporters in line. In the case of Inkatha, the ANC handled the situation badly: Buthelezi, an old friend of Mandela, had retained a personal link with him. Mandela had wanted to visit Natal not long after his release, but ANC militants in the province would not hear of it, insisting that nothing which enabled Buthelezi to acquire some vicarious legitimacy should be allowed.

Unlike other homeland leaders, notably Enos Mabuza of KaNgwane who made no secret of his support for the ANC, Buthelezi had not been prepared to subordinate his organization to the dictates of the ANC. Apart from serious policy differences, ANC media had launched a barrage of deadly invective against Buthelezi throughout the 1980s. Few gave him any credit for his outright rejection of independence for KwaZulu or participation in government-initiated negotiations involving homeland leaders. In doing so Buthelezi had struck a significant blow against whatever credibility apartheid may have had. Buthelezi undoubtedly wanted to be considered as one of the 'Big Three' – Mandela, de Klerk and himself – but this was unthinkable for the ANC, which wanted to be the unchallenged leader of black South Africa.

No doubt his exclusion from the early talks about talks further alienated him from the developing process, which he increasingly viewed as a ganging up of the ANC and the NP to the exclusion of all other interests – which in some measure it was. It would not be until the eve of the election in April 1994 that Mandela was allowed to work his magic on Buthelezi – and it succeeded. But thousands of lives had been lost in the intervening years.

A further meeting between ANC and government representatives took place near Cape Town on 12 February 1991 and resulted in the D.F. Malan Accord.[6] The delegations considered the report of a working group that had adumbrated the implications of the ANC's agreement to suspend the armed struggle. The Accord spelled out in detail what the suspension entailed, principally: no further armed attacks, infiltration and training of guerrillas and statements inciting violence. It was also agreed that 'in a democratic society no political party or movement should have a private army', and that the security forces take cognizance of the suspension of armed actions and that all allegations of unlawful activities or activities by the security forces contrary to the spirit of the agreement were to be promptly investigated.

It seemed that the preparatory work for negotiations had been successful, which it was, up to a point. Militants in the ANC, however, feared that they had been led into a trap; and Buthelezi warned that while he welcomed the agreements, violence in Natal and elsewhere would continue until he and Mandela had held a formal meeting. Buthelezi may have exaggerated his political importance, but there was truth in his warning – as Zuma (quoted earlier) had observed. A further serious factor was violence alleged to have been initiated by a shadowy 'third force' that was intent on weakening the ANC. Indeed, a murderous unit, the Civil Co-operation Bureau, operating clandestinely in the inner recesses of the military, had been exposed, as had a death camp at Vlakplaas, near Pretoria, which operated within the police force.

Further poisoning of the waters occurred in July 1990 when the police uncovered Operation Vula, an ultra-secret plan, approved by Tambo in 1986, to embed senior MK operatives inside South Africa to organize for a long-haul people's war. Large arms caches were discovered. Few in the ANC's NEC or in MK were privy to the operation. By 1990, when the situation had changed, Vula was described as an 'insurance policy' against the possibility that negotiations would founder and it was necessary to resume the armed struggle. The government, however, regarded Vula as evidence of the ANC's duplicity: negotiating, on the one hand, but preparing for war on the other.

The ANC leadership was unrepentant: indeed, it had long asserted that negotiations were another 'site of struggle' in a multi-pronged strategy. But many in the ANC, who were unaware of Vula's existence, were startled by the disclosures and inclined to dissociate themselves from the operation.[7]

The poisoned waters accounted for the uncompromising tone of the ANC's document *Advance to national democracy: guidelines on strategy and tactics of the ANC*, published in February 1991.[8] The significance of the document is that it set the stage for the ANC's participation in the formal negotiations that began in December 1991. It began with an analysis of the crisis of the apartheid state, arguing that the 'space won by the liberation movement and the possibility of negotiations do not change the essence of apartheid power relations', which meant that the strategic aims of the struggle remained unchanged. Transfer of power to the people as a whole and the construction of a socio-economic system that met popular aspirations remained central objectives.

Deep suspicions of the government's strategy indicated how difficult bridging the gap would be:

Underpinning the regime's approach is a perspective to impose, by hook or by crook, a constitution which entrenches apartheid in a new and disguised form. Attempts to limit the powers of the new government, and entrenchment of white privilege in property and land ownership and distribution of income, are cunningly designed cloaks under which to perpetuate the system of white minority domination.

The guidelines proceeded to insist on the establishment of an interim government, acceptable to the widest spectrum of the population, to supervise the transition to democracy. An election by universal franchise should elect a constituent assembly which should then draw up a democratic constitution. The modalities of forming an interim government and electing a constituent assembly should be decided upon by a 'congress of all parties with a proven constituency convened to work out the broad and basic principles to underpin the new constitution . . .'.

The ANC acknowledged that it had entered negotiations as a viable mechanism for transition, but warned that if negotiations failed the option of 'seizure of power – armed and/or otherwise' would be pursued. MK, now an unbanned and hence lawful organization, was being maintained, including its underground structures. The implication was quite clear: what could not be won at the negotiating table would be won on the streets by mass action.

For the NP government much of what the ANC demanded was unacceptable. It would not countenance a constitutional vacuum during which an unelected interim government ruled; nor could it accept that an elected constituent assembly could draw up the constitution. De Klerk and his colleagues realized that the ANC would win such an election and could thereupon write its own constitution. It was, as a cabinet minister observed, 'putting the political cart before the constitutional horse'.

In the election of September 1989 the NP, while emphasizing that it wished to remove racial discrimination and negotiate a new constitution, had made no mention of unbanning the ANC and other organizations. Nor had it spelled out what constitutional proposals it would take to the negotiating table. During 1990, however, de Klerk and other ministers insisted that they were opposed to 'simple majoritarianism' in a unitary system. Power-sharing, with appropriate protection for minorities, would have to be a component of any new constitutional system.

Subsequently, a more detailed set of proposals was introduced at CODESA. Its core was that a Westminster system, based upon the principle of 'winner-take-all', could result in a party's winning 51 per cent of the vote but obtaining 100 per cent of the power which, in de Klerk's words, 'would be the worst possible model for a country like South Africa . . .'.[9] The alternative should be a system that prevented excessive power from being concentrated in the hands of a single party. At the apex of the system should be a small executive council consisting of the leaders of between three and five of the most important parties, who would reach decisions by consensus. The presidency of the country would vest in the chairman of the council who would be appointed on a rotational basis for six months to a year. Further protection for minority parties would reside in the second house of a bicameral parliament: each party that won a certain minimum level of support would have equal representation.

The proposals were a variation of consociational democracy, particularly of the Swiss version in which majority rule is tempered by institutionalized coalition government and an ongoing quest for consensus in decision-making. But neither the Swiss system nor most of the other consociations included these components as part of a written constitution: the rules were informal, being underpinned by a cross-party understanding that these admittedly cumbersome provisions were the price that had to be paid for viable democracy – and, in some cases, the avoidance of serious conflict.

The NP's provisions evoked hoots of derision from the ANC which saw them as a disguised form of apartheid that was antithetical to the ANC's quest for hegemony. It was probably true that a political system based on the proposals would have proved unworkable, but it was equally true that a system based upon the 'winner-take-all' principle, even if qualified by a proportional representation electoral system, was unlikely to establish durable democracy in a society as divided as South Africa. This was especially so since voting preferences were likely to mirror the divisions.

The ANC, having seen the profoundly undemocratic consequences of the one-party system elsewhere in Africa, favoured a multiparty system, but they were leery of minority safeguards other than broad-gauged expressions of respect for minority cultures. For Afrikaners the critical issue would be the protection accorded to Afrikaans, and since many Africans regarded it as the 'language of the oppressor' (despite its also being the language of a majority of Coloured people), its pre-eminent position in the old order was unlikely to survive.

The wide differences on constitutional proposals and the severe tensions caused by ongoing violence did not augur well for CODESA, which opened in a huge hangar-like structure near Johannesburg Airport on 20 December 1991. Critical ancillary issues, such as mutual allegations of complicity in violence and amnesty for political offenders, remained unresolved; but 16 of the participating parties, including the ANC and the NP, nevertheless signed a Declaration of Intent that committed them to setting in motion the process that would lead to the drafting of a constitution embodying the principle 'that South Africa will be a united, democratic, non-racial and non-sexist state' in which the constitution would be the supreme law, guarded over by an independent judiciary. Inkatha did not sign the Declaration until it had been reassured that its terms did not preclude federalism. The 'independent' Bantustan of Bophuthatswana refused to sign on grounds that it was a sovereign state whose government would have to ratify the Declaration. Ciskei, another pseudo-independent Bantustan, also jibbed at signing until reassured that the word 'united' did not rule out a federal system.

The Declaration expressed in broad terms a commitment to a classic liberal-democratic state. It was broad enough to encompass the divergent proposals of the ANC and the NP, as well as Inkatha's demand for a highly decentralized federal system. If it was seen as the prelude to a smooth process this would have been mistaken: fierce conflicts lay ahead. Nevertheless, that so wide a spectrum could have signed on to the Declaration would have been unthinkable even two years earlier.

The opening session of CODESA featured a blazing row between Mandela and de Klerk that dispelled some of the earlier optimism. De Klerk, who was supposed to be the final speaker at the opening, took the opportunity to accuse the ANC of violating the D.F. Malan Accord by not ending the armed struggle: unless the problem of MK was resolved, 'we will have a party with a pen in one hand while claiming the right to have arms on the other'. Prior to the opening of CODESA, there had been urgent discussions among NP ministers, with thought even being given to not going ahead with CODESA. The Minister of Justice, Kobie Coetsee, who had acted as an intermediary with the ANC, had reported that it was using delaying tactics. He was charged with the task of issuing an ultimatum to the ANC. Coetsee reported back that the ANC had agreed to make rapid progress to ensure their compliance with the Accord. He was thereupon instructed to inform the ANC that de Klerk would make some 'sharply critical remarks' about its breaches of the Accord. Coetsee later reported that he had conveyed the message to Thabo Mbeki who had promised to pass it on to Mandela.[10]

For reasons that remain obscure, the message never reached Mandela, who heard de Klerk's criticisms in silent fury, before grabbing the microphone to deliver a savage personal attack on de Klerk, describing him as 'the head of an illegitimate, discredited minority regime'. He accused the government of colluding with those who stoked the fires of violence and declared that the ANC would hand in its weapons only when it was part of the government responsible for collecting them.[11] He made no reference to the provisions of the D.F. Malan Accord or to NP allegations of violations, which, according to Coetsee, had been brought to the ANC's attention.

Some who witnessed this fiery encounter wondered whether the negotiation project would survive, but the two combatants formally shook hands on the following day: a kind of peace had been restored. But de Klerk acknowledged that their relationship would never be the same again. For his part, Mandela recognized that de Klerk was the only leader who could lead whites out of the corner into which apartheid had painted them. He may also have recognized that de Klerk's political position appeared to be increasingly parlous: the ultra-rightwing was making increasingly bellicose utterances and there were reasons to doubt the loyalty of significant elements in the security forces, over and above the assassination squads that lurked in their midst.

What exactly was CODESA intended to achieve? As far as the ANC was concerned it was emphatically not to be a constitution-writing process: that was to be the exclusive prerogative of an elected constituent assembly. CODESA should confine itself to preparing the way for an interim government and an election; and it could also consider broad principles for inclusion in the constitution. The NP, on the other hand hoped that CODESA could produce an interim constitution that would be adopted by parliament and in terms of which a fully inclusive election would be held, returning a parliament that would also act as the (final) constitution-making body, *but* the final constitution would have to incorporate constitutional principles agreed to by CODESA. The final constitution would thereupon have to be certified by a still-to-be-created constitutional court as complying with those principles. It was an ingenious, if cumbersome, way of bridging the wide gap between the ANC's and NP's different approaches. The ANC acquiesced. The trajectory of the constitution-making process closely followed the NP's template.

From the outset it was clear that CODESA had a tough task ahead of it. Not only was it a cumbersome institution that included a large number of small parties from the Bantustans and the Tricameral Parliament, none of them with serious electoral prospects, but the gulf between the major parties was huge. It would have been even bigger had the radical parties of the ultra-right and the PAC and Azanian People's Organization (AZAPO) not opted to boycott the process.

The business of CODESA was conducted by five working groups. Four of these dealt with more practical – though by no means unimportant – issues, and all managed to reach 'sufficient consensus', the ill-defined concept that meant, in practice, that when the ANC and the NP agreed, the process could go forward.

Working Group 2, however, had the crucially important brief of constitutional principles and the constitution-making body. It struggled from the start and ultimately deadlocked in mid-May 1992, at which point the proceedings were adjourned. The point in contention was the percentage vote in the constitution-making body to adopt the final constitution. The NP demanded that a 75 per cent vote be required for the bill of rights and other provisions aimed at safeguarding minority rights. The ANC refused to accept this, arguing that the NP was trying to build minority vetoes into the constitution, which the NP denied.

In the event, a deadlock occurred in Working Group 2, and the ANC delegation withdrew. It was believed in opposition circles that underlying the withdrawal was a deliberate stratagem to halt CODESA's proceedings, in the belief that the secret negotiations were alienating its support base, which feared that too many concessions were being made. It was time to break off relations and reinvigorate mass action.

Stirring events had taken place prior to the breakdown. A string of by-election defeats and slashed majorities caused de Klerk to wonder whether his party retained sufficient support among the white electorate to push forward with negotiations. The crunch had come on 19 February 1992 when the CP won a by-election in Potchefstroom, turning around an NP majority of nearly 2,000 in 1989 to a CP majority of 2,140. It was a bad omen, and several pro-NP newspapers even predicted that, were a general election to be held, the CP might win – and bring disaster down upon the country.

On the following day, 20 February, de Klerk took his courage in both hands and decided that a referendum would be held on 17 March to test white support for continuation of the negotiating process. When he informed his caucus of the decision, there was 'shock and consternation'. De Klerk writes:

It was clear to me that if I had put my decision to the vote the majority of the caucus would have opposed what they then regarded as an over-hasty and risky decision. However, under the caucus rules and the conventions governing the powers of the party leader, I was not required to put the matter to a vote. I decided to bite the bullet and to resign as leader of the National Party if the referendum did not produce a positive result.[12]

What followed was a short, fierce and furious campaign, while the country held its breath: defeat for the 'Yes' campaign spelled imminent disaster. NP members at CODESA were decidedly nervous, some believing that the 'Yes' vote would be won by 55 per cent to 45 per cent, which would have been a hollow victory, with an insufficient margin to be convincing.

The ANC opposed the referendum because it excluded black voters, but, as Mandela acknowledged, the ANC was realistic enough not to try to disrupt it and thereby push white voters into rejecting de Klerk. Accordingly, it urged voters to vote 'Yes'.

With the assistance of the Democratic Party, which enjoyed the support of about 20 per cent of the white electorate and ran its own campaign, the 'Yes' vote triumphed, winning 68.7 per cent of the vote. During the campaign the NP had punted power-sharing, rejecting simple majority rule, rights to private ownership of property, and a free enterprise economic system. It was perhaps the simpler message 'Do you want to talk or shoot?' which had the biggest impact on wavering whites.

The CP and its allies had also fought a vigorous campaign, but they succeeded in only one of the electoral regions into which the country had been divided for the referendum. This was the far north of the country, the heartland of the ultra-rightwing. The CP, while continuing to rage about de Klerk's 'sell-out', suffered a severe deflation after its defeat, which carried with it the danger that the initiative would now pass to the hard men of the ultra-right who spoke of violence and war.

It was, in the ANC's view, a cocky NP that returned to the negotiating table, strengthened in their resolve to insist on power-sharing and other minority safeguards. But the violence rumbled on, exacting large death tolls, particularly in Natal and on the Witwatersrand, where urban dwellers and Zulu migrants frequently clashed.

The pot boiled over on the night of 17 June 1992 when a group of Zulu migrants, Inkatha supporters it was presumed, raided the township of Boipatong (35 miles south of Johannesburg) and indiscriminately slaughtered 48 people, many of them women and children. Allegedly, the killers had been driven from a nearby hostel on police vehicles. It was yet another ghastly episode in a series of killings. De Klerk immediately issued a statement expressing his shock and revulsion, and promising to do everything in his power to bring the killers to justice. He attempted to visit Boipatong on 20 June to express his condolences to the community. But a hostile crowd made it impossible and de Klerk's convoy had to flee.[13] Mandela's reaction was swift, and brutal:

The police did nothing to stop the criminals and nothing to find them; no arrests were made, no investigation began. Mr de Klerk said nothing. I found this to be

the last straw, and my patience snapped. The government was blocking the
negotiations and at the same time waging a covert war against our people.
Why then were we continuing to talk with them?[14]

Mandela's comments, fuelled by his rage, were precipitate: investigations
were begun, arrests *were* made (and resulted in convictions), and de Klerk
had immediately issued a statement deploring the senseless killings. No
evidence of police complicity was found, as even the Amnesty Committee
of the Truth and Reconciliation Commission acknowledged.

The ANC broke off direct dealings with the government, and not long
thereafter rolling mass action commenced, culminating in a two-day strike.
The ANC leadership had been forced to take a tough line by its followers,
who were shouting 'Mandela, give us guns'; and some, who had been opposed
to the idea of negotiation, felt themselves to have been vindicated.

There followed an extremely rough exchange of letters between Mandela
and de Klerk, including one that accused de Klerk of behaving like a Nazi.[15]
Mandela's dismay at what had happened was understandable, but his
reaction was intemperate, partly, no doubt, because he had to satisfy ANC
supporters that he was being tough with his opponent.

The Boipatong massacre proved to be a turning point in the negotiations,
even though no police complicity was proved and several of those responsible
for the killings were convicted and jailed. Whereas previously the ANC
and the NP had been fairly evenly balanced, the scales now tipped in the
ANC's favour. Rolling mass action and talk of the 'Leipzig Option' (referring
to the demonstrations that ousted several Eastern European governments)
exacerbated the widespread despondency in the country, causing some
to fear civil war. Pessimism was deepened by an episode that occurred at
Bisho, capital of the Ciskei Bantustan, on 7 September when trigger-happy
Ciskei soldiers opened fire on protesters, who were demanding abolition of
the Ciskei government. Altogether 29 marchers were killed after they had
ignored prearranged agreements on an approved route.

The dangerous downward spiral of the economy – which made an impact
on the ANC economic team when they saw the figures – and heavy diplomatic
pressure forced the ANC and the NP to resume bilateral negotiations. These
resulted in the signing by de Klerk and Mandela of the Record of Understanding on 26 September 1992.[16] The Record followed agreements reached
at CODESA: that the constitution should be written by an elected body,
which would serve also as an interim parliament; that it would be bound
by constitutional principles agreed to at CODESA; that adequate deadlock-
breaking mechanisms would operate in the constitution-making body; and

that a government of national unity govern on an interim basis. Other significant agreements included: a phased release of political prisoners, although determining those who were eligible for release would receive further attention; the fencing and policing of migrant labourers' hostels; prohibition of carrying dangerous weapons; and acknowledgement of the right to participate in peaceful mass action.

The Inkatha leader, Mangosuthu Buthelezi, was angered by the implicit assumption of NP–ANC control of the negotiations. In particular, he objected to the provisions regarding hostels, in which many Zulu lived and the ban on carrying dangerous weapons, without consulting him. The Record was decisive in further alienating him from the negotiations. In a fit of pique he joined the Concerned South Africans Group (COSAG), consisting of various homeland governments and ultra-rightwing organizations, including the CP. COSAG's aim was to act as a counterweight to the perceived 'unholy alliance' between the ANC and NP. From now Buthelezi would play a perilous game of brinkmanship.[17]

Formal multiparty negotiations were resumed in April 1993, now being termed the 'Multiparty Negotiating Process' (MPNP). It was a more streamlined forum and, in view of the prevailing tension, it was imbued with a sense of urgency.

On 10 April 1993 the country was again brought to the brink of widespread violence by the assassination of Chris Hani, a popular SACP and MK leader, who was gunned down in front of his home. It took Mandela's public appeals for calm to avert disaster. He pointed out that a young Afrikaner woman, who witnessed the killing, had noted the registration number of the assassins' car, and reported it to the police, resulting in quick arrests of two ultra-rightwingers, one of whom had been a former CP MP. Hani might well have been Mandela's successor as President of South Africa. Although initially opposed to negotiations, he overcame his objections and played a powerful role in persuading many reluctant ANC supporters to support the negotiating process.

Hani's death had been a severe blow, but it enabled the ANC to extract an important agreement that the founding election be held on 27 April 1994. Effectively this imposed a deadline on the negotiators since an interim constitution would have to be enacted into law by the existing parliament before the end of 1993.

An important bridging of differences between the NP and the ANC had occurred in November 1992 when the ANC accepted a strategic repositioning devised by Joe Slovo of the SACP and one of the ANC's leading theoreticians. Slovo argued that while the apartheid power bloc had been weakened, the

ANC and its allies did not have the immediate capacity to overthrow it. Although the ANC commanded majority support, it suffered persisting weaknesses of capacity, while the 'regime' had the capacity 'to endlessly delay while consolidating its hold on power'. Slovo recommended a 'sunset' clause whereby a government of national unity (GNU), comprising the major parties, would govern for a five-year period, with the proviso that parties that had lost the election would not be able to paralyse the government. Slovo also drew attention to the 'vast potential' of the bureaucracy and security forces to destabilize a fledgling democracy, unless guarantees of job security or retrenchment packages were offered.

The NP was still holding out for permanent multiparty government, but the ANC's concession went some way to meeting their demand. Roelf Meyer, the Minister of Constitutional Development and the NP government's chief negotiator, acknowledged subsequently that the government of national unity concept was not a coalition 'but a forced agreement of co-operation between opponents and not between two parties who have found common ground'. The GNU proposal was to be temporary, which some of Meyer's colleagues opposed, wanting it to be permanent. With de Klerk's backing, Meyer's view prevailed, thereby neutralizing a major source of division.[18]

Although the principle of a GNU had been accepted, agreement on how it should take decisions proved elusive. The NP wanted two-thirds support for cabinet decisions, which the ANC rejected. It was not until November 1993 that agreement was reached when the NP abandoned its demand. De Klerk recognized that an impossible situation would be created if the cabinet had to vote on every decision: 'If the minority parties [of which there would be two] consistently thwarted the will of the majority it might in the end impose intolerable strain on the whole constitutional edifice'.[19]

The formula for the composition of the GNU eventually agreed to and embodied in the interim constitution was that every party winning at least 80 seats (out of 400) would be entitled to a Deputy Presidency; and every party winning at least 20 seats would be entitled to cabinet seats proportionate to the number of seats held by it in the National Assembly. The prescribed mode of decision-taking was included in the interim constitution: 'The Cabinet shall function in a manner which gives consideration to the consensus-seeking spirit underlying the concept of a government of national unity as well as the need for effective government.'

Slowly and painfully the ANC and the NP edged closer together. Initially, while the NP wanted maximum decentralization of government, the ANC wanted a strong central government. Examination of the German federal system, which featured a strong central government and strong *lände* (regions), had impressed ANC constitutional experts. This paved the way for the ANC's acceptance of regional governments whose powers could not be removed by the centre.

The ANC's concession should have cleared the way for the IFP to return to negotiations in view of its insistent demand for a highly decentralized federation. Indeed, in December 1992 the IFP published a *Constitution of the State of KwaZulu/Natal* which embodied proposals that were virtually confederal in character (though not secessionist as some claimed). All along Buthelezi had opposed the principle of an elected constitution-making body and the practice of 'sufficient consensus' in the negotiations. He feared that a victorious ANC would impose its hegemony over South Africa and also destroy the scaffolding of his power-base in KwaZulu, namely the traditional leaders. It was only on the very eve of the election that Inkatha decided to participate, a decision that was no doubt prompted by the possibility that non-participation would hand KwaZulu-Natal to the ANC on a platter and consign Inkatha to oblivion.

First, constitutional principles had to be agreed to. These principles would require the constitutional assembly (the new parliament sitting as the constitution-making body) to incorporate them into the final constitution, and a constitutional court, still to be established, would certify that this had been done. Second, regions (later called provinces) had to be demarcated. Third, legislation had to be prepared for 'levelling the playing field' prior to the election.

The constitutional principles, of which there were eventually 34, were enshrined in the interim constitution that was enacted into law in December 1993. In summary, the most important principles were:

- A constitutional democracy in which all forms of racial, gender and other forms of discrimination were prohibited and equality was promoted.

- Equality before the law, making allowance for affirmative action.

- Separation of the powers between the legislature, executive and judiciary, with appropriate checks and balances.

- An independent, impartial judiciary vested with power of judicial review.

- The diversity of language and culture to be protected.

- The recognition and protection of civil society.

- Provision for the participation of minority parties in the legislative process in a manner consistent with democracy.

- Exclusive and concurrent powers to be vested in the national and provincial governments, with an explicit directive that provincial powers under the final constitution were not to be substantially less than, or inferior to, those provided for in the interim constitution.

- Provincial boundaries could not be changed in the final constitution from their demarcation in the interim constitution.

- Special procedures were to be required to amend provincial boundaries or powers.

- The allocation of powers to the national and provincial governments to be determined by:

  1 The level at which decisions can be taken most effectively.

  2 The national government could intervene where it was necessary to do so for the maintenance of essential national standards or for the establishment of minimum standards.

  3 Where it was necessary for South Africa to speak with one voice, powers should be allocated to the national government.

  4 Where uniformity across the state was required for a particular function, legislative power over that function should be vested predominantly, if not wholly, in the national government.

  5 National economic policies were to be vested in the national government.

  6 The national government should not encroach upon the geographical, functional or institutional integrity of the provinces.

- A Financial and Fiscal Commission was to recommend equitable financial allocations to the provinces and local governments from the national treasury.

- The public service was to be efficient, non-partisan and broadly representative of the public; and members of the security forces were to be prohibited from furthering or prejudicing party political interests.

- There was to be an independent Reserve Bank, Public Service Commission, Auditor-General and Public Protector.

Two late additional principles sought to appease Buthelezi and the IFP, whose participation in the election was in doubt right up until the eve of the election; and General Constand Viljoen of the Freedom Front. Viljoen had emerged as the most popular leader of the ultra-right forces and had become convinced that it was necessary to seek an Afrikaner *volkstaat* by participating in the negotiations for the final constitution – which meant participating in the election. His decision to participate further weakened the ultra-rightwing and virtually extinguished their ability to wage a counter-revolutionary uprising.

Traditional leadership was to be recognized and protected, and provisions in a provincial constitution relating to the role, authority and status of a traditional monarch were to be recognized and protected in the constitution. Referring to the quest for a *volkstaat*, principle number 34 acknowledged the right of a cultural community to self-determination, provided there was substantial proven support for this within the community concerned.

The independent 'homelands' of Transkei, Bophuthatswana, Ciskei and Venda had little option but to be reintegrated into South Africa: Transkei and Venda, whose military dictators supported the ANC, agreed willingly. Bophuthatswana and Ciskei were reluctant but, faced with popular unrest and pressure from the South African government, were both forced to acquiesce.

Significant legislation drafted by the MPNP and passed into law by parliament created institutions designed to level the playing field in the run-up to the election. These included:

- The Transitional Executive Council (TEC) came into operation in January 1994. It was a multiparty body with a wide brief to facilitate at all levels of government the transition to democratic government by creating and promoting a climate for free political participation. It was also to ensure that no government or administration exercised its powers so as to advantage or prejudice any political party. To achieve this watchdog function sub-councils were appointed to oversee: regional and local government and traditional authorities; law and order, stability and security; defence; finance; intelligence; and foreign affairs.

  In effect, the TEC was a quasi-government. The ANC hailed it as a major advance towards democracy, declaring that the NP could no longer act as player and referee. The IFP and CP vehemently opposed the TEC.

- The Independent Electoral Commission (IEC), chaired by Judge Johann Kriegler, was required to ensure that the election was free and fair, to determine the result, to adjudicate disputes, and to supervise the conduct of parties during the campaign. It was a formidable task, made even more difficult by the absence of voter lists and the refusal of the IFP to participate in the election, until reversing this decision a mere six days before election day, which required pasting a slot for it onto the ballot papers.

● The Independent Media Commission's task was to contribute to a climate conducive to free and fair elections and, particularly, to ensure that state information services and the SABC were impartial in their treatment of the parties.

The NP and the ANC had agreed that the electoral system for both national and provincial elections should be based on list system proportional representation, which has the advantage of simplicity and of enabling minority parties to obtain some representation. The details of the system were set out in Schedule 2 of the interim constitution: the National Assembly was to consist of 400 members, 200 of whom would be elected from national lists submitted by registered parties, and 200 from provincial lists. Pressure from the DP led to an amendment requiring separate ballot papers for the national and provincial elections.

An unavoidable weakness was the absence of voter rolls for the 1994 election: insufficient time remained to compile them. Instead, eligible voters were required to produce an identity document – which millions did not possess. Accordingly, the IEC was empowered to issue temporary voting cards. Its statistics showed that by 29 April over 3.5 million such cards had been issued, nearly 1.5 million during the four voting days. It was obviously a system liable to abuse since many applicants were unable to provide proof that they were 18 years old.

Another potential weakness in the electoral mechanics was the so-called anti-defection clause (section 43(b)) of the interim constitution, which required that a member of the National Assembly vacate his or her seat on ceasing to be a member of the party on whose list he or she was elected. Ostensibly, there were two reasons for this clause: first, that members were elected via party lists, and not as individual candidates in constituencies; and second, it was held to be a measure that would contribute to the cohesiveness of parties, which was necessary while the fledgling democratic polity was being consolidated. In fact, the anti-defection clause, even though later modified, exacerbated a weakness of proportional representation systems, namely that they give excessive power to party bosses to determine the order in which candidates' names appear on party lists. Expulsion from a party meant vacating one's seat, which, in turn, made independent-mindedness of MPs a risky business, and thereby tended to undermine the oversight role that parliament was supposed to play vis-à-vis the executive. The anti-defection clause was retained in the final constitution as a 'transitional arrangement'.

The election was held over three days, 26, 27 and 28 April – and was extended to 29 April in six areas that had been seriously affected by logistical problems. The challenges facing the IEC were formidable. The magnitude of the task is conveyed by some of the statistics: an estimated 22.7 million persons were eligible to vote (according to the dubious figures contained in the 1992 census) for which 10,000 voting stations were required. The IEC employed a short-term staff of some 300,000, including nine provincial electoral officers, a district election officer for each of 1,200 voting stations, and 21,000 monitors. Remote areas had to be reached prior to the election for purposes of voter education, and then staffed by officials.

The problem of violence haunted the country. There were reports of housewives stockpiling food in case there was a general breakdown of law and order. The IEC was especially worried by the possibility of intimidation: research reports prior to the election suggested that there were 165 no-go areas across the country. But the worst did not happen: the IEC's official account of the elections says that 'the incidence of frustration of political activity was minimal and that the degree of election violence was negligible throughout the country'. That there were irregularities and cheating is undoubted – de Klerk says, plausibly, that as many as 1 million illegal votes were cast, mostly because towards the end of the election temporary voting cards were being issued virtually on request.

Of the 22.7 million eligible votes, 19.7 million voted in the national election and 19.6 million at the provincial level. These figures indicated an 86 per cent poll. Very few spoilt votes were recorded in spite of the substantial number of illiterate voters especially in the rural areas. The ballot papers were simple: they depicted each party's name and crest in party colours, together with a mug-shot of the leader. Perhaps the major reason for the remarkably high turnout was that for many voters, especially Africans, the election was a joyful catharsis and a symbolic affirmation of their new-found rights as citizens.

Nineteen parties contested the election at national level, but only seven gained representation, despite the absence of a minimum threshold. The results were announced by the IEC on 6 May, although the NP had conceded defeat on 2 May. The seven parties and their percentage share of the vote and seats were:

ANC:	62.65	252
NP:	20.39	82
IFP:	10.54	43
Freedom Front:	2.17	9
DP:	1.73	7
PAC:	1.25	5
African Christian Democratic Party:	0.45	2

At the provincial level, the ANC won outright control of six provinces, the NP winning Western Cape and the IFP KwaZulu-Natal. In Northern Cape, the ANC won a plurality of the votes (49.7 per cent), fractionally more than the combined total of votes won by the NP, FF and DP.[20]

Among African and white voters especially, votes cleaved largely to the racial divide. According to Andrew Reynolds's estimates, 94 per cent of the ANC's national votes came from Africans, with only 0.5 per cent from whites. The NP, proportionately to its overall vote, showed the widest spread of cross-racial support: 49 per cent from whites, 30 per cent Coloured, 14 per cent African, and 7 per cent Indian. An estimated 65 per cent of Coloured and Indian voters, respectively, voted for the NP.

In terms of the interim constitution's provisions for the composition of the GNU, the ANC and the NP were each entitled to an Executive Deputy President. Nelson Mandela was duly elected President by the National Assembly, and the NP and the ANC designated F.W. de Klerk and Thabo Mbeki, respectively, as Deputies.

South Africa's constitutional negotiations were unique in several respects, notably the two-phase approach whereby the final constitution was to be drawn up by an elected Constitutional Assembly (CA), the final draft having to be certified by the (new) constitutional court as complying with the 34 constitutional principles laid down in the interim constitution.

The CA, consisting of 400 members of the National Assembly and 90 members of the senate, met for the first time on 24 May 1994 and proceeded to elect Cyril Ramaphosa (ANC) and Leon Wessels (NP) as chairperson and deputy chairperson, respectively. The CA appointed a constitutional committee consisting of 44 members appointed by the seven parties on a proportional basis. It was the critical engine driving the process, though supplemented by numerous bilateral negotiations, especially between the ANC and the NP. Six theme committees were established to examine the constitutional implications of the constitutional principles.

The CA had to work against a tight deadline: it was required in terms of the interim constitution to pass a new constitutional text within two years of the date of the first meeting of the National Assembly, namely 9 May. A deadlock-breaking mechanism could be invoked if required. The CA required a two-thirds majority for passing the text (including a two-thirds majority of all members of the senate in respect of provisions of the text relating to the powers, functions and boundaries of provinces). A panel of five recognized constitutional experts who were not office-bearers in any party, was on hand as an advisory body, and could be invoked in the event of a deadlock. If the draft text were to be passed by a majority, though less than the required two-thirds majority, the draft could be referred to the panel for its advice to be given within 30 days. An amended draft text unanimously recommended by the panel was to be considered by the CA and if passed by the requisite two-thirds majority would become the constitution.

Should the panel fail to reach unanimity or should it recommend a text that the CA failed to pass, the CA could approve any draft text approved by a (simple) majority. Such a text, after certification by the constitutional court, would be referred by the President to a referendum, in which the electorate was asked to accept or reject the text. A majority of at least 60 per cent of the votes cast would ensure that the draft constitution could be submitted to the President for approval and promulgation.

With over 62 per cent of the votes in the founding election, the ANC possessed considerable weight in the CA's deliberations, but even with the possible support of the PAC, its majority fell short of two-thirds. Compromises would be necessary if a text were to be agreed on.

The 34 principles, already largely woven into the text of the interim constitution, provided a fairly elaborate framework of a constitution, but many details required to be elaborated or expanded – and in those details lurked many devils.

The CA sought to operate as transparently as possible and to engage public interest by extensive media reportage and an invitation to submit proposals. In addition, individuals and organizations were invited to address particular theme committees. A constitutional public meetings programme was launched early in 1995 and many meetings were held around the country. Despite efforts to draft a 'people's constitution' and the submission of numerous proposals by the public, the eventual constitution was inevitably based on a series of pacts, especially between the ANC and the NP. The attempt to draw in the public extended to protracted, but unsuccessful, efforts to draw the IFP into the proceedings after it had walked out of the CA in late February 1995, having failed in its quest for 'international mediation' to resolve its demands.

The difficult issues in the negotiations related less to the structure of the executive and the concept of a GNU, which had been resolved at the MPNP, than to a range of seemingly more technical issues, which, in fact, turned out to be both highly important and difficult to resolve. The looming deadline of 8 May 1996 imposed great stress on the principal negotiators. The issues were:

- The relationship between the national and provincial governments.

- The extent to which – if at all – property should enjoy constitutional protection.

- Whether the rights of trade unions to bargain collectively and to strike should be matched by a right of employers to enforce lockouts.

- The death penalty.

- The procedure for appointing judges, the Attorney-General, the Auditor-General and other officials, whose posts required strict impartiality and security of tenure, in such a way that the political factor in their appointments was circumscribed.

- The official language(s).

- Whether the constitution should allow single-medium schools (which, in practice, meant principally Afrikaans-medium schools).

- Whether the Bill of Rights should include 'second-generation' or socio-economic rights, and whether rights could be limited during states of emergency.

Disagreements on these obviously critical issues continued until near the deadline, when the CA was due to vote on the text. The ANC let it be known publicly that if agreement on the full draft could not be reached it would invoke the deadlock-breaking mechanism, going all the way to a referendum – which it knew it would win – and thereafter consider reverting to its own original draft, and not the negotiated text.

That general agreement was reached in the nick of time was little short of miraculous, but it was achieved partly by fudging issues, ambiguous clauses, or qualifying principles by means of 'escape' clauses. For example, the text appeared to have certain federal characteristics, such as the vesting of some exclusive powers in the provinces; but these were largely negated by the retention of the 'overrides' that could be employed by the national government to ensure that provinces stayed basically in line. Moreover, the revenue-raising capacity of provinces was severely circumscribed. The description of the constitution as a hybrid federal-unitary model was misplaced: it was little more than a unitary constitution with federal fig leaves.

The school medium issue provided an example of using an 'escape' clause. Schools were permitted to offer single-medium tuition, but subject to considerations of: equity, practicability, and the need to redress the results of past discrimination. Comparable clauses qualified the principle of equality and non-discrimination by permitting affirmative action; and the right to own property, which was subject to expropriation but only in terms of a general law and with payment of compensation.

The text of the constitution was put to the vote on 8 May 1996: the ANC, NP, DP and PAC voted in favour – 421 votes (327 votes were required for a two-thirds majority); the Freedom Front abstained, the IFP boycotted the proceedings as it had done for much of the CA's negotiations; and the African Christian Democratic Party voted against.

The next hurdle to be faced was certification by the constitutional court. The court was widely reputed to be an 'ANC court' since it was informally designed to be a counterweight to the existing judiciary, the great majority of whose judges had been appointed during the pre-democratic era. None of the 11 judges of the constitutional court had been known as a supporter of apartheid. Indeed, its president, Arthur Chaskalson and another judge, Albie Sachs, had been advisors to the ANC in the earlier rounds of negotiation; others, such as Judges John Didcott and Richard Goldstone, were sturdy liberals who had handed down judgments that struck significant blows against apartheid laws. Whatever their backgrounds, nothing militated against the overall high legal calibre of the court.

The court was faced with a unique task, unprecedented in constitution-making history. It began hearing argument on 1 July 1996. A dominant concern of the court was that it was being asked to consider not only strictly legal issues, but also political ones that were unavoidable. After 10 days of hearings the court retired to consider its verdict. When the verdict emerged on 6 September, there could be few doubts that the court had done its work thoroughly and judiciously. It found that eight sections and much of the constitution's chapter on local government did not fully reflect the 34 constitutional principles and therefore required revision. The most important finding was that the powers allocated to the provinces were less than those prescribed by the constitutional principles. Nevertheless, the court concluded, the basic structure of the constitution was sound, and the instances of non-compliance should present no significant obstacle in the Constitutional Assembly to formulating a text that was fully compliant.[21]

None of the parties wanted to reopen old questions, despite the IFP's blowing hot and cold. The issues were accordingly reduced to technical amendments and were dealt with relatively easily by 11 October. The constitutional court approved the revised text, and the constitution was signed into law by President Mandela as *The Constitution of the Republic of South Africa*, Act 108 of 1996.

Notes

1 Seekings, *The UDF*, pp.260–84.

2 Carolyn Jenkins, 'Economic Implications of Capital Flight', in Liz Clarke, Karen MacGregor and William Saunderson-Meyer, *The Industrial Trade Union Guide* (Durban, 1989), p.180.

3 De Klerk, *The Last Trek*, pp.70–1.

4 Mandela, *Long Walk to Freedom*, p.553.

5 *Idem*, p.578.

6 For the texts of the Groote Schuur, Minute, the Pretoria Minute and the D.F. Malan Accord see Ebrahim, *The Soul of a Nation*, pp.485–97.

7 Padraig O'Malley, *Shades of Difference – Mac Maharaj and the Struggle for South Africa* (New York: Penguin Books, 2007), p.381.

8 For the full text see Ebrahim, *The Soul of a Nation*, pp.498–521.

9 De Klerk, *The Last Trek*, p.237.

10 *Idem*, pp.219–20.

11 Mandela, *Long Walk to Freedom*, pp.588–9.

12 De Klerk, *The Last Trek*, p.232.

13 *Idem*, p.241.

14 Mandela, *Long Walk to Freedom*, p.595.

15 See Ebrahim, *The Soul of a Nation*, pp.540–81.

16 *Idem*, pp.588–94.

17 Johann van Rooyen, *Hard Right: The New White Power in South Africa* (London: I.B. Taurus, 1994), pp.109–11.

18 Roelf Meyer, 'From Parliamentary Sovereignty to Constitutionality: The Democratisation of South Africa, 1990 to 1994', in Penelope Andrews and Stephen Ellmann (eds), *Post-Apartheid Constitutions: Perspectives on South Africa's Basic Law* (Johannesburg: Witwatersrand University Press, 2001), p.61.

19 De Klerk, *The Last Trek*, p.290.

20 For the official account of the election see the Independent Electoral Commission, *An End to Waiting: The Story of South Africa's Elections – 26 April to 6 May 1994* (Johannesburg: IEC, 1995).

21 Carmel Rickard, 'The Certification of the Constitution of South Africa', in Andrews and Ellman, *Post-Apartheid Constitutions*, pp.224–301.

CHAPTER 6

South Africa and the world

In this chapter we examine the role that external factors played in the demise of apartheid focusing on three related and relevant themes:

1 The changes that occurred – particularly after the Second World War – in the structure, process and norms of international society; we note, too, the emergence of new norms which governments, opinion-moulding elites and influential publics could increasingly not ignore in dealing with so-called 'pariah' states like South Africa.

2 The responses of the South African government to these changes and the extent to which foreign policy was dictated by the constraints of domestic policy.

3 An extrapolation from the historical account of South Africa's changing role in international relations of the relative weight of a variety of external pressures and their individual contribution to the establishment of a 'new' South Africa. This will involve, *inter alia*, a discussion of the role of the Great Powers; the exiled liberation movement; international organizations; the Third World and African states in particular; the impact of sanctions; 'soft power' diplomacy; and the attitudes and policies of key personalities.

The international context

The inter-war years: 1919–39

The Union of South Africa was a beneficiary of the international order created by the victorious allies at Versailles in 1919: its government was assigned

South West Africa as a 'C'-class Mandate and the territory was administered as an integral part of South Africa, despite occasional rumblings in the Mandates Commission of the League of Nations about its record. There was, nonetheless, a general expectation at home and abroad that incorporation of the territory into the Union would eventually take place. Further, South Africa remained a respected and conscientious member of the League in the establishment of which General Smuts had been influential. In the 1930s the government stood firm on the issue of collective security against aggression. (Indeed, in 1935 South Africa, with New Zealand, remained committed to sanctions against Italy long after other states had retreated to a less demanding position.)

The truism that foreign policy begins at home is nowhere better exemplified than in the case of South Africa, where domestic preoccupations defined and limited the scope of foreign policy and dictated the pattern of national interests. This was evident in the influence of Afrikaner nationalism in general, and Hertzog's views in particular, on the structure of Commonwealth relations and South Africa's place within that structure in the inter-war period. Indeed, the great debate between Smuts and his Nationalist opponents on South Africa's constitutional status was in one profound sense an argument over what constituted South African nationhood. For D.F. Malan and his Nationalist followers (in opposition from 1934 to 1948), continued membership of the Commonwealth could not be reconciled with the achievement of political supremacy for the Afrikaner *Volk*, the establishment of a republic and, by implication, revenge for the injuries and humiliations of the past. For Hertzog, who with Smuts led a United Party government in office from 1934 to 1939, the struggle to give South Africa equality of status with the other Dominions was an extension into the realm of external affairs of the domestic struggle to gain recognition of the Afrikaners' equality with English-speakers in the political, economic and cultural life of the nation. For Smuts, the Commonwealth concept of 'unity in diversity' (which he did much to frame) was the only means of reconciling white South Africans of both language groups to each other and to continued association with the mother country and the member states. The influential domestic factor was the Afrikaner group, split between the camps of Smuts's party and the Nationalist minority. Depending for electoral support on members of both language groups, Smuts could never afford to antagonize either. This in large part explains his particular conception of the Commonwealth and South Africa's place in it.[1]

Moreover, South Africa felt confident enough to assert a claim to the Bechuanaland Protectorate, Basutoland and Swaziland (both crown colonies), the continued existence of which – in view of geographical indivisibility and economic interdependence – seemed an affront to the Union's recently acquired sovereignty in international affairs. Successive British governments resisted these overtures for incorporation with varying degrees of firmness but the process was nonetheless assumed by the Union's leaders to be inevitable.[2]

At this stage, too, South Africa was the most important state on the continent. Her interests were closely linked with those territories inhabited by white settler minorities, and despite the refusal of white Southern Rhodesians to accept in 1923 the offer of provincial status within the Union, there is evidence suggesting that as late as 1935 many South African politicians, led by Smuts, still aspired to the creation of two or three federations between the Limpopo and the Sudan, 'linked to the Union by a common Native Policy . . .' and 'directly flowing from the common Native Policy, a common defence policy'.[3]

In general, the Union's standing in this period was unquestioned: Britain regarded South Africa:

as a vital military and industrial base, a link in the Commonwealth chain of defence whenever Africa was threatened by outside powers. Moreover in the 1920s and 1930s South Africa's voice on the treatment of racial problems was a respected one, whether in the calm of an Oxford lecture hall, in evidence before a Royal Commission, or as a source of mute encouragement to East African settlers, angered by the idiosyncrasies of Whitehall. Her technicians were at the disposal of less developed areas, her educational institutions the nurseries of a generation of African nationalists, and her cities the venue of a host of inter-African conferences on a variety of subjects.[4]

External discussion of South Africa's black majority was muted: the decision in 1936, for example, to remove a minority of Africans from the common voters' roll in the Cape, excited little hostile comment abroad, although a hint of trouble to come was inherent in Hertzog's insistence that 'native policy . . . is and must remain a matter of *purely domestic concern*'.[5]

Space will not permit an elaborate discussion of the changing nature of international society in the first half of the twentieth century. Certainly, the tumultuous events of the 1920s and 1930s – the rise of totalitarian dictatorships, the failure of the League of Nations to stem the tide of aggressive behaviour by Nazi Germany and Fascist Italy and the outbreak of the Second World War – absorbed the energies of the Great Powers to the exclusion of major concern with the segregationist policies of the South African government. There were – as we shall see – the first hints of what was to come after

1945 by way of external criticism of South Africa's domestic policies; nevertheless throughout this period, the sovereign state – the traditional bulwark of international order since the Treaty of Westphalia in 1648 – maintained its traditional role as the source of law, authority and power in the international system and this despite liberal aspirations insisting that sovereignty be legitimized by the principle of national self-determination and efforts to institutionalize the principle of collective security as a means of deterring and defending against the threat of interstate war.

Yet the international context in which South African policy-makers had to operate varied in the 1920s and 1930s from one of benign global indifference to the problems of a small state geographically distant from the main centres of power and influential international society to one – in the post-1945 world – in which its domestic policies aroused passionate concern and hostility together with a high and unwelcome salience in a host of international organizations.[6]

One consistent theme in the story of this descent from 'paragon to pariah'[7] (Sara Pienaar's expressive phrase) is the interaction between domestic and foreign policy. South Africa was, of course, by no means unique in this respect, but what is striking in this particular case especially after 1945 – is how far the formulation and conduct of foreign policy was concerned with defending the country's domestic political arrangements. Hence our editorial decision to concentrate – in the first instance – on analysis of internal developments in the expectation that the reader will then be hopefully well equipped to understand the incentives and constraints that governed the responses of external actors to South Africa's domestic policies.

Change in the structure, process and norms of international society: 1939 and beyond

The values underpinning the 'classical' state system (again the legacy of Westphalia) – sovereign equality, non-interference in the internal affairs of states and the separation of foreign from domestic policy – came increasingly under attack in the decades after 1939.

Thus the states that went to war in 1939 were not simply concerned with redressing an unfavourable balance of power brought about by Germany's appetite for conquest, but were also concerned with destroying a state whose domestic policies were an affront to all civilized people and a potent threat to the maintenance of order in international affairs. Hence the Allied insistence on unconditional surrender and the self-conscious effort to instil new values in the defeated states in order to underpin the democratic systems of Italy, Germany and Japan – the establishment and maintenance of which systems were the price of readmission to the international society of states. This radical departure from the time-honoured principle of non-interference in the internal structure of a defeated state, and the punishment meted out at Nuremberg and elsewhere from 1947 to war criminals for 'crimes against humanity' – in particular, the barbarous treatment of European Jewry – clearly indicated that this traditional distinction between foreign and domestic policy no longer held good.

Thus, however much international law might assert that a state's claim to sovereignty protected it from criticism or intervention, a crucial precedent had been set with respect to the treatment of minorities – or, indeed, majorities – within its boundaries. It is true that a domestic jurisdiction clause (Article 2:7)[8] was written into the Charter of the United Nations, but the belated recognition of the horrors of the concentration camps in Nazi Germany ensured that human rights and, in particular, those of racially persecuted groups, would over time become the subject of intense international concern. No Western state, however conservative and however wedded to traditional assumptions of power politics, could ignore this new dimension in world politics which was to become a source of ideological conflict in a world already polarized by competing Western and Soviet conceptions of what constituted a desirable international order. Thus a significant tension emerged between the need for order and claims for justice by oppressed peoples.

A second legacy of the Second World War was the emergence of two superpowers – the US and the USSR. Both were anti-colonial in outlook, indeed the declaration of the Atlantic Charter by Roosevelt and Churchill in 1941, and in particular Article 3 which endorsed 'the right of all peoples to choose the form of government under which they will live' was – despite British reservations – interpreted as signalling the end of empire by the nationalist movements of Asia and Africa. Their supporters took heart from the early defeats of Britain and France at the hands of the Japanese, which had clearly demonstrated that white men were not psychologically, morally or indeed technologically, superior, nor had they a God-given right to rule 'lesser breeds without the law'.

Third, the human and material costs of the war sapped the will of the European colonial powers to maintain imperial rule: the abandonment of Palestine and the granting of independence to India and Pakistan in 1947 set a precedent which could hardly be denied to those who claimed the right to national self-determination elsewhere – and in Africa in particular.

Thus by 1945 the stage was set for a new phase in the evolution of the international system. European dominance of that system had effectively come to an end, and succeeding decades were to witness major changes in structure, process and values. As Hedley Bull argues:

The old Western-dominated international order was associated with the privileged position of the white race: the international society of states was at first exclusively, and even in its last days principally, one of white states: non-white peoples everywhere, whether as minority communities within those white states, as majority communities ruled by minorities of whites, or as independent peoples dominated by white powers, suffered the stigma of inferior status.[9]

The struggle to eradicate this stigma was to become a central theme in the politics of the post-war world.

This struggle had both a conservative and radical dimension. Again Hedley Bull's insight is instructive:

The non-European or non-Western majority of states in the world today . . . played little role in shaping the foundations of international society to which they belong . . . [but] . . . by securing a place in the society they have given their consent to its basic rules and institutions . . . they themselves have sought the right of membership of it and the protection of its rules, both vis a vis *the dominant European powers and in relation to one another.*[10]

This acceptance of a Western definition of statehood was paralleled by the emphasis placed (for example by the Organization of African Unity established in 1963) on the traditional norms that underpinned it: sovereign equality: the inviolability of existing frontiers: and non-intervention.

But if nationalist elites were conservative with regard to the structure of the international society they sought to enter, they were revolutionary in terms of the demands made upon it. The achievement of statehood and the recognition of their formal sovereign equality left much unfinished business: political independence without economic viability and succour for deprived millions represented only a half-won victory, which the West – it was claimed – exploited to its own advantage and for its 'unjust enrichment'. In this sense the new states were dissatisfied with the existing global distribution of power and resources: and an insistence on justice, for redress for the evils of decades of colonial neglect, therefore, dominated the external posture of the 150 new states which entered international society after 1945. It was, however, couched in terms different in kind and degree from claims made in earlier periods, and provides one more telling example of the perennial tension between the values of order and justice in international politics.

In the post-war era, however, justice for new states was defined as the achievement of economic and racial equality: indeed, the two were fused together to provide a potent anti-colonial ideology which explained past miseries, analysed present discontents, and offered hope of a better future. Further, the experience of economic deprivation and of racial stigma provided a degree of cohesion for the poorer states of three continents which otherwise might have had little in common in terms of culture, tradition and political complexion.

The claim for economic justice has been global, embracing the great majority of states of the southern hemisphere – many of them poor and underdeveloped – and pitting them against the rich, industrialized countries of the north. And superimposed on this economic division was a racial one: the rich were white, the poor non-white: hence the assertion that racial inequality buttresses economic disparity. Finally, a demand was made for a global transfer of resources from north to south, and an end to the arms race between the Great Powers which was perceived as a wasteful diversion from the moral obligation to aid weaker states.

Thus, in the perceptive words of A.N. Johnston:

third world states seek to transform aspects of the international order . . . (to) . . . challenge the nation state values and sovereignty-dominated image of international values . . . African and Asian states have attempted to instil anti-colonialism and anti-racism as the central values of an evolving world community.[11]

The question remains: what impact did the twin demands for economic and racial equality have on the international system? Certainly, South Africa and its apartheid policy became a crucial and indeed the most salient test case in international debate about these issues.

The United Nations proved to be the main forum for the articulation of these new values and the developing world's interests reflecting them, despite the view of the founders of the UN who saw its utility largely in security terms. The Security Council, for example, was an attempt to institutionalize the Concert of Great Powers that had won the war – on the assumption that if they had remained united and willing to employ the enforcement procedures laid down in the Charter, no power would dare to resort to war in defiance of the Council – by definition – the international community.

But the Afro-Asian states that joined the organization in increasing numbers in the two decades after 1945 defined the role of the UN in radically different terms. For them the Charter was a 'global Bill of Rights' (the phrase is Ali Mazrui's), the most important of which rights was national self-determination.

The UN, therefore, became an organ for the collective legitimization of statehood for ex-colonial territories and, as their numbers increased, the General Assembly became 'more and more a channel for the expression of the demand for the definite termination of Western colonialism'.[12]

The fact that this objective was largely achieved by 1960 is a tribute to the strength and pervasiveness of the anti-colonial ideology and its influence on the tone and substance of debate in the General Assembly. It affected the policies of the great colonial powers no less than their nationalist opponents in dependent territories: the French eventually succumbed, despite – or perhaps because of – the costs of bitter rearguard actions in Indo-China and Algeria; the British quickly abandoned the achievement of political and economic viability as criteria for statehood, for, by 1960: 'all that mattered was that an indigenous elite, with some degree of local support, should exist and be willing to take over'.[13]

For nationalist movements, on the other hand, the UN and its Special Committees on Colonialism and Apartheid effectively internationalized the indigenous struggle for independence, providing a forum for receiving petitions and a platform for liberation movements to state their cases against colonial powers. Thus the UN, in effect, legitimized anti-colonialism both as ideology and strategy, and, in doing so, elevated racial equality and national self-determination to the status of norms by which the action of states in both domestic and foreign policy would be judged.

In this climate, colonialism became indefensible, and although we must be wary of exaggerating the influence of the UN on the process of decolonization, there can be no doubt that the organization helped accelerate the transfer of power by giving Third World nationalism a moral and legal status, the validity of which even the most conservative governments could not easily deny without repudiating those liberal values which informed their own political theory and practice.

Indeed, so far had the pendulum swung that, by 1961, India would justify its forceful annexation of the Portuguese colony of Goa on the grounds that colonialism constituted aggression, that UN practice (and the declarations and resolutions legitimizing that practice) had effectively 'abrogated the legal right of European states to rule non-European territories'.[14] Thus, on matters colonial the traditional legal constraint against aggression did not operate and had been replaced by a legal right to take even forcible action against colonialism.

In explaining the West's moral ambivalence on the issue of colonialism, Cold War considerations must also be taken into account – expressed in its reluctance to challenge the dominant ethos of the UN. At the height of the

Cold War in the 1950s and 1960s, the allegiance of 'neutralist' Third World states was seen as a valuable prize in the competition between East and West. Hence denying the right of subject peoples to independence – or prolonging resistance to that goal – was perceived as playing into the hands of the Soviet Union which everywhere spared no effort to denounce the iniquities of colonialism. (The imposition of Soviet rule on Eastern Europe in the 1940s and nineteenth-century Russian imperialism across the eastern landmass were rarely, if ever, equated with Western imperialism. What mattered to the new elites of Asia and Africa was the prospect of exploiting East–West competition to their advantage in terms of development and military assistance.) This coincidence between the emergence of Cold War rivalry and the major phase of decolonization was undoubtedly helpful to the anti-colonial cause. In the late 1960s, however, the utility of neutralism as a ploy for bargaining between East and West weakened somewhat under the pressures of détente between the Soviet Union and the United States, the emergence of China as a 'third force', the failure of the Soviet economic model to take productive roots in Asia and Africa, and, too, Western disillusion with the political and economic performance of many Third World states.

Thereafter, the thrust of anti-colonialism altered course: continuing white rule in Rhodesia, in the Portuguese colonies and South Africa still provided a major source of Third World unity on the issue of racial equality and national self-determination. But in the 1960s at the UN and elsewhere the pursuit of economic equality meant that accusations of neo-colonialism became more frequent. A coalition of states – the Group of 77 – was established in 1964 at a meeting of the UN Conference on Trade, Aid and Development (UNCTAD) and the West responded with the doctrine of partnership, defined by Hedley Bull 'as the rich having a stake in the development of the poor, and the poor in the further development of the rich'.[15]

The failure of aid programmes devised under this rubric hardened Third World attitudes, while the oil crisis of 1973/4 and the economic recession that followed led to corresponding disillusion with liberal doctrines of economic aid, reinforced by the frailty of government in many Third World societies. Radical elites now perceived the economic relationship between rich and poor states as a zero-sum game: what was required was a global redistribution of wealth rather than handouts from the affluent states. The success of the OPEC states in improving their position at the expense of consumers in the Western world initially raised hopes that other raw material cartels could do likewise. This proved illusory, but the new mood and, in particular, the bitter hostility directed at multinational corporations was reflected in the 1974 Declaration of a New International Order and in the Charter of the Economic Rights and Duties of States, both of which received massive support at the UN.

The struggle for racial equality has followed a similar path: an expression of a global concern with the promotion, the assertion and protection of human rights in general. Here too the UN played a vital role in the creation of new norms and values to the extent that, as Geoffrey Goodwin remarks: 'the United Nations has become a mechanism through which race relations are apt to be transformed into international relations'.[16]

The contrast with the pre-war international system is instructive: Japan in 1919 had failed to persuade the founders of the League to include a clause on racial equality in the Covenant. Their successors in 1945, no doubt reflecting the universal revulsion aroused by the mass extermination of 6 million Jews, inserted in the Charter references to human rights and fundamental freedoms of all without distinction as to race, sex, language or religion. In the course of the next 30 years the Third World majority at the General Assembly of the UN succeeded in mobilizing support for a series of declarations and covenants, all affirming the sanctity of human rights and legitimizing resolutions for obtaining them – for example, in 1967 the right to use force in a war of liberation. Other pertinent examples are the Declaration of Human Rights (1948), the Declaration on the Granting of Independence to Colonial Peoples (1966) and the UN-sponsored Convention on the Elimination of All Forms of Racial Discrimination (1965). What this demonstrated was the capacity of the organization – unlike its predecessor – to evolve as circumstances changed and reflect in its debates and discussions the new emerging values of the post-war period.

The post-war emphasis on human rights – and racial equality in particular – had several important consequences: first, the Third World coalition stressed the importance of collective, rather than individual, rights: hence the emphasis on the rights of 'subject peoples to be liberated from colonialism, subject states from neo-colonialism, and subject races from racial discrimination'.[17] Secondly, UN-sponsored declarations on human rights have been interpreted by an influential school of legal theorists as a source of customary international law and therefore binding on all states, whether or not they are signatories to such declarations. As Rosalyn Higgins writes: 'Collective acts of states, repeated by and acquiesced in by sufficient numbers with sufficient frequency, eventually attain the status of law'.[18]

These developments, especially with respect to UN resolutions on racialism and national self-determination, had important implications for the policies of the South African government.

Third, individuals and groups – it is claimed – are subjects of international law with corresponding rights and duties. Fourthly, sensitivity to the human rights issue has affected Western practice on the issue of the rights of individuals within the EU where the European Court of Human Rights grants access to aggrieved individuals in terms of the European Convention for the Protection of Human Rights and Fundamental Freedoms. Similarly the signatories to the Helsinki Final Act (and they included the NATO powers as well as the members of the Soviet bloc) were, and still are, enjoined continually to review the state of human rights in their respective countries. The incorporation of a 'human rights' dimension into Western policies, while no doubt useful in the ideological competition with the Soviet Union, nevertheless exposed policy-makers to the accusation of double standards if derelictions of human rights were ignored in states – such as South Africa or Chile – traditionally regarded as part of the Western camp. And, however much European and American conservatives jibbed at accepting the legally binding status of UN declarations and resolutions, influential elites – especially those of a liberal or socialist persuasion – came to accept the Third World view that:

human rights have long since . . . passed into that realm which is of legitimate interest . . . (that) . . . specific resolutions directed at individual states . . . (are) . . . a legitimate method of bringing pressure upon a state and yet not falling foul of the prohibition against interference in Article 2, paragraph 7, the domestic jurisdiction clause of the UN Charter.[19]

Thus a Third World majority successfully injected new values into the international system and new issues into the domestic debate within Western states. Few could be found to defend the traditional view that what occurs inside a state should remain a matter of indifference to the world at large: before 1945, this, and its corollary of non-intervention, were regarded as a major source of order in international affairs on the grounds that relations between states were difficult enough without the added complication of making the state's internal political arrangements a subject for dispute.

It is one thing, however, to assert values which appear to transcend those which traditionally underpinned the states-system. Certainly it is true, as A.N. Johnston remarks that: 'when the legitimacy of domestic, social, political and economic systems is called into question, no doctrine of non-intervention can hope to survive'.[20]

But agreement on how the values of economic and racial equality could be translated into practice, whether between or within states, was less easily forthcoming in an international system where the states – as in the case of

South Africa – remained for so long strong enough to resist their imposition short of defeat in war.

To sum up: after 1945 the global environment in which South African policy-makers had to operate was one very different from its pre-war counterpart. True, the state still retained its traditional status as the key actor in international relations, as the sole provider of security (both internal and external), the source of welfare and – above all – a focus for the maintenance, enhancement and assertion of national identity.

But following decolonizations its number had increased dramatically with many of the newly independent states joining a loose and ill-defined coalition – the so-called Third World. Many were small, poor and insignificant in terms of regional let alone global influence, but the United Nations, and in particular, the General Assembly provided a forum for asserting their self-proclaimed rights for redress from the evils of colonialism.

The so-called 'neutralist' Afro-Asian bloc purported to play an influential role admonishing the two rival superpower coalitions for their seemingly wasteful and unproductive absorption in power politics and arms races in particular to the exclusion of the welfare needs of the poor and deprived in the Third World. This posture had profound benefits in terms of aid and arms sales as both power blocs competed for support from key members of the neutralist camp.

Perhaps the most fundamental change in post-war international relations was the elaboration over time of new norms such as the high salience given to the principle of racial equality both within and between states. And this development encouraged an erosion of the traditional divide between foreign and domestic policy: thus the emphasis on values such as the sanctity of domestic jurisdiction and the principle of non-intervention was undermined – albeit haphazardly rather than consistently in favour of intervention where there was clear abuse of human rights in particular countries. And it was this combination of factors – new states, new institutions, new values – which were to complicate the foreign policy calculations of the major powers and a variety of non-state actors in their reaction to the apartheid policies of the post-1948 South African government.

The mass media

There have, of course, been other changes in international society beside those in structure and values. We refer to one in particular which does have importance and about which white South Africans felt strongly and bitterly – the technological revolution in mass communication. The role of the media in promoting consensus on the new values which have been articulated in international society over the last 40 years has been crucially important. The late Raymond Aron, the distinguished French sociologist, argued that:

The diplomatic universe is like an echo chamber: the noises of men and events are amplified and reverberated to infinity. The disturbance occurring at one point of the planet communicates itself, step by step, to opposite sides of the globe.[21]

Media presentation is highly and inevitably selective. The tone of the Western media in the post-war period has been predominantly liberal, reflecting, indeed reinforcing, that post-war consensus on such issues as racial discrimination and social and economic deprivation. Equally, the media have been important in reflecting that consensus which stresses the state's responsibility to remedy the evils of deprivation and inequality: that the rich and the powerful have an obligation to help the poor and the weak. It has been very difficult, understandably, for Western conservatives to argue against this consensus. Few can be found to defend racial discrimination or economic injustice.

South Africa and the media

Moreover, South Africa in media terms – unlike many other oppressive regimes – was a 'penetrated' state: it was relatively easy to report on apartheid, given the efficiency of communications with the outside world and the government's acknowledgement that banning all media reporting would only strengthen external hostility to its policies. Consequently, apartheid earned far more publicity than other regimes with poor human rights records. Those who suffered knew that their plight was known in every corner of the globe and was universally recognized and pitied. Moreover, their expectations were fuelled by the fact that: 'Newspapers from abroad, broadcasts from overseas, the television screen, video films, popular music that brings ambiguous messages of love and freedom as part of the youth culture of the 20th century, cannot be blanketed out despite government control of the media.'[22] And paradoxically the state's willingness to accept the consequences of media exposure could not be translated into political capital in its contest with the outside world. The bleak and disturbing message, however selective, carried by the world's media prevented any acknowledgement of virtue for permitting it to be conveyed at all.

What, in effect, media coverage did was to link black opposition at home with a global constituency to which it could appeal for redress of grievances, where spokesmen in abundance existed willing to point an accusing finger at South Africa in international forums. Oppressed groups elsewhere had their supporters in Western countries, but none were subjected to the 'publicity war of debate, surveillance, conferences and reports . . . conducted against the Republic.'[23] Russian Jewry, for example, had the backing of the American Zionist movement, but the Soviet Union's legitimacy – its right to rule – was not questioned in international bodies. South Africa, by contrast, became the subject of an international convention – the Suppression and Punishment of Apartheid (1973) – signed by some 52 states.

To sum up the growth of anti-racist sentiment in Western societies, the proliferation of anti-apartheid groups in churches, trade unions, political parties and educational institutions meant that few could be found to defend apartheid, for to do so was to fly in the face of an international morality which found racial discrimination repugnant. But the mere denunciation of racialism was not enough: the question was pressed further: what are you – the politician, the banker, the churchman – going to do about it? Moral pressure of this kind gathered strength from a perception of mounting crisis in South Africa. Whether the pressure emanated from the United Nations, the House of Commons or Trafalgar Square, it compelled a change in Western perceptions and an attempt to redefine what could and should be done over the long term. For these reasons, Western governments found it increasingly difficult to treat the republic 'as simply one among the world's many oppressive states . . . as a familiar, if disagreeable, member of the international community on the same footing as other areas of the world whose governments are sometimes friendly, sometimes hostile, to Western interests'.[24]

South Africa versus the world: 1945–90

In this section of our analysis we do not propose to offer a year-by-year, blow-by-blow account of South Africa's foreign policy and its reaction to the cumulative weight of criticism that over four decades was directed from a variety of sources at the apartheid policy.

Rather we propose to examine particular episodes demonstrating their impact on both domestic and foreign policy and in particular the government's reaction – whether defensive or offensive – depending on circumstances. Thus special attention will be paid to key events, for example, the 1960 Sharpeville massacre; the 'outward movement' in foreign policy in the late 1960s; the short lived 'détente' phase in the early 1970s designed to improve relations with South Africa's neighbours in the immediate region; the Soweto disturbances of 1976; the declining state of the economy in 1985 and after and the ratcheting up of sanctions in the same decade.

(a) The immediate post-war period: 1945–60

The Union had emerged from the Second World War with its status enhanced following its contribution to the Allied war effort; its government was perceived as a highly respected member of international society and in the Commonwealth, in particular, to the evolution of which General J.C. Smuts, the wartime Prime Minister had made a notable contribution. Moreover, his role in the Second World War as the confidant of Churchill, his country's role as a source of British investment and trade and the Western perception that the Union retained strategic significance (on the assumption that a war between the East and West would be a conventional replay of 1939–45) – all these factors gave South Africa a degree of influence and prestige out of all proportion to its position as a small power at the southern tip of the African continent. To this end its government contributed to overcoming the Berlin blockade (1949) and to the Korean war (1950–53).

Throughout the 1950s, South Africa – despite the election of an Afrikaner Nationalist government committed to apartheid – managed to maintain its favoured position in Western circles as a potential ally and a reliable business partner. True, the government refined its instruments of social control through a barrage of repressive legislation – including the 1950 Suppression of Communism Act – which came under increasing attack at the United Nations from the Soviet Union and a relatively small number of newly independent states including India, Pakistan and Ghana. Western governments were reluctant, however, to join in this condemnation until the shock of the Sharpeville killing of 69 black protesters against the pass laws in March 1960.

As Nigel Wordern has rightly stressed 'the Sharpeville shootings marked a dramatic turning-point in South African history'.[25] A month earlier, Harold Macmillan, the British Prime Minister, had warned the South African government in his Cape Town 'Wind of Change' speech that the United Kingdom could not be counted on to support apartheid or to defend apartheid in international forums, that the traditionally close relationship could no longer be sustained given Britain's recognition of the strength of African nationalism and its critical impact on white minority rule on the African continent.

These two events – Macmillan's speech and the Sharpeville killings – together with the banning of the African National Congress and the Pan-Africanist Congress, received massive media coverage across the globe; the consequence was a severe short-term economic crisis with capital leaving the country at the rate of R12 million a month and falling gold and foreign currency reserves from R312 million (in January 1960) to less than R153 million by May 1961.

Throughout this period criticism mounted at the United Nations where the possible use of sanctions against the Union was debated for the first time in the Security Council but vetoed by Britain and the United States. Thus 1960 might be described as an 'annus horribilis' for the South African government. It was also Africa's year and South Africa's situation was made worse by the coincidental increase in the number of independent African states whose leaders were vociferous at the UN and in Commonwealth gatherings in their criticism of the apartheid policy and the government's refusal to prepare South West Africa/Namibia for independence. Indeed, Pretoria had provided for six white MPs from the territory to sit in the South African House of Assembly. Ultimately this weight of hostility was sufficient to engineer South Africa's forced resignation from the Commonwealth – a decision which led in 1961 to the establishment of a republic.

The full significance of these events will be examined in our concluding section; what should be stressed at this juncture is the role that the Sharpeville crisis played in giving South Africa an unenviable place on the international agenda of concern with the plight of oppressed groups – whether minorities or majorities and reflected in the annual debates on South Africa in the UN General Assembly. This is not to say that at this stage South Africa was a pariah state; what must be emphasized is that the country's foreign policy would increasingly be concerned to find ways and means of defending the self-proclaimed merits of its domestic policies.

(b) The 'golden' years: 1962–75

Yet despite the setbacks of the 1960/1 period, the newly established republic rode out the storm of criticism.

There was little the UN or, indeed, the Soviet Union could do to force change on Pretoria. The absence of economic leverage, the Soviet inability to project power at long range (as demonstrated by the 1962 Cuban missile crisis) and the military and economic weakness of its putative allies in the Organization of African Unity meant that Soviet policy towards southern Africa – while high on rhetoric – was low in terms of current achievement in the region. Recovery from the Sharpeville crisis was swift and the 1960s saw an astonishing economic performance with growth rates averaging some 6 per cent per annum. The government devoted considerable effort to the consolidation and extension of economic links with Western powers on the shrewd assumption that the more the republic integrated itself into the international economy, the less prospect there was of economic sanctions against it. Western political and business leaders helped reinforce this strategy, given their conviction that violent revolution by the black majority was improbable. Moreover, economic growth was regarded as the solvent of political ills, on the assumption that racial barriers would eventually collapse as an expanding economy required new sources of skilled manpower and a larger consumer market.

So confident was the Nationalist government of its capacity to withstand external pressure, that in 1965 it launched an 'outward' movement in foreign policy designed to break down the ideological barriers that divided its country from the rest of the continent. Exploratory talks were held with a variety of states in the southern African region and beyond, but only Malawi took the bait and established diplomatic relations with Pretoria. Nor did the government succeed in its attempt to win incorporation into Western alliance structures or to reverse the voluntary arms embargo imposed in 1963, although there were many in conservative ranks in Western Europe who sympathized with both these aspirations.

Nevertheless, throughout this period, despite apparent domestic calm, South Africa remained a major source of concern for its critics at the UN. The organization provided the Soviet Union with a platform for the assertion of solidarity with the Third World and the apartheid regime was an obvious target. Moreover, the Soviet–Third World alliance was instrumental in persuading the General Assembly to pass a series of covenants and declarations on human rights issues. South Africa provided a crucial benchmark in this context: the country was perceived as the last outpost of a decadent Western colonialism, given the concentration of political power in the hands of the white minority and the dependence of the latter on the labour of the black majority for the production of wealth in a capitalist economy. In effect, the republic was perceived in microcosm as a reflection of the profound divisions between rich and poor, black and white in international society as a whole.

Yet this perception was not universal. Afro-Asian hostility could be endured provided important economic links with the Western powers could be maintained – indeed enhanced. Thus, from 1968 onwards, the republic was tacitly accepted as a sound candidate for inclusion in the Nixon Doctrine which assigned a security and development role to regional states which had the resources and commitment to underpin it. Thus a *realpolitik* analysis might suggest that South Africa's 'isolation' was more apparent than real.

Trade and investment flourished to produce an impressive growth rate; the black opposition was seemingly dormant; overt and covert links with significant areas of black Africa were fostered, while arms deals with maverick suppliers made good the shortfall of a rapidly growing domestic arms industry. Afro-Asian hostility expressed in cumulative resolutions at the UN was perhaps an acceptable price to pay for a foreign policy which had staved off the worst – Western intervention in deference to the claims of the Third World. On this reading of events, the state had been preserved intact by a combination of draconian security measures at home and, abroad, by the assiduous cultivation of those powers whose support really mattered on the crucial issue of white self-preservation in a hostile world.

In the late 1960s the South African government tried to capitalize on its strategic position at the junction of the Indian and Atlantic Oceans, arguing that the newly established Soviet naval presence in the Indian Ocean in 1968 constituted a major threat to the security of Western shipping lanes around the Cape.[26] This claim aroused fierce debate in Britain in particular and revived the case for resuming the sale of naval capability to the republic. Yet ultimately, South Africa's projected image as the 'bastion of the free world' failed to convince Western policy-makers. This scepticism was based on the argument that what the Soviets sought by projecting naval power in distant waters was political influence rather than the means to pro-voke military confrontation with the West. Hostile action against Western shipping in the South Atlantic would rapidly – it was argued – escalate into a major conflict with the West. What mattered ultimately was the efficacy of nuclear deterrence which was, after all, indivisible and designed to deter threats – whether conventional or nuclear – whenever and wherever they occurred. Finally, Western governments recognized that in the improbable event of a shooting war in the southern oceans, South Africa would have little alternative but to place its ports, harbours and military facilities at the West's disposal. Thus, because of its strong anti-communist posture, the republic's government could not 'threaten unfaithfulness'[27] to the West. Thus the latter had the best of both worlds: a near-certain guarantee of South Africa's availability in a crisis without the political costs to be incurred by closer political and military cooperation.

This failure to impress the West with its military value led to a shift in South Africa's position. Following the oil crisis of 1973, Pretoria argued that the country's value as a supplier of key raw materials (platinum, manganese, chrome and vanadium) entitled it to explicit Western acknowledgement of its role in the anti-communist struggle. Several Defence White Papers in the 1970s and 1980s stressed that the Soviet Union was committed to a long-term strategy of resource denial to the West. But again, this argument failed to convince; it assumed the Soviet leadership was bent on implementing a grand strategy deriving from some profound sense of historical mission exemplified in the tenets of Marxist-Leninist ideology. A more accurate interpretation of Soviet policy during the Brezhnev years suggested that what moved Moscow was the desire to maintain and assert superpower status in competition with the United States. Certainly, during the 1970s the Soviet Union became a truly global power but it did so by 'pursuing low risk and low cost adventures without a major danger of confrontation with the United States'.[28]

However, despite the setback to the aspiration to become a major outpost of Western defence against Soviet ambitions, there was a brief period in the mid-1970s when South Africa earned a degree of recognition as a state with a positive and dynamic regional role and when domestic policy no longer seemed to inhibit Western and indeed African acceptance of that role. This opportunity arose because of the need for the republic's cooperation in achieving a negotiated settlement of the Rhodesian issue: the resulting 'détente' between South Africa and the frontline states, enhanced by Henry Kissinger's (the US National Security Adviser) visits to Pretoria, gave South Africa the status of a major actor whose views and capability could not be ignored. And for once the government found itself doing business with a statesman whose conservative assumptions about international politics were perceived as helpful and sympathetic: in particular, Kissinger's emphasis on order as the prerequisite for any sensible and rational conduct of international affairs; his hostility to moralistic foreign policy postures; his search for détente at the regional and global level between states, regardless of ideological complexion.

This reaffirmation of the traditional values of Western statecraft by the representative of the world's most powerful country was a source of comfort to a South African government which had always attempted to make a clear distinction between foreign and domestic policy, especially in a regional context.

Kissinger's theory and practice held out the prospect that South Africa's reiterated plea for 'tolerance, mutual respect, the recognition of the sovereign independence of all states, non-interference in each other's domestic affairs'[29] might become the dominant norms governing its relations with its neighbours. And were this to be reinforced by the demonstrated effect of South Africa's capacity to play a constructive economic role in the region as a whole, the legitimacy of the state – however peculiarly constituted – would be easier to defend in a wider international context.

(c) Unstable equilibrium: 1975–85

The high expectations entertained in the 1960s and early 1970s were by and large engendered by apparent stability at home and the long-term aspiration for a breakthrough in relations with the African states symbolized by the 'outward movement' in foreign policy.

But this aspiration was short-lived and collapsed in the wake of the abortive South African military intervention in Angola in 1975. This followed Soviet-Cuban intervention in the territory, created by the Portuguese withdrawal and the outbreak of civil war between the rival liberation movements – UNITA, FNLA and the MPLA. Now, Soviet intervention indicated a more self-conscious and substantial assertion of its capability made easier by America's impotence following a decade of fruitless and costly intervention in Vietnam. Some 20,000 Cubans backing the newly established MPLA government in Luanda were supplied with a considerable array of weapons: aircraft, mechanized units, small arms, and a 22 mm rocket launcher (worth in all some $225 million). Any prospect of American help to aid South Africa's counter-intervention failed following a Senate vote against further covert CIA assistance in December 1975. The United States was thus confronted with what it perceived as a major challenge at a time when it appeared least able to respond.

The consequences of the Soviet-Cuban deployment in Angola were profound:

- The Soviet Union established a claim to have its voice heard in a region where hitherto it had relatively little influence;

- Moscow's standing with the OAU rose, while Fidel Castro justified his credentials as a defender of Third World interests against the hated apartheid regime;

- China's standing in Africa was reduced after its failure to sustain initial support for the UNITA/FNLA forces in the Angolan conflict.

Success in Angola encouraged a similar intervention in Ethiopia to recoup the losses incurred when the Somali government expelled its Russian advisors in November 1977, and thereby helped consolidate a Marxist regime occupying a critically important strategic position in the Horn of Africa. The ill-fated South African attempt to counter the Cuban intervention spelled an end to its efforts to promote détente with its African neighbours. Equally, Henry Kissinger's grander vision of détente with the Soviet Union collapsed.

Regional insecurity in general increased as Pretoria perceived the Soviet-Cuban bridgehead in Angola as clear evidence of Moscow's 'total onslaught' against white rule in the southern third of the continent – the objective of which (it was argued) was to gain exclusive access to South Africa's extensive mineral resources. The liberation movements – the ANC and SWAPO in Namibia in particular – thus acquired new and threatening significance for the Nationalist government in South Africa, which saw them as tools of Moscow now rejuvenated for the task of the 'armed struggle' by the support of an active Soviet policy in the client states of Angola and Mozambique.

The achievement of Soviet-Cuban gains in southern Africa coinciding with widespread black unrest reinforced the Nationalist government's perception that Moscow was engaged in a 'total onslaught' against the republic. This generated a response – the so-called total strategy – which, in effect, gave the military increasing influence on decision-making via the mechanism of a State Security Council which subjected virtually every facet of government policy to scrutiny in terms of its implications for security and the country's political stability. To this end, an elaborate National Security Management System was devised based on a technocratic faith in a capacity to manipulate the twin instruments of reforms and repression in the expectation that once order was restored and economic grievance redressed, suitable black candidates for negotiation over the country's political future would become readily available. Yet what was missing from this attempt at counter-insurgency theory and practice was an alternative vision of society (an essential requirement for any government attempting to compete for popular support against its opponents). Short-term military tactics became long-term strategy, and the prospect of a political solution receded still further. This, then, was the consequence of defining security needs in the context of a 'total onslaught' where opponents were – wittingly or unwittingly – perceived as the dupes of a malevolent conspiracy centred on Moscow.

The threat represented by the ANC and SWAPO in the early 1980s appeared to give ample scope to the implementation of a 'total strategy' in a regional context. Hence the pattern of military intervention in the 1980s in support of proxies such as the Mozambique National Resistance Movement (MNR) in Mozambique, UNITA in Angola and the Lesotho Liberation Army – all ostensibly designed to counter the 'armed propaganda' of the ANC operating from bases beyond South Africa's borders. But the strategy of 'destabilization' also had the wider objective of to 'actively . . . turn back the tide of foreign (or Marxist) influence' seen to be penetrating the region, and as the 1984 Defence White Paper emphasized, to allow 'black

African states to experience the dangers of Russian involvement in their countries, as well as the suffering and retrogression that follows upon the revolutionary formula'.

Yet despite this bellicose policy, the government was also active on the diplomatic front: in the early 1980s South Africa made 'informal and secret' agreements with Zimbabwe, Botswana, Lesotho and Swaziland to 'thwart ANC operations from or through Zimbabwe'. But the most dramatic example of this diplomatic démarche was the signing of the Nkomati Accord with Mozambique on 16 March 1984. Jan Heunis in his book *The Inner Circle* gives a vivid account of the negotiations, the outcome of which was an undertaking by South Africa to halt military attacks on the ANC bases in Mozambique and to suspend the supply of weapons to Renamo, an anti-government movement active in Mozambique. There was, in addition, a corresponding commitment by the Mozambique government to rein in the ANC guerrillas and forbid their infiltration into the republic in pursuit of the 'war of liberation'. As Chester Crocker remarked: 'by any measure, it was a great accomplishment for South Africa's diplomats and security bureaucrats, so eager for external recognition of its legitimate security interests against guerilla infiltration and terrorist violence'.[30]

Indeed, the agreement received widespread publicity abroad and was perceived to be a major breakthrough in relations between South Africa and the rest of the region. Sadly, the ink was hardly dry on this non-aggression pact before arms shipments to Mozambique were removed once more with the active support of some senior officers in the South African Defence Force. As Crocker rightly maintains:

One moment, he (Machel) received contrite noises and pledges of tangible aid from top levels in Pretoria who were visibly scrambling to 'save Nkomati'; at the next, he was given fresh evidence of unauthorised flights and intensive unidentified radio transmissions emanating from across the eastern borders, from Malawi in the south to South Africa's Transvaal Province. Anyone who knew the region knew that such activity could only have one source . . . How could the government in Pretoria have committed one of its most striking accomplishments to be so promptly discredited? What purpose could be served, short term or long term, by acting to destroy what confidence existed in one's solemn word.[31]

The regional setback represented by South Africa's forced withdrawal from Angola in early 1976 had its domestic counterpart in the Soweto disturbances of June 1976: the willingness of the new generation of militant young blacks to challenge the state's authority led to a change in Western perceptions of South Africa's long-term capacity to survive, free of the threat

of black revolt against apartheid. Few disputed the government's commitment to using the considerable resources at its command in defence of law
and order; what was abundantly clear, however, after 16 years of relative
domestic calm, was the erosion of the state's deterrent capability, its failure
to prevent violence.

Thus for many, both inside and outside South Africa, Soweto then
represented the fundamental break with the past. Internally, this provoked
a debate on the utility of reform; externally, Western policy-makers were
forced to recognize that it was not enough to place one's faith in the long-
term ameliorative impact of economic growth on the structure of apartheid.
Instead, a more positive, self-conscious involvement was required on the
assumption that recurrent violence would probably be the pattern of the
future, with all that implied in terms of increasing pressure for drastic action
against the republic from anti-apartheid lobbies. In the past, Western governments had been able to live with an ostensibly stable and economically
productive South Africa. Once that image of stability was threatened by
internal violent dissent, however, foreign ministries were forced into the realm
of public debate and it became increasingly difficult to justify inaction –
especially when many lobbies, especially the anti-apartheid movement, were
demanding decisive action. As George Shepherd has argued: 'There are
hundreds of human rights groups, largely based in the Western World, who
represent church, civil, ethnic, racial, economic and humanitarian zones.'[32]
There was also a tacit acknowledgement that sooner or later (and as the
periods of calm between disturbances shortened) a major sustained confrontation would probably occur and one which would not easily, if at all,
be amenable to crisis management from the outside. Western economic
interests would be put at risk and – in the event of severe unrest – be damaged
beyond hope of recovery in the short run.

There was also the Soviet role in the region to be considered: would
the threat of conflict escalation with the West over the republic's future act
as a constraint, or serve as a 'window of opportunity'? That no clear, convincing answers could be given to these questions reinforced the Western
imperative to move the republic along the road to reform before the worst
happened and options were foreclosed.

(d) The beginning of the end: 1977–89

In the mid-1980s events reached a climax with the outbreak of disturbances
in the Vaal Triangle – the major industrial conurbation of South Africa. As
we argued earlier, this development followed a six-year period of piecemeal

reform initiated by P.W. Botha (Prime Minister from 1978 and State President from 1983) and designed to ameliorate the social and economic plight of the black majority. Recognition of black trade unions, the erosion of the colour bar in employment culminated in the establishment of a Tricameral Parliament representing the interests of white, Indian and Coloured voters but making no provision for Africans. By 1985, black opposition had been resuscitated in the form of the United Democratic Front, a loose umbrella organization of social and economic groups allied to the exiled ANC.

The government responded by declaring two states of emergency – in July 1985 and March 1986 – and external pressure – in part generated by widespread media coverage of the security forces in action in black townships – mounted swiftly. Overseas banks, led by the Chase Manhattan in New York refused to roll over South Africa's $14 billion-worth of external debt; the United States Congress, the Commonwealth and the European Community passed a variety of sanctions packages, in effect weakening the Western commitment and characteristics of Western policy during the early 1980s. This was a setback for the policy of constructive engagement, the brainchild of Chester Crocker, Assistant Secretary of State for African Affairs. The task, he argued, was to 'steer between the twin dangers of abetting violence in the Republic and aligning ourselves with the cause of white rule'.[33]

Throughout the 1980s South Africa appeared to be in a state of 'unstable equilibrium'. Yet constructive engagement still had its uses, witness the pro-tracted negotiations over the status of Namibia, the successful conclusion of which led to Namibian independence in 1990 and the ultimate with-drawal of both Cuban and South African troops from Angola and Namibia respectively. The Namibian initiative was made possible by the emergence of 'new thinking' about superpower cooperation in settling issues of Cold War dispute in areas such as southern Africa, following the accession of Mikhail Gorbachev to power in the Soviet Union in 1985. The absence of public hostility in the republic to withdrawal from Angola and the pre-paration for Namibia's independence gave F.W. de Klerk, Botha's successor as President (from September 1989) a degree of flexibility in his search for a new deal between black and white. Soviet cooperation in producing the Namibian agreement and – more important – the collapse of the Berlin Wall in November 1989 (the most potent symbol of the end of the Cold War) reinforced his conviction that the Soviet Union's 'total onslaught' was no longer a credible threat to South Africa. As he put it, 'it was as if God had taken a hand – a new turn in world history . . . we had to seize the opportunity. The risk that the ANC was being used as a Trojan horse by a superpower had drastically decreased.'[34]

And while the collapse of communism in Eastern Europe provided a major incentive for speeding up the process of domestic change, the constraint of economic sanctions on the country's beleaguered economy offered another compelling reason for releasing Nelson Mandela, the imprisoned ANC leader and lifting the ban on that organization's political role within South Africa. This was the substance of de Klerk's momentous speech to the Cape Town parliament on 2 February 1990. As he argued, the impact of sanctions had made 'people realise that we were in a dead end street'.

Similarly, in May 1991 he argued that South Africa was falling into an 'absolute impasse'. And this view had long been espoused by Nelson Mandela: as long ago as 1985 he had argued that:

We had been fighting against white minority rule for three-quarters of a century. We had been engaged in the armed struggle for more than two decades. Many people on both sides had died. The enemy was strong and resolute. Yet even with all their bombers and tanks, they must have sensed they were on the wrong side of history. We had right on our side, but not yet might. It was clear to me that a military victory was a distant if not impossible dream. It simply did not make sense for both sides to lose thousands if not millions of lives in a conflict that was unnecessary. They must have known this as well. It was time to talk.[35]

Thus, by the end of the 1980s South Africa was set on a new course, involving initially covert negotiations with the ANC, its erstwhile opponent, which led to the creation of a new constitutional dispensation and South Africa's first fully democratic election in April 1994.

The range of pressures on South Africa

In this concluding section of our analysis we offer a commentary on the role and relative significance of external actors in promoting the end of apartheid. What now remains – without doing injustice to the complexities of the historical record – is to analyse the separate contributions of the major actors in moving South Africa to the turning point of 1990.

The role of the Great Powers

It is, however, important to recognize that the process that led to 1990 was tortuous, seemingly haphazard and punctuated by periods of stalemate between the South African government and the forces ranged against it. Thus, it could be argued that South Africa's fortunes fluctuated throughout the post-war period with its government at times remaining passively on the defensive or, alternatively, attempting a proactive role in the hope of dis-arming criticism. The Nkomati Accord discussed earlier, is an example of the latter tendency both in the region and beyond.

In retrospect, one might claim that at the time of maximum isolation, when the degree of hostility was at its highest, South African decision-makers recognized that what they had to do was to sit tight; prepare for the long haul; cultivate and enhance critically important relationships with Western states – all in the hope that ultimately world opinion and policy would alter to provide a truer perspective of South Africa's position, rather than a biased one. The assumption behind this major thrust of South African policy was that Western elites in both political and economic spheres were essentially supporters of the status quo in southern Africa. They, therefore had little inducement to alter their perception of South Africa's domestic situation unless, and until, they were compelled to do so, because of some fundamental change in the southern African sub-system. For that to happen, the changes would have to be profound enough to threaten significantly Western political and economic interests in the region. Above all, the Western governments had no desire to devise strategies e.g. comprehensive sanctions to cope with an unknown future and one which might have unintended and unexpected deleterious consequences for their interests.

The West also aspired to avoid having to make hard choices about commitments to the republic in advance of any major social upheaval. Thus South Africa could take advantage of Western decision-making which tended inevitably to be concerned with short-term considerations, rather than long-term planning to meet future contingencies.

There was, furthermore, an implicit assumption in policy-making that if stability were to crack then clearly Western perceptions would change to the detriment of South Africa's security and seemingly invulnerable position. Certainly the Western powers were impressed with South Africa's stability and implicitly acknowledged that any attempt to intervene against South Africa, whether economically or militarily, would run into the most pro-found difficulties. Thus South Africa succeeded in impressing upon the West its capability to resist either internal subversion, covert infiltration, or indeed external intervention.

The South African government tried at times to reinforce this percep-tion of the Western powers: hence the outward movement in foreign policy devised in the mid-1960s. This was designed, according to Dr Hilgard Muller, South Africa's Foreign Minister, to improve economic and political cooperation with the African states in the expectation that 'the attitude of the West would improve . . . We must simply accept that our relations with the rest of the world are largely determined by our relations with the African states.'[36] Of course, this strategy assumed that the country's internal stability could be maintained, indeed, even enhanced if necessary by further measures of draconian legislation. As Larry Bowman explained the outward strategy was an attempt to establish an 'economically and militarily strong South Africa, surrounded by client states, befriended by the Great Powers and geographically isolated from any significant political enemy'.[37]

Similarly, the policy of 'détente' in the mid-1970s appeared to give South Africa breathing space in its relations with Western powers and encourage the perception that a policy of 'liberalism abroad and repression at home' could be sustained over the long run, given the West's dependence on South Africa's role to help engineer a settlement of the Rhodesian crisis. The most notable example of the success of the détente policy was the signing of a trade pact between South Africa and Malawi in 1967 and the subsequent agreement to exchange diplomatic representatives.

Yet throughout this period, up to 1974, it was clear that the failure to achieve a Rhodesian settlement and the long drawn out counter-insurgency in Angola and Mozambique were forcing choices on Pretoria, which in a sense had the effect of undermining the objectives of South Africa in the region as a whole. To begin with, the Rhodesian deadlock had the twin consequences of focusing world attention on South Africa, as repeated calls were made to extend sanctions to the republic; and second, and more important in the local context, Pretoria felt obliged to give economic support to the new regime and, from August 1967, military aid, by sending police units to help the fight against guerrillas operating from the Zambian side of the Zambezi.

Thus, throughout the period 1965–76 Western self-interest dictated constructive engagement with Pretoria, encouraging reformist trends internally and enlisting cooperation on a settlement of the Namibian issue. And all this against a background of events which complicated the calculations of South Africa and the West. The emergence of the ANC as an organization committed to a radical mobilization of black opinion via the strategy of the 'armed struggle' and the independence of Zimbabwe in 1980, achieved by a combination of sanctions and guerrilla war, was a potent reminder of what might happen in the republic unless reform were undertaken with speed and conviction.

At the time – the early 1980s – constructive engagement seemed appropriate, indeed, seemed to be the only choice for conservative governments antipathetic to the use of blunt instruments such as economic sanctions. The effects of such sanctions were uncertain, their impact difficult to monitor or control, the political objective often lacking precision. Those who pressed for their use argued that the strategy of the 'quick kill' was preferable on the grounds that things could only get worse, making negotiated solutions even more improbable. This argument had a certain logic to it, appealing in the abstract; but Western governments resisted its force not simply for reasons of economic interest, but because it assumed a capacity to take action well in advance of a crisis occurring. For most governments, however, the short term is all – or nearly all – and constructive engagement was a short-term response designed to deal with the here and now of South African politics in the hope of fending off some vaguely sensed apocalypse in the future.

Western preoccupation with apartheid was not, however, exclusively a matter of economic and political interest, important as both are in shaping perceptions and determining policy. Indeed – as we have seen – the pre-servation of those interests required a variety of responses over the last four decades, all of which have had to be justified as contributing to the end of apartheid. Testing policy for ideological virtue has rarely been required in relation to other states with oppressive regimes, and if it was, as in the debate over the political utility of trade and investment in the Soviet Union, the argument usually centred on the contribution which closer economic ties might make to détente *between* the superpowers rather than their potential for internal liberalization.

This is not to deny that Western governments were critical of the Soviet's human rights record, but it was usually the external record (the invasion of Afghanistan, for example) which led to the demand for punitive economic measures, rather than better treatment of dissidents within the regime. In the Soviet case, as James Barber remarks, the 'international order is given priority over individual justice'.[38] To do otherwise would have been to endanger international peace.

South Africa, however, enjoyed no such advantage. True, it had nuclear weapons, but these provided no strategic let alone political advantage in the country's dealings with the outside world. Indeed, it relied on a 'bomb in the basement' posture *à la* Israel and a system of deterrence by uncertainty about both its capabilities and intentions and this, if anything, strengthened distrust and hostility abroad.[39] It was not a great power capable of destroy-ing the world if pushed too far, and the application of a double standard in this context arose, therefore, from the assumption that in the South African case morality and interest coincide, pointing policy in the same direction, whereas plainly they did not with regard to the Soviet Union. In other words, double standards of moral judgement were not necessarily the product of malice and ignorance; they were the inevitable products of a state system in which considerations of force and capability, perceptions of threat to economic and political interests dictate the strength or weakness of a state's response to human rights issues elsewhere. And South Africa was a small power, out of step with the prevailing moral norms and unable to threaten unfaithfulness to a Western world with which it had long enjoyed close economic links. There was little, therefore, it could do to avoid scrutiny and criticism of its domestic policies.

Western declarations of interest in political change in South Africa and the relative indifference shown to abuses of human rights elsewhere derived also from the self-ascribed status of the republic as a Western state. The claim to be part of the West, standing for the defence of Western values, was often made by South Africa's leaders in their efforts to combat external criticism, but there the South African government was hoist with its own petard: as Mrs Thatcher pointed out, 'but since the South Africans assert that they belong to the Western world, they must be expected to be judged by Western standards'.[40]

This broad proposition neatly encapsulated the peculiar nature of the relationship between South Africa and Britain in particular. It was the product of a variety of historical links embracing cooperation in two world wars, a once-respected status for South Africa in the Commonwealth; the common heritage of a Westminster model of parliamentary government; close and productive economic relationships; a multitude of kinship ties. These ties – tangible and intangible – combined to produce a degree of 'cultural proximity', provoking expectations on Britain's part that South Africa should 'comply with Western standards and procedures of race relations'.[41] And when these expectations were not met, criticism was the result. On the other hand, the 'cultural distance' between Britain (together with the West in general) and many oppressive regimes in the Third World did not lead to similar expectations, and – by the same token – to expressions of repugnance. But in South Africa's case 'cultural proximity' cut both ways: it may well be (and this is difficult to support with hard evidence) that the traditional preference for constructive engagement rather than dramatic intervention involving sanctions could be explained in part as a reluctance to make economic war on a society whose close economic linkages with the West were reinforced by the more intangible ties of culture and political tradition. Certainly the Wilson government's unwillingness in the 1960s to intervene militarily against the Smith regime in Rhodesia was ascribed by some commentators to kith-and-kin connections between the two countries.

What then were the imperatives governing both the outward movement and the détente strategies? Those of a Marxist persuasion in Britain, and elsewhere, argued that the outward movement and indeed the détente strategy was forced upon the South African government because of domestic economic difficulties, that both policies were primarily a desperate search for new markets and outlets for investment.

This seems an oversimplification of a very complex process in which a variety of motives were clearly at work and were very difficult to disentangle into neat components required by the dialectic. Rather, it could be argued that for a combination of reasons which had to do with the emergence of a favourable domestic and international climate between 1965 and 1975 South Africa was primarily concerned to translate a traditional position of economic dominance in the region into political and diplomatic advantage. Hence the emphasis was on the contribution its government could make to the maintenance of security in physical and strategic terms in southern and central Africa by military and economic means. Hence, the related aspiration to establish a Southern African Economic Community as both symbol and practical expression of a new peaceful and constructive political dispensation for the region.

James Barber has pertinently argued that it was a misperception to see the South African government being driven by economic forces it could not control; rather it was attempting to use economic and military resources to gain political objectives.[42] In this sense it was the republic's economic strength not its economic problems which provided the foundation for both the outward movement and détente. This is not, however, to deny the possibility that over the long term significant economic advantages might well have accrued to the republic, measured in terms of access to hitherto untapped sources of water, power and outlets for capital and manufactured goods. In the last analysis if South Africa could become a benevolent hegemon for the region as a whole, that outcome could only strengthen its standing and influence in the West and deter any prospect of hostile action against the state.

So much then for policies – the outward movement and détente – designed to earn respite from external pressure. But, as remarked earlier, the Soweto disturbances of 1976 profoundly affected Western perceptions of South African capacity to maintain internal stability indefinitely. Thereafter, pressure mounted on the Western powers to take a more proactive role in promoting change in South Africa, culminating in programmes of limited sanctions.

The role of diplomatic actors

In this context it is appropriate to refer to the efforts of certain key diplomatic representatives of the Western powers in South Africa. Space will not permit a detailed account of the role of the Western diplomatic corps in their efforts – both public and private – to help break the stalemate in South African politics.

A detailed account of one such ambassador's role is that afforded by Robin Renwick in his book *Unconventional Diplomacy in South Africa*.[43] He had played a pivotal role in Zimbabwe's achievement of independence and as Ambassador to Pretoria he worked tirelessly to persuade influential economic and political elites to accept the need for fundamental political change.

He arrived in 1986 at a time when

Mandela and most of his senior colleagues remained in prison with no prospect of release, the ANC and Pan-African Congress (PAC) were banned, the press were heavily censored, a state of emergency was in force, nearly all demonstrations of political dissent were suppressed and 2500 people were in detention without trial.

Nevertheless he felt that as the representative of Margaret Thatcher, the British Prime Minister, and

through the presence of so many British citizens and as the largest foreign investor, we had a position of influence in South Africa and that we should try to use it more actively than, hitherto, we had seemed disposed to do. This was contrary to the received wisdom in the Foreign Office at the time where the sentiment was that we should keep our heads down and aim to engage in damage limitation. It was made clear to the South Africans that I was going there as the Prime Minister's appointment and that, I hoped, would give me some leverage with the regime: for they could hardly afford the complete withdrawal of her support, though they had been doing precious little to justify it.[44]

And in pursuit of this more positive objective of British foreign policy, Renwick quickly established contact with major players on both sides of the political divide. In particular, he concentrated his efforts

on the Afrikaners and the black leadership . . . to avoid falling into the trap of consorting mainly with the more liberal elements of the English speaking community who, unfortunately, with one outstanding exception [Mrs Helen Suzman] were even less likely than in Rhodesia to have any decisive political effect.[45]

Hence he talked, *inter alia*, to prominent Afrikaner journalists, editors, churchmen, Pieter de Lange, the head of the *Broederbond*. Renwick also had conversations with a number of the 'younger members of the National Party caucus . . . [who] were worried about the impasse in which South Africa found itself internally and externally'.[46]

At the same time he expanded diplomatic and personal contacts with prominent black leaders including, for example, Cyril Ramaphosa, charismatic leader of the National Union of Mineworkers, and a number of ex-Robben Islanders and members of the United Democratic Front who had served long sentences in prison with Mandela. Renwick also funded some 300 social and economic projects in the townships and their implementation gave him plenty of opportunity to meet local leaders – many of whom were *de facto* supporters of the ANC. His activities in this context (and we can only offer a brief summary) might be described as a variation of what has come to be called 'soft power' diplomacy as distinct from its 'coercive' counterpart. Thus calls for sanctions were denied in the knowledge that his role as a diplomatic activist was to a degree constrained by the generally hostile attitude of Mrs Thatcher to the ANC and indeed the use of economic instruments of pressure against the republic's government. With impressive skill and judgement Renwick managed to play an important role in the years leading to the release of Mandela and his colleagues early in 1990. It is also worth emphasizing that Renwick was an influential actor in the events leading to the settlement of the Namibian issue in the late 1990s.

One final vignette to illustrate the Ambassador's potent influence: he persuaded Douglas Hurd, the British Foreign Secretary, to rescind the ban on foreign investment in South Africa as a way of offering President de Klerk an inducement to release Mandela and unban the ANC. Thus de Klerk could more easily placate those in his own Party who needed convincing that radical steps could produce a positive reaction from one influential external actor. As Renwick explains 'de Klerk relayed this to the members of his Cabinet on the eve of the opening of Parliament' – a good example of what could be done using traditional methods of secret diplomacy – yet another example of 'soft power' at work.[47]

Similarly, what emerges from Ambassador Princeton M. Lyman's account is the intense interest and commitment demonstrated by key members of the resident diplomatic corps in prodding the protagonists in the negotiation process into continued talks following a breakdown caused by events beyond the control of the parties in the Multi-Party Negotiating Forum which convened in 1993. This diplomatic role was principally concerned with attempts at mediation between rival factions and, in particular, the conflict between Buthelezi's IFP and the ANC – an issue discussed at length in Chapter 4.[48] Their concern was to make the election in 1994 'as inclusive as possible' and as noted earlier this was achieved but only at the last minute when Buthelezi was finally persuaded by outside influence to participate in the election.

The exiled ANC

We focus now on the role the exiled ANC played in the transition from apartheid to democratic government. It is appropriate at this point to consider at the same time the role of international organizations and the UN in particular, and the impact of the African states both within and outside the organization. The roles of these actors – different as they were in terms of structure and impact – were nevertheless interrelated and merit, therefore, collective rather than separate analysis.

Consider first the role of the exiled ANC: Scott Thomas in his definitive study rightly stresses the survival capacity of the organization over a 30-year period from 1960 onward.[49] Thus the so-called External Mission of the ANC contrived to project a global image stressing the organization's exclusive claim to international legitimacy and representation of South Africa's black majority in the outside world. As Graham Evans has explained,

Indeed, the past four decades both supporters of the ancien régime and opponents of it were united in regarding the external world as essentially contested territory in the sense that a vital strategic component of the foreign policies of the government and of the ANC's International Department was to secure international recognition, legitimisation and support. And until February 1990 when de Klerk began the transition process away from apartheid, there is little doubt that of the two mutually competing sets of foreign policies, that of the ANC was the more successful, in that it succeeded in mobilising near-universal support for the imposition by the UN of mandatory sanctions against Pretoria.[50]

This was achieved by a variety of means: maintaining the armed struggle both at home and in the southern African region forcing the South African state to embark on repressive measures which singularly failed to win 'hearts and minds' in the conventional method of counter-insurgency strategy. True, the so-called war of liberation never had much prospect of toppling the South African state, but it did succeed in maintaining a perception among many blacks that the organization had a serious purpose and its reputation correspondingly rose. Equally, abroad the liberation campaign and the government's counter-response of destabilizing South Africa's neighbours for harbouring ANC insurgents in the 1980s enhanced the salience abroad of the ANC's claims to have just cause for its military campaign.

With regard to the UN, the ANC, according to Scott Thomas,

Exaggerated expectations of what the United Nations could accomplish. The
ANC and many Afro-Asian states wanted the United Nations, quite beyond
its capacity (and arguably, contrary to the Charter's principles), to become an
instrument of coercion, to force the Western powers to implement economic
sanctions by setting the General Assembly against the Security Council. Even
after the Special Committee on Apartheid was formed with this implicit role, the
UN's ineffectiveness became apparent because it was unable to force member
states to implement General Assembly resolutions, which is why the ANC
became disillusioned with the UN.[51]

Nonetheless, the organization played an important role in isolating South
Africa from the mainstream of international relations. True, it proved
impossible to translate the widespread hostility expressed in countless
anti-apartheid resolutions in the General Assembly into meaningful and
sustained practical measures against the South African state. One exception
was the voluntary arms embargo of 1963 which the Security Council made
mandatory on member states in 1978. This, however, had unexpected consequences; it hastened the development of the local arms industry to the
extent that by the late 1980s South Africa was the world's twelfth-largest
arms exporter.

But the real value of the UN to the anti-apartheid struggle was its success
as a forum for mobilizing support against apartheid from the Afro-Asian
bloc (as noted earlier) which dominated the General Assembly for much of
the post-war period. Many of the states – in Africa in particular – were small,
poor and lacking in international visibility once the heady moment of independence had passed. Yet membership of the UN offered the Afro-Asian
bloc an opportunity to unite behind an anti-colonial ideology which
identified South Africa as a prime target for condemnation. This strategy was
strengthened by the absence of any conflict of political and economic interest over the South African issue. In general, the states perceived themselves
as 'revolutionary' – i.e. as a dissatisfied group determined to change an
international status quo which, in their view, had been profoundly biased
against *their* interests.

As R.B. Ballinger argued the matter,

. . . the dispute over South West Africa and the Union's racial policy are now
so closely interwoven that they react one upon the other in ways which, if
not easy to define, nevertheless inflame the atmosphere in which either is
considered.[52]

Faced with this barrage of criticism South African delegates to the General Assembly initially invoked Article 2:7 – the domestic jurisdiction clause of the UN Charter claiming that the international community had no right to intervene in the internal affairs of a member state. After all, apartheid did not constitute 'a threat to international peace and security' but this defence made no real headway as resolutions criticizing South Africa became an annual event at meetings of the General Assembly.

Subsequently, South Africa tried a new approach: thus the South African defence of its policies presented the evolution of the Bantustans as a form of decolonization while at the same time rejecting the opposite principle of political and economic integration as a basis for a solution to the problems of a plural society. It cited in support of the policy the evidence of territorial partition in areas such as the Indian sub-continent, Ireland and Palestine, and, in defending the Group Area legislation, 'exposed' the failure of integrationist policies in Britain and the United States.[53] Neither justification was accepted by critics at the United Nations, who in the ideological debate appear to enjoy the best of both worlds. The republic's policies could be branded as colonialist and the government denied the one defence the European powers were able to offer – namely their evident willingness under nationalist pressures to forgo control over their colonial dependencies. In particular, opponents of South Africa denied the South African claim that independence was contemplated for the Transkei. If nothing else, anti-colonialism with its emphasis on the evils of imperialism and the moral responsibility of the colonial powers to rectify these evils was difficult for the Western powers to refute. After all, the values enshrined were precisely those which Western liberals had long espoused and, indeed, asserted against their own governments in the period of imperial rule. Western governments were invariably on the defensive having to recognize eventually that the principle of non-intervention enshrined in the domestic jurisdiction clause (Article 2:7) of the UN Charter was no longer sufficient or indeed respectable justification for refusal to act against South Africa. As the Pakistani delegate to the General Assembly claimed in 1952: 'it is better to be carried away by emotions rather than bogged down by legal sophistications'.[54]

This view carried increasing weight in the massed ranks of General Assembly delegates. Indeed, it could be argued that the claim that human rights should override judicial limitations finds current expression in the classic doctrine that the international community has 'a responsibility to protect'. To this extent, the apartheid issue was crucial in setting the pace for the subsequent elaboration of new legal and political doctrines for the better governance of the international society.

Thus with regard to international organizations – whether intergovern-mental or NGOs – South Africa found itself increasingly isolated. Sporting and cultural associations in abundance were targeted by the ANC and South Africa was either expelled or forced to withdraw.[55] The ANC won the struggle for 'hearts and minds' abroad and indeed at home to the extent that black opposition within South Africa was encouraged by the perception of a global constituency to which it could appeal for redress of grievances. Indeed, as we have noted, external spokesmen in abundance were readily available to point an accusing finger at South Africa in a wide variety of international forums. Oppressed groups elsewhere had their supporters but none was subjected to the 'publicity war of debate: surveillance, conferences and reports . . . conducted against the Republic'.[56]

It is fair to conclude that for much of the post-war period the ANC won the diplomatic and political battle for support from a variety of quarters in the external realm. Its efforts to promote a revolutionary war of liberation designed to overthrow the South African regime ended in stalemate but this was not a crucial failure given the success the movement enjoyed in denying the country a 'rectitude base' from which to pursue a vigorous and constructive foreign policy. (In this context the example of Canada and the Scandinavian countries as good citizens of international society provides a salutary contrast given their governments' capacity to follow strategies of niche diplomacy in areas like mediation, support for Third World causes, international peacekeeping, etc.)

This battle was, however, long and hard with fluctuating fortunes for the South African government; the latter – as argued earlier – did enjoy some short-term tactical successes with the policies of the outward movement and détente. As Evans argues

Tacit assurance of support from a superpower patron (the USA) which perceived the ANC to be a Soviet puppet organisation was, for South African decision makers, a powerful disincentive to change. In this period Cold War bipolarity protected South Africa and ring-fenced the state to the extent that regime survival was still conceived primarily in terms of military diplomatic initiatives rather than in terms of reform of domestic political institutions.

Yet, citing Evans again:

By the mid-1980s the South African conflict had reached what William Zartman calls a 'hurting stalemate'. In effect neither side had anywhere else to go but to the negotiating forum. The demise of the Cold War was a convenient moment for a new political dispensation for both sides since the ANC for its part

realised that although it could render South Africa ungovernable, it could not,
without the support of a powerful patron, succeed in bringing the state down.
As Joe Slovo, leader of the South African Communist Party, claimed, 'Neither
side had won the war. The NP couldn't rule any longer and we (the ANC)
couldn't seize power by force. So that meant both sides had to compromise.
That's the reality.'[57]

The sanctions issue: some theoretical observations

Clearly, on this issue both Western governments and corporations with interests in South Africa were in a difficult position. The middle ground between inaction and the adoption of punitive measures had been steadily eroded by the evidence of the increasing repression and the refusal of the South African government to take decisive steps on reform. Hence the (again reluctant) adoption of selective sanctions by the EC and Japan in the summer of 1986, followed by the more stringent package of the United States Congress which involved the overriding of a presidential veto. But there were three compelling reasons behind Western reluctance to impose mandatory comprehensive sanctions in the South African or almost any other case.

The first arises from a peculiar feature of the structure and process of modern government, namely the fact that Western governments are not well placed to engage in prophylactic action designed to forestall a crisis, however long predicted. For foreign ministers the short term is all: coping with the current flood of 'telegrams and anger' is hard enough without having to plan for contingencies which may never arise, and if they do may well assume a form and substance very different from that envisaged by contemporary scenario builders. By contrast, there is a general perception among Western leaders that comprehensive sanctions are a blunt instrument, with indiscriminate impact, which in any case, is only likely to be felt over the long term. By contrast, in the South African case supporters of sanctions such as Allan Boesak – a leading activist in the UDF – believed in quick and effective sanctions, 'not a long drawn out campaign that goes on for years, and leaves us with an economy that is a wasteland'.[58]

The second objection relates to the imprecise nature of the political objective sanctions are designed to achieve: it is one thing to use such instruments as a way of compelling a state to desist from aggressive action against a neighbour: that, after all, was the original intention of the sanctions rubric built into both the Covenant of the League of Nations and the Charter of the United Nations. But it is quite another matter if sanctions are designed to compel a state to abolish the *raison d'être* on which it is based and create in its place an entirely new political dispensation.

As in the case of military intervention, economic pressures only succeed if the objective is relatively limited and those responsible for its imposition have a commitment to monitoring and controlling the course of events induced by sanctions. Moreover, keeping means and ends both distant and limited in scope is difficult over the inevitable long term that sanctions require for their implementation. If economic measures fail to make an immediate impact, naval blockades and perhaps military intervention may be required as the crisis deepens. Thus the initial objective in the South African case – to force the protagonists to the conference table – was perceived as potentially widening to involve military occupation and the reconstruction of the target state by external agencies. What inhibited Western governments was the real possibility that means and ends would inevitably fuse, confronting the sanctioning states with commitments far removed in scope and substance from those originally envisaged. One influential study written in 1963 claimed that the enforcement of sanctions would cost some £60 million (for a six months' naval and air blockade of South Africa's 1,800 miles of coastline); casualties might be between 19,000 and 38,000 for a three–four-month period.[59] In these circumstances, it was claimed, a successor regime to the ruling National Party would inherit a wasteland.

These arguments might be regarded as deriving from a *realpolitik* critique of the utility of sanctions; they are in essence an example of a conservative (in a philosophical sense) version of statecraft, reflecting a sceptical view of what can be achieved in an uncertain and unpredictable world. They were and indeed could not be articulated in public defence of Western inaction and caution with respect to the use of economic coercion against South Africa. Their substance – however true – rang hollow as compared with the liberal reasoning of those who believed that united action on behalf of human rights transcended the Clausewitzian niceties constraining the limits of political intervention in defence of a good cause. Nevertheless, considerations of this kind were deeply embedded in the thinking of those responsible for policy and constituted a major inarticulate premise of the case for rejecting comprehensive sanctions as a straightforward and relevant solution for South Africa's ills.

Over the long term, however, it must be acknowledged that the arms embargo paid off, in the sense that South Africa was eventually forced to the conference table on the Namibian issue partly because its ageing aircraft capability proved inferior to the Russian-supplied aircraft and SAM missiles of the Angolan government and their Cuban surrogates. It could also be argued that the diversion of resources to military manufacture over a 25-year period meant that more productive and civilian state enterprises were denied the means to improve black living standards and thus soften the impact of apartheid.

Yet another example of the ambiguous impact of sanctions was the sports boycott. True, some local sporting associations were forced to integrate their activities with their black counterparts (cricket and athletics being prime examples in this context). On the other hand, as the external world shifted the goal posts and insisted on the principle of no normal sport in an abnormal society, South Africa reacted by resorting to the power of the purse and, in effect, bought overseas rebel cricket and rugby tours. These enterprises lacked legitimacy, not to mention any sense of genuine *international* competition.

The impact of sanctions in practice

Sanctions of various kinds (economic, political, military, cultural and sporting) were applied spasmodically against South Africa over a period of 40 years (beginning with India in 1946). Their application was usually the result of a domestic crisis (Sharpeville 1960; Soweto 1976; the disturbances of 1984–6). Those sanctions with a limited objective – e.g. the arms and sports boycotts – did clearly make an impact, the outcome of which can be measured in terms of results achieved – even if there were unintended consequences – as we have seen – in the case of the arms embargo. This is less easy in the case of sanctions designed to achieve more grandiose objectives such as the replacement of one regime by another.

Following F.W. de Klerk's epoch-making decision in February 1990, both sides in the sanctions debate claimed victory for their respective arguments. The pro-sanctions lobby argued that the cumulative effect of growing economic isolation produced by massive disinvestment (and the threat of more to come), together with the denial of key markets for exports (e.g. coal and steel) and the loss of new technologies, led to a fundamental reconsideration of government policy on the issue of black advancement. Certainly, the statistics of disinvestment were stark; by June 1988 150 US firms had withdrawn from the South African marketplace, more than one-third of the total involved in South Africa in 1984. Similarly, some 150 non-US companies (49 of which were British) had withdrawn.

Moreover, the pro-sanctions lobby could point to the oft-repeated statements of South African finance ministers during the 1980s that the republic
required R3 billion a year to support a growth rate of 6 per cent per annum
and this was simply not forthcoming in that troubled decade. They could
also cite the evidence of the electoral debate in 1989 when F.W. de Klerk
made it abundantly clear that South Africa had no choice but to seek a
restoration of its traditional links with overseas traders and investors if
economic and political disaster was to be avoided. But, it was too easy to
draw the conclusion that sanctions alone had the desired effect of moving
de Klerk into new and radical reform in the early months of 1990.

The impact of sanctions varied. Certainly, there is still disagreement over
what damage was caused to the economy and how much unemployment
was generated by their imposition. For example, Hufbauer, Shott and Elliott
claimed that 'post-1985 sanctions cost (South Africa) less than 1 per cent of
GNP'[60] while de Klerk claimed that the economy grew by an annual rate of
2.7 per cent between 1986 and 1989. But the crucial factor was that overseas
confidence was badly damaged not only by external pressures to disinvest,
but also doubts about the republic's long-term political stability.

Nevertheless, a variety of factors – other than the sheer and direct pressure
of sanctions – must be taken into account for an understanding of what
moved the de Klerk government away from apartheid. First, it is clear that
the South African economy was in severe difficulties for much of the 1980s
well before major sanctions were launched. What sanctions did, in effect,
was to make a bad situation worse. Consider, for example, what happened
to the South African economy in the 15-year period between 1972 and 1987
when a combination of internal and external pressures accelerated the process of change. 'Each trade agreement, each bank loan, each new investment,
is another brick in the wall of our continued existence'.[61] This assertion in
August 1972 by B.J. Vorster, South Africa's Prime Minister, neatly encapsulates
the dominant thrust of his country's foreign policy for much of the post-war
period. Closer integration into the Western political economy had as one of
its primary objectives the inhibition of Western policy-makers against any
attempts to apply economic pressures against the republic as a means of
inducing political change in the structure and process of apartheid, leading
to a weakening of white control on the levers of state power.

Fifteen years later, the Vorster strategy appeared to be in ruins: new
foreign investment had virtually dried up; South Africa had been forced
to negotiate new terms for repayment of more than half of its $24 billion
debt to creditor banks overseas; and the negotiation of new trade agreements with traditional customers and the securing of new credit was proving

increasingly difficult. This combination of private and public sanctions had been induced by nearly two years of black unrest (starting in September 1984). In turn, all these developments contributed to extraordinary measures of state repression via the declaration of two states of emergency in July 1985 and June 1986.

Second, it has been argued that, the 'private' sanctions of many overseas bankers and corporations were based on a calculation of South Africa's long-term stability; that it was the violent events of the 1985–8 period and the general weakness of the economy rather than external pressure on banks and companies to disinvest which led to withdrawal and the sale of assets; that these 'private' sanctions were based by and large on straightforward calculations of risk and were far more important in persuading de Klerk to change direction. The reduction in profits and the decline in the rand's value which began in late 1981 helped to negate the importance of their South African investments for a growing number of MNCs.

Third, the so-called 'hassle' factor and the pressure on universities, state governments and local authorities in the United States and elsewhere to disinvest from corporations with interests in South Africa cannot be ignored. These developments, must therefore, be regarded as an example of pressure on a variety of economic actors to withdraw for reasons other than those based on orthodox calculations of economic and political risk. Moreover, the cost of adherence to the voluntary codes of conduct in terms of black employee support programmes also induced some companies to disinvest. This, of course, could be indirectly attributed to the sanctions controversy in the sense that the creation of the codes was an attempt to demonstrate commitment to an alternative strategy.

Another line of defence adopted by governments and by companies was the emphasis placed on codes of conduct designed to improve the wages and working conditions of black workers employed by foreign companies in South Africa. The EC Code and the Sullivan Code (for US companies) were often cited as good examples of the policy of constructive engagement, but it has to be remembered that their creation was in large part inspired by their critics and the adverse publicity given to MNC employment practice in a series of newspaper articles in Britain and the United States in the late 1970s. No doubt the codes did make a contribution of some substance but, given their voluntary nature, Jesmond Blumenfeld is surely correct in his assertion that the codes 'relied almost exclusively on public pressure and "moral suasion" for their impact, with official attitudes stopping well short of the employment of fiscal incentives and penalties, such as subsidies and taxes, as a means of enforcement'.[62]

Blumenfeld also argues that:

Even in the EC, where the codes were supposed to be officially monitored, there was much criticism of governmental half-heartedness and of the reluctance to publish the results. Indeed the monitoring process reflected little official commitment to the aims and objectives of the codes. This non-interventionist approach to enforcement and monitoring of the codes effectively minimised their impact on economic and social conditions in South Africa and gave the lie to the claim that Western governments were serious in their professed attempts to promote non-racialism and power sharing within South Africa, even within the relatively narrow confines of the labour market.[63]

Blumenfeld concludes: 'Many Western-owned firms in South Africa did not . . . fully subscribe to the objectives of the various codes and this severely undermined the benefits of the exercise and thereby exposed even the most committed signatories to the continuing charge that Western investment in South Africa was not contributing to real reform.'[64] Indeed, it is worth asking why more was not done to encourage, or enforce compliance with the codes, especially as both governments and companies were understandably anxious to 'rid themselves of the allegation that they supported apartheid policies'. Blumenfeld argues that there were two reasons: first, an absence of electoral and economic advantage, and second that until the upheavals of the mid-1980s,

Western governments tended merely to accept the predominant judgement of international markets on the issue. Prior to the mid-1980s, this judgement clearly was that the likelihood either of revolution in South Africa or of enforced Western disengagement was too remote to warrant heavier discounting of the expected returns on trade with an investment in, the Republic.[65]

These were compelling arguments for Western inaction, but there can be no doubt that governments and companies missed a trick in not publicizing their efforts (which in some cases were considerable, e.g. Shell and Unilever in South Africa) more widely. Even so, the implicit assumption behind the codes – enforced or not – was that the evolutionary change over the long term was to be preferred to complete disengagement and here the argument fell foul of the opposite assumption underpinning the work of the anti-apartheid movement that change was required quickly and that sanctions of all kinds offered a powerful short-term solution. They might well have cited Keynes's famous dictum: 'in the long run we are all dead'.

It was this combination of private sanctions and public pressure from the anti-apartheid movement and its NGO allies which provoked the crisis of the mid-1980s and weakened the capacity of the South African state to hold on indefinitely. If nothing else, sanctions (however haphazard in terms of cumulative impact and however limited in scope and substance) served as a potent symbol of the world's disapproval of the apartheid regime. The republic could not, therefore, aspire to international legitimacy until apartheid was no more. Internally, too, sanctions had a psychological impact: a siege mentality and a high degree of uncertainty about the future were characteristics of the 'white minority' mindset – especially in the late 1970s following the Soweto rebellion and for much of the 1980s after the resurgence of black opposition in the form of the United Democratic Front and a variety of other organizations.

In assessing the impact of sanctions (or any other single element of policy), we must allow for the 'play of the contingent and unforeseen in human destiny' (the historian H.A.L. Fisher's evocative phrase). A good example in the South African context was the forced withdrawal of the hardline President P.W. Botha from politics and his replacement by F.W. de Klerk, a more pragmatic and flexible leader.

We have already examined the reasons why de Klerk was willing to do a deal with the ANC. And we should bear in mind that the coincidental ending of the Cold War in 1989 gave de Klerk a degree of flexibility in the wider arena of foreign policy. Clearly the notion of a 'total onslaught' by the Soviet Union against South Africa was now absurd and the traditional arguments of rightwing elements both within and outside the National Party lost their potency.

Finally, de Klerk, unlike Botha, was convinced that continuing economic weakness coupled with a massive increase in population would wreck South Africa unless a new political dispensation could be agreed, one, moreover, strong enough to restore the confidence of foreign investors and international funding agencies in South Africa's future.

In this context it is worth quoting de Klerk's own views on the role of sanctions:

There is, however, no doubt that sanctions seriously harmed and distorted the South African economy – and probably reduced its economic growth rate by about 1.5% per annum. In general, South Africa could obtain virtually everything that it required – including oil – but at a premium. South Africa was also forced to make enormous and uneconomical strategic investments, such as its investment of some 13 billion Rand in a huge refinery near Mossel Bay which converted gas from marginal off-shore fields into petroleum. . . . Even more seriously, the world's major banks, led by Chase Manhattan, sensing the *inability of the South African government to control the situation, refused to roll over about $14 billion of short-term loans. South Africa was faced with the extremely serious prospect of being forced to default on its international commitments and was able to save the situation only at the last moment through the negotiation of a draconian repayment agreement. The banking crisis was perhaps the most serious economic threat that South Africa ever had to deal with – and ironically it was precipitated by market forces caused by a collapse of confidence rather than by government-imposed sanctions.*[66]

The banks were also responding to threats from domestic customers to take away their business unless the banks withdrew from South Africa.

However, by 1988 South Africa appeared to have weathered the storm. De Klerk again:

The government's strict state of emergency had successfully restored order throughout the country. Despite tightening sanctions and growing uncertainty, the economy actually grew at an annual rate of 2.7% between April 1986 and February 1989. There is every reason to suppose that the government would have been able to maintain control of the country for at least the next ten or twenty years.[67]

It seems reasonable, therefore, to conclude that sanctions played some part in producing change in South Africa. But their role was not unique and solely decisive. Other factors were at work as well, difficult as these may be to quantify in the same way as purely economic indicators. As Merle Lipton argues, we have to take into account 'a mixture of domestic and international pressures and economic and political factors' in assessing the reasons for de Klerk's change of direction in February 1990.[68] And the components of this mixture have in effect been the substance of this study.

The damaged prize

While white living standards did not decline catastrophically even at the height of the sanctions campaign from 1984 onwards, influential white elites – especially in the business community – recognized that the long-term future of the economy was bleak unless and until foreign investment on a significant scale could be induced to return. And that was unlikely unless and until the sanctions programme was lifted. And when that did occur in the course of the 1990s as South Africa moved towards democratic rule, those who inherited the state found that attracting much needed investment was more difficult than expected, given the competition from many competing emerging markets and new states in the former Soviet Union, Eastern and Central Europe and the Asia-Pacific region.

Alongside the assessment of the short-term role of sanctions, it is therefore worth quoting the conclusion (written in 1987) of Jesmond Blumenfeld, a leading authority on the South African economy:

While sanctions and disinvestment have undoubtedly resulted in some losses of current output, incomes and employment, their major economic impact has been in further undermining investor confidence and the current rate of economic growth, and hence in reducing the future levels of these variables. This effect cannot be precisely quantified, for the obvious reason that the internal political upheavals have also been destructive of investor confidence. Even so, the external pressures, and the associated exceptional rise in uncertainty, have undoubtedly been major contributory factors in this accelerated collapse of confidence.

The conclusion that the external pressures have caused economic damage will doubtless give comfort to those who actively seek such a result. But, the reduced availability of investable resources, both domestic and foreign, has worrying long term implications for black living standards. For, regardless of future political developments, meaningful and non-cataclysmic political and social change in South Africa . . . will simply not be possible without a substantial – indeed unprecedented – injection of new resources.[69]

True, the 'Government of National Unity' did not inherit a wasteland, as so many in the anti-sanctions camp predicted. Yet it is not unreasonable to assume that the dislocation caused by sanctions to the South African economy – the damage induced by being cut off from best practice in a host of professional, commercial and technological fields, and the effort required to evade the worst effects of sanctions in the 1980s in particular – distracted the South African government and the local business community from the crucial task of liberalizing and deregulating a highly *dirigiste* economy. And this at a time when governments elsewhere were actively engaged in this enterprise to meet the pressures of globalization.

Whether – if sanctions had not been applied – South Africa could and would have made substantial progress leading to a gradual evolutionary change in the political status of the black majority is a question that cannot be answered with any certainty. To the detached external observer the sanctions legacy may, therefore, be regarded as ambiguous in its consequences. Yet it was no doubt deemed a price worth paying for those who suffered under apartheid and who finally achieved the goal of democratic rule in 1994 – an outcome unthinkable just a decade earlier.

Conclusion

What we have tried to do in this penultimate chapter of our study is to single out from the 'booming buzzing confusion' of international relations those external factors which contributed to the demise of apartheid. It would be difficult (and not really sensible) to attempt a precise weighting for any one of these factors; it was rather their cumulative effect which ultimately undid the efforts of successive South African governments to preserve apartheid – a perverted and profoundly humiliating system of governance, the cost of which in terms of deaths and damaged lives is incalculable.

What can be asserted with some confidence is that the changes that occurred in the norms governing state behaviour in the post-1945 period were crucial. Western governments, in particular, had to pay at least some deference to these new norms, the effect of which was to give South Africa a unique status in the international society of states. It was the legislative enshrinement of racial inequality 'in all the spheres of living' that distinguished South Africa from other repressive regimes. To respond as South African ministers did with *tu quoque* arguments in defence of apartheid and by so doing accuse its critics of double standards made little if any impact abroad. Some influential elites in the West might have shared that view; but it was not one which could be easily articulated or defended in the councils of international society or the forums of domestic debate in Western societies.

Moreover, throughout the years of apartheid white South Africans enjoyed an enviable standard of living in contrast to their black counterparts; nevertheless, a price had to be paid and one that was measured in the accumulation of external hostility and pressure. That price was bitterly resented by many whites, but they could hardly have expected apartheid to be condoned or indeed accepted by critics abroad, given the prevailing climate of opinion on racial issues. Indeed, one might argue that in a globalizing world the domestic politics of virtually all the member states of international society have consequences for their foreign policies – both favourable and unfavourable. South Africa was no exception to this proposition either then or now. After all, it is a truism of international relations theory that the traditional divide between domestic and foreign policy has been greatly eroded. Thus it is fair to say that foreign policy begins at home as South Africa found to its cost.

What can be asserted with some conviction is that the international milieu in which South Africa had to operate provided a context for promoting change within the country. External distaste, indeed the outright hostility which manifested itself with varying degrees of passion and commitment were not in themselves sufficient to produce fundamental reform of the South African political system. What was required was a combination of circumstances including *inter alia* heightened black protest often resulting in sporadic outbreaks of violence at ever decreasing intervals; 'a mutually hurting stalemate' between the ANC and the National Party capital government which reached its climax as this volume has tried to show in the course of the 1980s; a botched effort at reform during the Botha regime (the de Toequeville effect); and finally a profoundly depressing economic outlook which economic sanctions threatened to make much worse.

All these developments taken together produced a mood of weariness verging on despair about the future. This is not to say that revolution was 'just around the corner': far from it. The state was still intact, but it was becoming increasingly difficult to deliver the social and economic goods that the black peoples of South Africa increasingly demanded. Thus, the prospect of slow decay into an increasingly troubled and insecure future seemed real enough with the state stumbling from one crisis to another. What, in effect, prevented this bleak outlook maturing, as Chapter 5 makes clear, was the emergence of inspired leadership in the persons of de Klerk and Mandela and their close and loyal associates. Their mutual recognition that compromise was essential meant that, despite conflicting interests and expectations, there was nonetheless in Hedley Bull's phrase 'an overlapping interest' without which success in negotiation is impossible.[70]

What constituted that 'overlapping interest' in the South African case was the recognition on both sides of the political divide that failure to arrive at an acceptable negotiated settlement would be the worst result of all. It was in this particular context that the pressures exerted by outsiders especially in the four-year period 1990–4 were very important; they contrived to keep the negotiations on course despite occasional disturbing setbacks. This was soft diplomacy at its best – a true fusion of external diplomatic influence and local skill, commitment and political conviction. It was this extraordinary outcome that might really be called a turning point in South Africa's turbulent history.

Notes

1 For a fuller discussion of this issue see J.E. Spence, *Republic under Pressure – A Study of South African Foreign Policy* (London: Oxford University Press, 1965), pp.11–23.

2 *Idem*, pp.89–99. For a detailed discussion of this divisive issue in Anglo-British policy towards South African issues see J.E. Spence, 'The High Commission Territories', *Journal of Modern African Studies,* vol. 2, 1960, pp.221–46.

3 Speech by Oswald Pirow, Minister for Defence in the Union Cabinet, 1935–9, quoted in Eric Walker, *History of Southern Africa* (London: Longmans, 1956), p.685.

4 Spence, *Republic under Pressure,* pp.2–3.

5 See Basutoland, the Bechualand Protectorate, and Swaziland, *History of Discussions with the Union of South Africa, 1909–39* (London: HMSO, 1952), p.87. Hertzog's statement in the 1937 meeting between him and Malcolm MacDonald, British Dominion Secretary at the time.

6 See J.E. Spence, 'The Most Popular Corpse in History', *Optima* (Johannesburg: Anglo-American Corporation, 1986), pp.3–21.

7 Sara Pienaar, *South Africa and International Relations between the Two World Wars: The League of Nations Dimension* (Johannesburg: Witwatersrand University Press, 1987), p.175.

8 This article reads 'Nothing contained in the present Charter shall authorise the United Nations to intervene in matters which are essentially within the domestic jurisdiction of any state or shall require the Members (of the UN) to submit such matters to settlement under the present Charter; but this principle shall not prejudice the application of enforcement measures under Chapter VII.'

9 Hedley Bull, in Hedley Bull and Adam Watson (eds), *The Expansion of International Society* (Oxford: Clarendon Press, 1984), p.221.

10 *Idem*, p.124.

11 A.N. Johnston, 'Domestic Concerns and International Pressure: The Evolution of the New International Relations', in F. McA. Clifford-Vaughan (ed.), *International Pressures and Political Change in South Africa* (Cape Town and New York: Oxford University Press, 1978).

12 For a full discussion of this theme see Inis Claude, *The Changing United Nations* (New York: Random House, 1967).

13 D. Goldsworthy, *Colonial Issues in British Politics: 1945–1961* (Oxford: Oxford University Press, 1971), p.361.

14 Claude, *The Changing United Nations.*

15 Bull and Watson, *The Expansion of International Society*, p.222.

16 Geoffrey Goodwin, *Britain and the United Nations* (London: Oxford University Press, 1957), p.259.

17 Bull and Watson, *The Expansion of International Society.* See pp.118–124 for an elaboration of this theme.

18 Rosalyn Higgins, *The Development of International Law through the Political Organs of the United Nations* (London: Oxford for the Royal Institute of International Affairs, 1963), p.2.

19 Rosalyn Higgins, 'Intervention and International Law', in Hedley Bull (ed.), *Intervention in World Politics* (Oxford: Clarendon Press, 1984) pp.35–6. (In this context see, for example, the objections of the late Enoch Powell to the Higgins view in *The Times*, 24 June 1977.)

20 Johnston, 'Domestic Concerns and International Pressure'.

21 Raymond Aron, *Peace and War: The Theory of International Relations* (Garden City, NY: Doubleday, 1966), p.373.

22 Dennis Austin, *South Africa 1984* (London: Royal Institute of International Affairs, 1985), p.19.

23 Dan Keohane, 'South Africa', unpublished MS. I am grateful for permission to quote from the text.

24 Austen, *South Africa 1984*, pp.4, 63.

25 Nigel Worden, *The Making of Modern South Africa: Conquest, Segregation and Apartheid* (London: Blackwell, 1994), p.107.

26 For more discussion of this scene see J.E. Spence, *The Strategic Significance of South Africa* (London: Royal United Services Institute, 1970), pp.16–23. See also J.E. Spence, 'The Cold War in Africa', *History Today*, vol. 49, no. 3, 1999, pp.43–9. I am grateful to the editor, Mr Peter Furtado, for permission to quote from this article.

27 The phrase is the late Colin Webb's in his 'Foreign Policy of the Union of South Africa', in J.E. Black and K.W. Thompson (eds), *Foreign Policies in a World of Change* (New York: Harper and Row, 1964), p.444.

28 Seweryn Bialer, 'The Harsh Decade: Soviet Politics in the 1980s', *Foreign Affairs*, vol. 59, ch. 5, 1980/81, p.1001.

29 Dr Hilgard Muller, South Africa's Foreign Minister, quoted in *Report from South Africa*, December 1969, p.8.

30 Chester Crocker, *High Noon in Southern Africa: Making Peace in a Rough Neighbourhood* (New York: Norton, 1992), p.244. Crocker, as America's Assistant Secretary of State for African Affairs led the negotiations which resulted in Namibia's independence in 1989.

31 Crocker, *High Noon in Southern Africa*, p.246.

32 George Shepherd, *Anti-Apartheid – Transnational Conflict over Western Policy in the Liberation of South Africa* (Santa Barbara: Greenwood Press, 1977).

33 For a full discussion of the concept of 'constructive engagement' see Crocker, *High Noon in Southern Africa*, pp.74–82.

34 Quoted in Patti Waldmeir, *Anatomy of a Miracle: The End of Apartheid and the Birth of the New South Africa* (London: Penguin Books, 1997), pp.136–7.

35 Quoted in Abdul Minty, *South Africa's Defence Strategy* (London: Anti-Apartheid Movement, 1969), p.15.

36 *Idem.*

37 Larry Bowman, 'The Subordinate State System of Southern Africa', *International Studies Quarterly*, vol. 12, no. 3, 1968, p.259.

38 See James Barber, *The Uneasy Relationship – Britain and South Africa* (London: Heinemann for the Royal Institute of International Affairs, 1983), p.42.

39 J.E. Spence, 'The Republic of South Africa: Proliferation and the Politics of the "Outward Movement" ', in R.M. Lawrence and Joel Larus (eds), *Nuclear Proliferation Phase II*, (Lawrence/Manhattan/Wichita: University Press of Kansas for the National Security Educational Programme, 1974), pp.209–38.

40 Letter to Mr Ian Lloyd, MP, 2 September 1985.

41 R.H. Jackson, 'International Legitimacy in Sub-Saharan Africa' (Paper presented to the British International Studies Association, Bristol, 1985). The author is grateful for permission to quote from this paper.

42 Barber, *The Uneasy Relationship*, p.90.

43 Robin Renwick, *Unconventional Diplomacy in Southern Africa* (Basingstoke and London: Macmillan Press, 1997), pp.112–13.

44 *Idem*, p.112.

45 *Idem*, p.113.

46 *Idem*, p.114.

47 *Idem*, p.142.

48 Princeton M. Lyman, *Partner to History: The US Role in South Africa's Transition to Democracy* (Washington, DC: United States Institute of Peace Press, 2002). This book contains a full discussion of the US role in the pre-election period.

49 Scott Thomas, *The Diplomacy of Liberation: The Foreign Relations of the ANC since 1960* (London: I.B. Tauris, 1996).

50 Graham Evans, 'The International Community and the Transition to a new South Africa' *Round Table*, vol. 330, 1994, pp.178–9.

51 Thomas, *The Diplomacy of Liberation*, p.236.

52 R.B. Ballinger, *South West Africa: The Case against the Union* (Johannesburg: South African Institute of International Affairs, 1961), p.48.

53 See the author's contribution to volume II of the *Oxford History of South Africa* (Oxford: OUP, 1971) for amplification of this theme.

54 Quoted in Martin Wight, *The Power Struggle within the UN* (London: Proceedings of the Institute of World Affairs, 1956), p.255.

55 For example, the Olympic movement; a large number of sporting associations; and a wide range of civil society organizations, for example university and legal associations.

56 Dan Keohane, *South Africa*, unpublished manuscript. I am grateful for permission to quote from this helpful paper.

57 Evans, 'The International Community and the Transition to a new South Africa', p.180.

58 Quoted in Merle Lipton, *Sanctions and South Africa – The Dynamics of Economic Isolation* (London: Economic Intelligence Unit, 1988), p.120.

59 Amelia Leiss, *Apartheid and Forceful Measures* (Mimeo, 1963).

60 G. Hufbauer, J. Schott and K. Elliott, *Economic Sanctions Reconsidered* (Washington, DC for the Institute of International Economics), quoted in Margaret Doxey, *International Sanctions in Contemporary Perspective* (Basingstoke: Macmillan, 1996), p.25.

61 Quoted in J.E. Spence 'Foreign Policy Retreat into the Laager', in J. Blumenfeld (ed.), *South Africa in Crisis* (London: Royal Institute of International Affairs, 1987), p.155.

62 J. Blumenfeld, 'Western Policy Towards South Africa: Empty Rhetoric or Real Interest?', 6th Bradlow Lecture, Jan Smuts House, Johannesburg, Nov. 1987, pp. 16–17.

63 *Idem*, p.17.

64 *Idem*, p.17.

65 *Idem*, p.18.

66 Speech by F.W. de Klerk at a conference at the Institute Choiseul, Paris, 14 June 2004, pp.3 and 5.

67 *Idem*, p.5.

68 Lipton, *Sanctions and South Africa*, p.67.

69 Blumenfeld, *South Africa in Crisis*, p.4.

70 Hedley Bull, *The Anarchical Society – A Study of Order in World Politics* (Basingstoke: Palgrave, 1977), p.174.

Epilogue

The central theme of this book has been the downfall of apartheid and its replacement by a fully inclusive democratic polity. What follows is a broad overview of how democracy has fared since 1994, a topic that has already spawned a rich literature, some of which is cited in the references.

South Africa's internal diversity, its massive inequalities and the legacy of bitter conflict make it a difficult society to govern. Sustaining democratic political systems in the face of severe racial or ethnic divisions is always difficult; moreover, political competition offers insuperable temptations to mobilize support along racial/ethnic lines, as was largely the case prior to 1994 when political participation was effectively confined to whites.

The strength of the parties

Since (and including) 1994 there have been four elections, each of which has returned the ANC with a share of the vote that has not fallen below 60 per cent. Such electoral dominance suggests that South Africa is following a familiar African path of single-party dominance. The current President, Jacob Zuma, claimed a few years ago that the ANC would govern 'until Jesus comes'. While this was hyperbole, there is no serious challenger on the horizon: opposition parties remain relatively weak – in the 2009 elections the Democratic Alliance (DA), which ran second, won only 16.7 per cent of the vote, while a breakaway faction from the ANC, the Congress of the People, could manage a mere 7.4 per cent. As has been stressed in this book, the ANC is a 'broad church' that was able to unify many Africans (and to a lesser extent Coloureds and Indians) in the struggle against apartheid; but the binding force of common opposition and the emergence of divergent class and other interests is beginning to fray the previous unity. For much of the past 15 years there have been regular spats between the ANC and its alliance partners COSATU and the SACP, mitigated to some extent by the judicious cooptation of senior SACP figures into government. The partners' charge against the ANC was principally its perfunctory consultation with them on policy issues, while sharp differences on the conduct of macroeconomic policy have been frequent (see below). COSATU has been an effective mobilizer of voters at election times – but it accuses the ANC of ignoring it thereafter. Speculation about a breakaway to the left of the ANC surfaces periodically, but the ANC's alliance partners know that for the foreseeable future a socialist party is unlikely to make much headway. The more sensible strategy – which they are following – is to seek to gain control of the ANC from within the structure of the alliance.

The failure of the government of national unity

Having failed in its efforts to secure a constitutionally mandated permanent form of power-sharing, the NP had to content itself with a much-diluted and temporary 'government of national unity'. In terms of the interim constitution the election results in 1994 entitled the NP to six cabinet seats and Inkatha to three, as well as a Deputy Presidency, filled by de Klerk. Although the provision for a GNU lowered the stakes of the founding election, the cabinet that emerged was, inevitably, an 'unnatural constitutional coalition', and never 'a marriage of love', as de Klerk said.

Although the GNU worked reasonably smoothly at first, severe conflicts emerged by the end of the first year of its operation. The NP's discontent emerged by the end of the first year of its operation. Its hopes that policy would flow from a negotiated consensus on each issue did not materialize. Several clashes between the NP and the ANC occurred during 1995, leading de Klerk to conclude that

. . . we were increasingly confronted with majority government positions with which we disagreed and with which we did not want to be associated. We accordingly insisted on the right to oppose publicly policies which had been adopted in the cabinet – despite our opposition. This led to the untenable position where we were at one and the same time part of the government, as well as being the government's main opposition, attacking it in public.[1]

Despite efforts to patch up the problem, matters did not improve. It is evident that Mandela was eager to keep the GNU alive, as were some of the NP ministers (notably Pik Botha). De Klerk withdrew the NP in June 1996, leaving the three Inkatha ministers as the only non-ANC members. He retired from politics in 1997, being succeeded by Marthinus van Schalkwyk as leader of what was now called the New National Party. Its ignominious decline and eventual dissolution in 2006 forms no part of this account, save to remark that it signified the break-up of the once-mighty force of Afrikaner nationalism that had dominated South Africa.[2] At least six former ministers or deputy ministers subsequently joined or intimated support for the ANC.

Mandela and Mbeki

Mandela insisted that he would serve only one five-year term. He was less a 'hands-on' President than a symbol of reconciliation. His reassuring presence contributed greatly to the stability and calm of the transition:

I told white audiences that we needed them and did not want them to leave the country. They were South Africans just like ourselves and this was their land, too. I would not mince words about the horrors of apartheid, but I said, over and over, that we should forget the past and concentrate on building a better future for all.[3]

Under Mandela much of the day-to-day business of running government was in the hands of Thabo Mbeki, who was also a Deputy President, having elbowed aside his principal rival for the post, Cyril Ramaphosa.[4] Mbeki was an entirely different political figure from Mandela: whereas Mandela was a warm 'man-of-the-people', Mbeki was aloof, preferring to address small groups rather than large crowds, and intolerant of criticism.

Mandela was a hard act to follow, but this did not faze Mbeki, who had his own firm ideas on policy and the operation of government. He told his biographer, Mark Gevisser, that he and Mandela had conflicting approaches to racial reconciliation. Gevisser writes:

Mbeki felt that the way Mandela dealt with the issue negatively affected his own acceptability as his successor, and thus his ability to effect real transformation. South Africa just could not 'sustain a view of national reconciliation of the kind of which the media approved' and with which 'Madiba [Mandela] co-operated,' he told me. I have seldom seen Mbeki as exercised, or impassioned, as when he spoke about this: 'You just couldn't do it! It was wrong! Just wrong!'[5]

There was, he insisted, a 'dialectical relationship' between reconciliation and transformation: 'They are interdependent and impact upon each other. None is capable of realization unless it is accompanied by the other.'[6] In Mbeki's mind, transformation meant a frontal attack on the entrenched bastions of racism and a relentless assault on the inequality that scarred society. His inordinate sensitivity to race and racism would be the goad that drove the two principal instruments of transformation, affirmative action and black economic empowerment. Hand in hand with his views on racism went a strong identification with Africa, which he regarded as the victim of injustice at the hands of the imperial powers. Africa's problems, he insisted, should be solved by Africans themselves, and the imperialists should keep their noses out of the continent's affairs.

Mbeki's hypersensitivity to racial issues impacted every aspect of the policies that he sought to implement, most catastrophically in relation to the HIV/AIDS pandemic that was sweeping through South Africa. He aligned himself with dissident scientists who denied that HIV causes AIDS, insisting instead that AIDS was a disease of poverty. Moreover, the anti-AIDS drugs were 'toxic', and were being promoted by pharmaceutical companies in search of profits. There was also a racist dimension since some white Westerners are 'convinced that we [Africans] are but natural-born, promiscuous carriers of germs, unique in the world, they proclaim that our continent is doomed to an inevitable mortal end because of our unconquerable devotion to the sin of lust'.[7]

It took a court order to compel Mbeki and his eccentric Minister of Health, Manto Tshabalala-Msimang, to begin distributing anti-retroviral drugs, a process that began tardily and has reached 700,000, but at least as many still need them. Mbeki, in a huff because of the derision that was heaped on him, opted to withdraw from debates about AIDS, thereby denying the country what was vitally needed, namely firm leadership from the top in the fight against a deadly disease. By 2009 over 5 million were HIV-positive, more than 1,000 per day becoming infected, and over 2 million had died from AIDS – a figure that is far higher than the total number who died in the struggle against apartheid. Apart from his 'quiet diplomacy' that effectively gave protection to President Mugabe of Zimbabwe (see below), nothing did more to diminish Mbeki's stature as a world statesman than the AIDS debacle.

Affirmative action and black economic empowerment

One of the founding provisions of the constitution is non-racialism, but the Bill of Rights allows that to promote the achievement of equality, 'legislative and other measures designed to protect or advance persons, or categories of persons, disadvantaged by unfair discrimination may be taken' (clause 9(2)). Employment equity legislation, adopted in 1998, opened the way for a major exercise in social engineering, which critics have called 'job reservation in reverse'. The ANC has interpreted affirmative action to mean 'demographic representivity', i.e. that the public service should proportionately reflect the respective sizes of each population group as distinguished by race or colour. The ANC seeks to implement the representivity principle across the board, from the public service to national sporting teams.

During the constitutional negotiations there was widespread agree-ment that some form of affirmative action was necessary to make up for the deprivations of the past, but also to ensure that public institutions such as the judiciary, the defence force and police services acquired greater legitimacy by being broadly representative of the population at large. Affirmative action and black economic empowerment, however, have to be understood in the light of what the ANC terms 'cadre deployment', which is a project aimed at increasing its hegemony over society. Its implications were candidly spelled out in 1998 in a discussion document which stated that transformation requires

. . . *first and foremost, extending the power of the NLM [the National Liberation Movement, i.e. the ANC] over all the levers of power: the army, the police, the bureaucracy, intelligence structures, the judiciary, parastatals, and agencies such as regulatory bodies, the public broadcaster, the central bank and so on.*

Progress along these lines is far advanced. The public service has been extensively politicized by the deployment of ANC-aligned people to key positions, but at considerable cost to capacity. While relatively few white civil servants were dismissed, many accepted retirement packages and others were sidelined into positions that offered no hope of promotion. It was understandable that the ANC would be suspicious of a bureaucracy that had served the apartheid order, though many of the senior officials were prepared to serve an ANC government. Brian Pottinger writes: 'In all my discussions with old-era administrators . . . all without exception said they were willing to continue, but had little illusion that they would be allowed to do so'.[8] Their loyalty was never tested. An estimated 120,000 white bureaucrats left public service – and few young whites showed interest in joining. For the ANC, on the other hand, filling vacant and new posts offered a huge field for cadre deployment and for patronage.

In many cases assumed political loyalty trumped competence as a criterion for appointment, and often consultants had to be called in at considerable cost to help struggling departments. The most egregious case has been Home Affairs, whose inefficiency and corruptness have assumed major proportions. Other departments, as well as the police, hardly fare much better. The critical weakness lies in the lack of competent managers. Qualified blacks, moreover, are tempted by the higher salaries paid in the private sector and many quit the public service for these greener pastures. There is a vacancy rate averaging 30 per cent of all posts across the public service at national level. The situation is even worse in the provincial and local spheres of government, especially in those provinces that incorporated former Bantustans or local authorities situated in former Bantustans. Of the 283 local authorities countrywide most are officially described as 'dysfunctional' and 'paralysed'. Many are heavily indebted. Over the past few years thousands of demonstrations have occurred in many local communities, aimed at poor service delivery and corrupt councillors.

The Black Economic Empowerment (BEE) programme, introduced in the 1990s, was intended to reduce inequality in the ownership of assets and to promote the rise of black managers in the private sector. BEE has generated a complex set of targets with which firms should comply, or face being handicapped in dealings with government, notably in the matter of procurement of goods and services. The majority of BEE deals involved paper transactions in terms of which firms offered a share of equity to black businesspeople, usually funded by loans repayable by dividends. Although it was intended to be 'broad-based', it has benefited only a small group of African elites, some of whom have become fabulously rich. Many of BEE's beneficiaries have links to the ANC, a political connection which firms hoped would facilitate their dealings with government. Moeletsi Mbeki maintains that 'the black elite don't see themselves as producers and therefore do not envisage themselves as entrepreneurs who can initiate and manage new enterprises'.[9] Thus far, the 'trickle-down' effect has been minimal, while poverty and unemployment remain huge problems. BEE has also provided a cover for corrupt activities, often involving black businessmen with political links and bureaucrats with insider knowledge of tender arrangements.

Wider issues are raised here: a notion of entitlement is widespread among Africans. It nourishes a sense of dependency, and encourages 'playing the race card', which refers to the tendency to accuse critics of a policy of being 'racist' rather than addressing the criticism. These phenomena are understandable in the light of the past, but they do nothing to mitigate inequality or to promote interracial cooperation.

Corruption

Corruption is a major problem. South Africa is some way from being a 'kleptocracy', but hardly a day goes by without reports of corruption somewhere in government. Courageous investigative journalism, notably by the *Mail & Guardian* and the quirky *Noseweek*, has uncovered many instances of dodgy tender awards and other corrupt activities. The major case, which has since been a cancer in the body politic, is the arms deal concluded in 1998, whereby various European arms manufacturers were contracted to supply a range of weaponry to South Africa.[10] The original cost was estimated to be R43 billion (2000 rand value) and is now significantly higher. Why South Africa needed submarines and fighter aircraft has never been explained. The deal has long had a stench of corruption about it, allegedly implicating Jacob Zuma and his (financial) patron Schabir Shaik, who was sentenced to 15 years' imprisonment for soliciting bribes from a French arms manufacturer. Zuma, who was categorically implicated by the judge in Shaik's trial, was dismissed from his position as Deputy President by Mbeki. He thereafter spent eight years seeking to avoid charges being preferred against him, eventually succeeding, thanks to the intervention of a political appointee, the acting director of the National Prosecuting Authority. Zuma's 'reprieve' came in the nick of time – a fortnight before the elections of 22 April 2009. Zuma had faced multiple charges of corruption, racketeering, tax evasion, money-laundering and fraud; if convicted he could have faced a lengthy prison sentence. Fortunately for Zuma, by this time the internal dynamics of the ANC had changed radically.

The decline of Mbeki and the rise of Zuma

Mbeki was ousted as ANC president at the ANC's conference in December 2007, and forced to resign as President of the country in September 2008, to be replaced by Kgalema Motlanthe as an interim appointment until the election. The tide within the ANC had turned decisively against Mbeki and he was forced into a humiliating retirement. Zuma was to be the new man. How did it happen?[11] It was a combination of Mbeki's alienating personality traits and policy failures that produced a hostile reaction among many senior and rank-and-file ANC members.

Mbeki was both aloof and arrogant, especially concerning his own intellectual abilities, bitterly resentful of criticism coming from within the ANC-led alliance. Over time he became paranoid about alleged plotters against his leadership, even using the intelligence agencies to spy on his supposed rivals. These tactics alienated powerful people, including Cyril Ramaphosa, Mathews Phosa, Tokyo Sexwale, Winnie Mandela and various COSATU and SACP leaders. Within the (much-enlarged) presidency he surrounded himself with 'yes-men', further distancing himself from the grassroots. For

Mbeki, loyalty trumped competence, which explains why he declined to dismiss ministers whose incompetence not only incapacitated their departments but became national embarrassments.

He stripped away whatever federal possibilities the constitution may have offered, and ensured that premiers in ANC-controlled provinces were his own nominees. Parliament's constitutionally mandated oversight responsibilities, exercised through portfolio committees, faded, and the committees, dominated by ANC MPs, became little more than rubber stamps for the executive. Tony Leon, the pugnacious leader of the Democratic Alliance from 1994 to 2007, observed that within the brief span of a dozen years parliament 'became little more than a ceremonial relic, more engaged in all manner of pageants and celebrations of state power than in a serious-minded or substantive checking and balancing of governmental power'.[12]

The opposition was regarded more as 'the enemy' than the 'loyal opposition' of stable parliamentary systems; and its ability to put parliamentary questions was severely circumscribed. Mbeki only rarely appeared in parliament to face opposition questioning: the British Prime Minister's weekly grilling by opposition questioners was unthinkable. Underpinning the executive's control over MPs was the 'anti-defection' clause (see pages 137–8). MPs who switched party allegiances or were expelled from the party on whose list they were elected lost their seats – and the reasonably lucrative salary paid to an MP. This was a strong inducement to conformity.

Mbeki enjoyed some success in one area of policy: with the able assistance of Trevor Manuel as Minister of Finance, he was able to reorient ANC economic policy away from its traditional embrace of nationalization as an instrument for reducing economic inequality. Mbeki, who had been on the central committee of the SACP, had allowed his membership to lapse: it was evident that he now favoured Scandinavian-style social democracy. With Mandela's support, Mbeki pushed through in 1996 a new, market-friendly policy, Growth, Employment and Redistribution (GEAR).[13] It immediately evoked a hostile response from COSATU and some SACP members, who insisted (correctly) that they had not been consulted prior to the release of the new policy. GEAR, they claimed, embodied the dreaded 'neoliberalism'. The reaction signified the hardening of differing economic views inside the alliance, and marked a widening of the rift between Mbeki and the left.[14]

GEAR was supposed to enable GDP to attain a growth rate of 6 per cent p.a., while reducing unemployment and South Africa's reliance on the IMF and the World Bank. It was also intended to calm investor (domestic and foreign) fears that hardline socialist policies were being contemplated. A growth rate of 6 per cent has not been attained, although between 2004 and 2009 it nudged 5 per cent; and before the recession hit in 2008–9, 14 successive quarters of growth had been recorded. Unemployment remained stubbornly high: an estimated 25 per cent in 2009, but nearer 40 per cent if those who have given up looking for work are counted. The hard truth is that many of the unemployed, mostly young people, are virtually unemployable through lack of skills and abysmal education. South Africa's growth rate has been constrained by a chronic shortage of managerial, professional and technical skills, a situation that has been exacerbated by the emigration of an estimated 800,000 whites since 1994. Most are said to have left because of crime and affirmative action.

Mbeki should have seen the writing on the wall, when, in defiance of his dismissal of Zuma as Deputy President in 2005, the ANC's national general council reinstated him as deputy president of the ANC. It was a calculated rebuff that marked an escalation of hostilities between pro-Mbeki and pro-Zuma factions in the ANC.[15] The dénouement came in December 2007 at the ANC's conference in Polokwane. Mbeki had been assured by his close associates that he would win re-election for a third term as ANC president. Their – and Mbeki's – confidence showed how out of touch with grassroots sentiment they were: Zuma was voted in as president by 2,429 votes to 1,505. It was a conclusive but not overwhelming victory since Mbeki won nearly 40 per cent of the votes. Despite Zuma's general popularity, the vote was more of an anti-Mbeki protest than a positive affirmation of Zuma.

A number of Mbeki loyalists broke away from the ANC and formed the Congress of the People (COPE) in December 2008. There had been previous splits, but without exception the parties formed thereafter had fizzled out. Would COPE prove to be different? With little time to organize branch structures, raise funds, and an unseemly squabble over the leadership, it seemed unlikely that COPE would be able to capitalize on the widespread dissatisfaction with the ANC's poor record of service delivery. Pre-election opinion polls predicted that COPE would win between 9 per cent and 15 per cent of the vote in the April election, but it could only manage less than 8 per cent. It did, however, prevent the ANC's winning a two-thirds majority and, perhaps, denied the ANC sufficient votes in the Western Cape to give the DA outright control of the province.

Speculation about how a Zuma presidency will fare is obviously premature. He is 67 years of age and it is unclear whether he will seek a second term of office after the 2014 elections. He is of humble rural Zulu stock and had little formal education. During the apartheid era he spent long periods in prison (10 years) and in exile. As head of intelligence for MK he was deeply involved in the armed struggle. He was criticized for failing to stop abuses in the MK camps. After 1990 he tried hard to end the conflict in Natal, but his efforts to persuade provincial ANC leaders to accept Buthelezi as 'one of us' were rejected. By 1996, however, his efforts were rewarded, and a (brittle) peace was secured.

Zuma is affable, conciliatory, at ease with large crowds and capable of easily switching roles from traditionalist to modern politician. He is a poly-gynist with three wives and is said to have fathered 20 children. (Whether polygyny, and the concomitant patriarchy, is compatible with the constitu-tional value of gender equality[16] was not raised as an issue.) Zuma's large household was expensive to run, and must have been partly responsible for his financial dependence on his old friend Schabir Shaik.

During Zuma's campaign to avoid prosecution, while simultaneously staking his claim to the presidency of the country, he did little to curb his followers from beating a Zulu ethnic drum. Thousands of T-shirts pro-claimed '100 per cent Zulu boy'. Alec Russell writes that Zuma 'had clearly led the ANC into a new era of politics in which tribal identity was no longer to be a taboo'.[17] The same emphasis on Zulu identity contributed to the ANC's smashing of Inkatha in the 2009 elections.

Zuma's followers also conducted a concerted campaign to denigrate the judiciary as 'untransformed' or even 'counter-revolutionary', insinuating that both the prosecution and the courts were part of a political conspiracy to deny him the presidency. Zuma would often lead crowds in singing his trade-mark song 'Mshini Wam', translated as 'Bring me my machine gun'. This was an old MK ditty, but inappropriate in a country grappling with a desperate problem of violent crime and protest. Zuma's 'reprieve', for reasons that were widely criticized on legal grounds, cleared the way for him to become President, but it did not clear his name. He had long protested his innocence; having it established by a court would have removed the dark cloud around his head. His victory has come at some cost to the credibility of democratic South Africa's institutions.

Post-apartheid foreign policy: 1994–2009

This brief survey of South Africa's external relations since 1994 examines two themes:

1   The initial emphasis on the protection and assertion of human rights both in Africa and the wider global environment in which the new South Africa had to operate; as Nelson Mandela, the 'new' South Africa's first President stressed 'human rights will be the light that

guides our foreign affairs'.[18] We note too the contradictions that attended the pursuit of an 'ethical' foreign policy, in large part induced by the sheer intractability of international politics.

2   Similarly, we analyse the incentives and constraints that govern South Africa's efforts to be taken seriously as an emerging power.

Realism versus idealism

The 'new' South African foreign policy in the first flush of liberation from apartheid was – to a considerable degree – based on the country's high reputation and – in particular – on that of its first President, Nelson Mandela, both then and now regarded as the world's most honourable politician. His probity, and his commitment to reconciliation and forgiveness, gave his country a degree of influence and salience in global politics out of all proportion to its real weight in terms of military and economic capability. Ironically, and in profoundly different international and normative context, Mandela compares with J.C. Smuts who during both world wars and until his death in 1948 enjoyed a high reputation as a Commonwealth statesman and part architect of both the League of Nations Covenant and the United Nations Charter.

That reputation was, of course, enhanced by the so-called 'miracle' of the constitutional settlement of 1994. Indeed, the structure and process of that settlement (which has been considered in this book) was seen as a model for transitions elsewhere. Thus South Africa was perceived to be a 'good citizen' of the international society of states: during the 1960s its representatives played a key role in the renegotiation of the Non-Proliferation Treaty and the Ottawa agreement on land-mines. Furthermore, its impact on the attempt to promote a non-proliferation regime received significant endorsement by the decision to deliberately abandon the ambiguous nuclear posture of its apartheid predecessor.

It is, therefore, not surprising that the worldwide acclaim the country and its ANC leadership enjoyed post-1994 was reflected in the general celebrations attending the end of the Cold War in the late 1980s. Thus historical experience, together with the creation of a new international climate emphasizing democratic self-determination for oppressed peoples, inevitably reinforced the Mandela government's aspiration to play a liberating role in international relations.

And while a degree of realism dictating acceptance of free market ideas for managing the economy was deemed essential (despite the ANC's traditional preference for state control of its commanding heights of the economy), a coldblooded realism in the conduct of foreign policy was hardly likely to appeal to a ruling elite flushed with success at liberation and perceived by external actors as having a peculiar responsibility to encourage good governance and economic regeneration in the southern African region and beyond.[19]

Moreover, this emphasis on human rights issues was explicitly articulated in Mandela's famous *Foreign Affairs* article where he argued that 'we must treat the local regional actors with sensitivity and respect'.[20] Reputation was however found to be a wasting asset over the long run. This was especially the case given the government's self-perception as a key conflict resolver, standard bearer for the poor and the dispossessed, and regional leader. But that was to set the bar very high for the conduct of foreign policy and inevitably – as we shall see – contradictions arose between ethical imperatives and realist pressures. Indeed, external actors – Western governments in particular – entertained great expectations of the 'new' South Africa as a role model for conflict-ridden societies elsewhere and a promoter of positive change across the continent. Furthermore, a 'whiff' of manifest destiny was detectable in the heady days of the first post-apartheid administration. Witness Mandela's vociferous intervention in Nigerian affairs following the execution of Ken Saro-Wiwa and his colleagues in November 1995. His protests and demands for action from the Organization of African Unity met with a hostile reception from his fellow African leaders who remained wedded to the Westphalian principle of non-intervention. Similarly, the military incursion into Lesotho in 1998 ended in near disaster demonstrating yet again how difficult it was to reconcile a Western-style concern for human rights with African commitment to the principle of domestic jurisdiction.

Yet another contradiction emerged between economic dependence on the rich northern states of Western Europe and North America for trade and investment and the pressure to offer a lead in the search for 'African solutions to African problems' via South Africa's key role in the African Union, the Southern African Development Community, and the Non-Aligned Movement. These twin objectives of foreign policy had somehow to be reconciled: appearing to be the West's African poodle was clearly unacceptable. And to this end the South African government has certainly made a considerable effort to broaden the pattern of its investment and trading ties. Hence, reasonably successful attempts to penetrate Africa and expand economic links with Japan, Latin America, China and India. It is worth noting, however, that South Africa's export of manufactured goods to African countries faces stiff competition in terms of price and labour costs from the emerging powers of Asia.

South Africa's record as a defender of human rights has been mixed. Like many states, whose leaders pin their colours to an ethical mast as a matter of ideological principle, the constraints at times outweigh and complicate the incentives to be consistent and avoid accusations of double standards. In South Africa's case ties of gratitude to friends in the anti-apartheid struggle – for example Libya, Cuba and Algeria – overrode concern for human rights derelictions and provoked fierce argument over, for example, the morality of arms sales to these regimes. (Interestingly in 2009 this issue resurfaced with accusations by the opposition Democratic Alliance party that the National Convention on Arms Control Committee has engaged in a number of 'dodgy deals' (some authorized, some pending authorization) with, for example, Libya, Syria, Venezuela, North Korea, Zimbabwe and Iran.) Another issue which provoked fierce debate arose over which China to recognize – Taiwan or the People's Republic. In all these cases principle clashed with pragmatism and the latter won.

On the other hand, both Mbeki administrations showed a sensible preference for soft power instruments of mediation, good offices and other forms of conflict resolution. These diplomatic techniques were employed to good effect in recurrent crises in, for example, the Democratic Republic of the Congo, the Great Lakes region and Côte d'Ivoire. In part, of course, this particular thrust of policy was dictated by a realistic acknowledgement that military intervention and peace enforcement as distinct from peacekeeping were commitments beyond the country's limited military and economic capability. No doubt failure in Nigeria and Lesotho taught a salutary lesson: he, Mbeki too, might have recognized the danger of becoming bogged down in Africa's intractable conflicts where the parties are often warlords, militias and/or rapacious criminal gangs deriving benefit from the continuation of a conflict rather than the creation of a stable political order via third-party intervention. And even creating a 'stable political order' in conflict-ridden Africa seems peculiarly difficult: truces often give way to renewed fighting followed by yet another cease-fire and attempts at diplomatic resolution. Too often, the cycle repeats itself and would-be conflict resolvers find themselves on a treadmill with no lasting prospect of peace, let alone post-conflict reconstruction. Thus South Africa inhabits a rough continental neighbour-hood; the existence of frail, collapsing and failed states – very often the object of ameliorative intervention – makes the use of orthodox diplomatic and military instruments profoundly difficult. The best that can, therefore, be achieved is short-term, band-aid, patchy solutions.

Yet nowhere – in South Africa's case – is the tension between liberal incentives and the real or apparent constraints better illustrated than in the Zimbabwean example. This prolonged crisis – it could be argued – was *the* test case of South Africa's capacity to enhance its reputation for decisive action in defence of human rights. It was (and is) after all, the regional hegemon with the means, via a combination of sanctions and coercive diplomacy, to force the pace of change in Zimbabwe. Certainly, many in the West assumed that the Mbeki government had the primary responsibility and the means for the task.

Reliance on 'quiet diplomacy' had little effect in the short to medium run, witness the Mbeki government's refusal to openly criticize those responsible for the crisis, not to mention the extraordinary behaviour of official South African delegations – on electoral monitoring visits to Zimbabwe – who found little if anything to criticize. Rightly or wrongly, South Africa's reputation has been tarnished by its government's failure to adopt a more proactive role. True, a precarious Government of National Unity (GNU) was established early in 2009 and no doubt Mbeki and his colleagues would claim credit for their strategy of waiting on time and circumstance to provide change however uncertain its implications for the future might be. In the last analysis, however, South Africa's performance in the Zimbabwean crisis demonstrated that liberation solidarity with Mugabe would inevitably trump human rights.[21] In this context, the mediatory skills of President Jacob Zuma honed in his successful intervention in the KwaZulu conflict in the 1990s will be severely tested in any attempt he makes to consolidate and strengthen the role of the GNU in Zimbabwe. This strategy will require a delicate balancing act between the protagonists, utilizing a combination of soft and coercive diplomacy. This is certainly the most important task facing the Zuma presidency in the foreign policy arena.

There are other examples illuminating the fall from grace as early aspirations to be a 'force for good' in international relations gave way on important occasions to a disturbing, indeed damaging, exercise of *realpolitik*. This is clearly illustrated in South Africa's behaviour at the United Nations; as a non-permanent member of the United Nations Security Council during 2009, its delegation voted against a US-sponsored resolution condemning the military government of Burma. Similarly, South Africa was reluctant to support a tough resolution at the Human Rights Commission over the Darfur issue. It also argued for the suspension of the International Criminal Court prosecution of the Sudanese President. As Archbishop Tutu remarked, such a posture was 'inconsistent with our history'.[22] Strong criticism, too, came from the distinguished judge, Richard Goldstone, who argued that 'South Africa chose to support [a weak statement on Burma] which deliberately avoided pointing a finger of blame. It is a disappointing and inexplicable failure.'[23] In this context we should also note the refusal to support UN proposals for sanctions against Zimbabwe and Iran (the latter for violating nuclear safeguards). One perceptive explanation for this departure from Mandela's initial emphasis on a human rights-based foreign policy is offered by *The Economist*, arguing that it notes

South Africa's ambivalent sense of identity, with one foot in the rich world, where its main economic interests continue to lie, and the other in the poor one, with which many of its people identify. Even after the end of white rule, some of South Africa's neighbours regard it as something of a Trojan horse for the West. Hence its desire constantly to affirm its African credentials while playing down any hegemonic ambitions.[24]

Inevitably, ethical imperatives clash with the constraints of national self-interest.

South Africa as an emerging power

The debate on this topic is extensive but most scholars agree on the following criteria for inclusion in this category of states: a reasonably stable democratic base; a substantial military capability; a sizeable economic capability and the capacity to deliver both 'guns and butter'; an enabling environment, i.e. a set of political, economic and judicial institutions which observe (to some degree at least) the accepted principles of good governance; and finally, a reasonably hospitable regional or continental environment in which the state in question can play a decisive and constructive role.

In this context South Africa might be compared with those other 'niche' players – Canada and the Scandinavian quartet – with the difference that the latter operate from an unassailable 'rectitude base' of universally recognized good governance and impressive economic performance. In addition, their governments can pick and choose when and where to exploit their moral advantage as sought-after mediators or skilful exploiters of soft power diplomacy. So-called middle powers, therefore, entertain relatively modest foreign policy aspirations; they are content to be good citizens of international society and their electorates feel at ease with their self-prescribed role and their record of achievement.

Measured against these criteria South Africa has a mixed record: true, the state is stable but the level of crime remains unacceptably high; the management of the economy has been prudent, but the rate of delivery of social goods and services to the black majority has not realized initial expectations and sporadic township violence has occurred; the enabling environment of political and judicial institutions (a crucial and positive inheritance from the past) has been preserved although there are clearly signs of stress and strain; and finally, the immediate continental environment is not propitious for the conduct of a successful foreign policy. Moreover, this applies particularly to the South African region where a group of small poor weak states look to South Africa for leadership and economic benefit.

One might fairly conclude that this attempt to project itself as an emerging power of substance has been over-ambitious. One abiding problem has been the difficulty involved in reconciling the pressure to play domestically by the rules of globalization and simultaneously to act as a spokesman for Third World interests in international forums. Hence the need to project an image of prudent economic management to the overseas investor and one based on an 'eclectic synthesis' of neorealist and neoliberal principals.[25]

Certainly South Africa has a 'rectitude base' but it is relatively fragile as compared with more well-developed 'niche' players pursuing more limited ambitions. Indeed, it could be argued that the election of Jacob Zuma to the presidency in 2009 on an overwhelming mandate to accelerate the pace of domestic reform suggests that the government may well have to concentrate resources on the home front rather than on grandiose external enterprises. He will ultimately be judged on how well he meets demands for the economic and social betterment of his domestic constituency.

In conclusion, what this brief analysis of South African foreign policy shows is that commitment to ethical goals in foreign policy does open a government to accusations of inconsistency and double standards. Perhaps in the last analysis, a cautious sceptical realism, focusing on concrete and specific national interests and eschewing grandiose schemes for global progress, would have made more sense. As one perceptive scholar, Kuseni Dlamini, has argued 'even if Pretoria can do something it cannot do anything and everything everywhere all the time. Choices are inescapable.'[26]

Thus whether the 'new' South Africa remains an inspirational example as it was perceived by many to be at its birth in 1994 or has, in effect, become 'just another country' is perhaps too sharp a dichotomy. True, it is a member of the G20; true it aspires to a permanent seat on a reformed United Nations Security Council, but its record in foreign policy, as we have tried to show, is by no means inspirational in ethical terms. Perhaps the best that can be said is that South Africa has become, indeed in most respects, 'just another country' facing the same ethical dilemmas in foreign policy as most other states. It, too, has frequently to choose between evils – an inevitable consequence of living in an anarchical international society where statecraft involves the protection and enhancement of the national interest, arguably an ethical imperative often at odds with absolute principle.

This brief survey of South Africa's development as a 'new' polity is offered in part as a corrective to the widespread view that the country's transition provided highly relevant guidelines to those divided societies aspiring to achieve something similar in terms of substantial and sensible outcomes.

There may well be general lessons to be learnt: the significance and crucial importance of a 'mutually hurting stalemate' affecting all the protagonists involved; the extent to which external pressures can be brought ot bear; a rational willingness to accept compromise; and, eschewing extreme ideological positions, a willingness to cultivate a belief in the validity and durability of constitutional government; a commitment to reconciliation by both formal and informal mechanisms.

But in the last analysis what counts is local circumstance, past traditions of governance and the personalities and perspectives of the key players in a negotiation process.

We have tried to examine all these pressures for change in our study. One key factor emerges in any attempt to explain the peculiar nature of South Africa's variant of democratic governance. We refer here to the institutional inheritance of the post 1994 government and the benefits it derived from:

- A tradition of strong statehood, going back many decades.
- An historical commitment to parliamentary governance, admittedly exclusive during the apartheid regime.
- A commitment to the rule of law, however battered it was during the apartheid years.
- A vigorous civil society which never completely lost its voice and capacity for critical scrutiny of the apartheid's government's policy.

All these factors taken together gave the new South Africa ideological and practical advantage following the demise of the apartheid regime. And it is these advantages which distinguish South Africa's mode of conflict resolution from other transitions elsewhere.

What the record of the last fifteen years demonstrates is that South Africa's transition did produce an imperfect democracy, but one which nevertheless which may avoid the pitfalls affecting its counterparts elsewhere on the continent.

Notes

1 De Klerk, *The Last Trek*, pp.347, 352, 347–8.
2 See Inus Aucamp and Johan Swanepoel, *Einde van 'n Groot Party* (Allensnek: Morrison-Befonds, 2007).
3 Mandela, *Long Walk to Freedom*, p.606.
4 For Mbeki's rise to power see William M. Gumede, *Thabo Mbeki and the Battle for the Soul of the ANC* (Cape Town: Zebra Press, 2005).

5 Mark Gevisser, *The Dream Deferred: Thabo Mbeki* (Cape Town: Jonathan Ball, 2007).

6 Thabo Mbeki, *The Time Has Come: Selected Speeches* (Cape Town: Tafelberg, 1998), pp.41–2.

7 Quoted in Virginia van der Vliet, 'South Africa Divided against AIDS', in Kyle D. Kauffman and David L. Lindauer (eds), *AIDS and South Africa: The Social Expression of a Pandemic* (Basingstoke: Palgrave, 2004).

8 Brian Pottinger, *The Mbeki Legacy* (Cape Town: Zebra Press, 2008), p.105.

9 Moeletsi Mbeki, *Architects of Poverty* (Johannesburg: Picador Africa, 2009), p.72.

10 Andrew Feinstein, *After the Party: A Personal and Political Journey inside the ANC* (Cape Town: Jonathan Ball, 2007); Paul Holden, *The Arms Deal in Your Pocket* (Cape Town: Jonathan Ball, 2008).

11 See Carol Paton, 'Things Fall Apart', *Financial Mail* (Johannesburg) 23 May 2008.

12 Tony Leon, *On the Contrary: Leading the Opposition in Democratic South Africa* (Cape Town: Jonathan Ball, 2008), p.690.

13 Alan Hirsch, *A Season of Hope: Economic Reform under Mandela and Mbeki* (Scottsville: University of KwaZulu-Natal Press, 2005), pp.98–108.

14 Gevisser, *The Dream Deferred*, pp.670–5, 690–5.

15 Barney Mthombothi, 'Accidental Hero', *Financial Mail*, 17 April 2009; see also Jeremy Gordin, *Zuma: A Biography* (Cape Town: Jonathan Ball, 2008).

16 H.J. Simons, *African Women: Their Legal Status in South Africa* (London: C. Hurst, 1966), pp.24–5, 84–5.

17 Alec Russell, *After Mandela: The Battle for the Soul of South Africa* (London: Hutchinson, 2009), p.236.

18 Nelson Mandela, 'South Africa's Future Foreign Policy', *Foreign Affairs*, vol. 72, no. 5, 1994, p.86.

19 For a fuller discussion of this theme see J.E. Spence, 'South Africa: An African Exception or Just Another Country?', *Conflict, Security and Development*, vol. 7, no. 2, 2007, pp.341–7. I am grateful to Ms Catherine Carney, managing editor of the journal, for permission to quote from its contents.

20 Mandela, *South Africa's Future Foreign Policy*, p.97.

21 J.E. Spence, 'South Africa's Role in the Zimbabwe Crisis', *Round Table*, vol. 95, no. 384, 2006, p.194.

22 *Business Day*, Johannesburg, 11 December 2006.

23 *Idem*.

24 'The see-no-evil foreign policy', *The Economist*, 15–21 November 2008, pp.65–6.

25 *Idem*, p.66.

26 K. Dlamini, 'Is Quiet Diplomacy an Effective Conflict Resolution Strategy?', *South African Yearbook of International Affairs*, Johannesburg, 2002–3, p.171.

Bibliography

Adhikari, Mohamed, *Not White Enough, Not Black Enough* (Cape Town: Double Storey Books, 2006).

Afrikanerbond, *Bearer of an Ideal 1918–1997* (Johannesburg, 1997).

Argus (Cape Town) 18 April 1975.

Arnold, Millard W. (ed.), *Steve Biko: No Fears Expressed* (Braamfontein: Skotaville Press, 1987).

Aron, Raymond, *Peace and War: The Theory of International Relations* (Garden City, NY: Doubleday, 1966).

Aucamp, Inus and **Swanepoel, Johan,** *Einde van 'n Groot Party* (Allensnek: Morrison-Befonds, 2007).

Austin, Dennis, *South Africa 1984* (London: Royal Institute of International Affairs, 1985).

Ballinger, R.B., *South West Africa: The Case against the Union* (Johannesburg: South African Institute of International Affairs, 1961).

Barber, James, *The Uneasy Relationship – Britain and South Africa* (London: Heinemann for the Royal Institute of International Affairs, 1983).

Barrell, Howard, *MK: The ANC's Armed Struggle* (London: Penguin Books, 1990).

Bernstein, Rusty, *Memory against Forgetting: Memoirs from a Life in South African Politics 1938–1964* (London: Viking, 1999).

Bialer, Seweryn, 'The Harsh Decade: Soviet Politics in the 1980s', *Foreign Affairs*, vol. 59, ch. 5, 1980/81.

Black Review 1972 (Durban: Black Community Programmes, 1973).

Blumenfeld, Jesmond, *South Africa in Crisis* (London: Croom Helm, 1987).

Blumenfeld, Jesmond, 'Western Policy Towards South Africa: Empty Rhetoric or Real Interest?' 6th Bradlow Lecture, Jan Smuts House, Johannesburg, November 1987 pp. 16–17.

Bowman, Larry, 'The Subordinate State System of Southern Africa', *International Studies Quarterly*, vol. 12, no. 3, 1968.

Bull, Hedley, 'Human Rights in World Politics', in Ralph Pettman (ed.), *Moral Claims in World Affairs* (London: Taylor & Francis, 1974).

Bull, Hedley, *The Anarchical Society – A Study of Order in World Politics* (Basingstoke: Palgrave, 1977).

Bull, Hedley and **Watson, Adam** (eds), *The Expansion of International Society* (Oxford: Clarendon Press, 1984).

Carmel, Richard, 'The Certification of the Constitution of South Africa', in Penelope Andrews and Stephen Ellmann (eds), *Post-Apartheid Constitutions: Perspectives on South Africa's Basic Law* (Johannesburg: Witwatersrand University Press, 2001), pp.224–301.

Chamber of Commerce, Johannesburg, *statement*, 23 July 1976.

Claude, Inis, *The Changing United Nations* (New York: Random House, 1966).

Coleman, Max (ed.), *A Crime against Humanity: Analysing the Repression of the Apartheid State* (Cape Town: David Philip, 1998).

Commonwealth Group of Eminent Persons, The, *Mission to South Africa: The Commonwealth Report* (London: Penguin Books, 1986).

Crocker, Chester, *High Noon in Southern Africa: Making Peace in a Rough Neighbourhood* (New York: Norton, 1992).

De Klerk, F.W., *The Last Trek – A New Beginning: The Autobiography* (London: Macmillan, 1998).

de Villiers, Dirk and **Johanna,** *Paul Sauer* (Cape Town: Tafelberg Press, 1977).

de Villiers, Dirk and **Johanna,** *PW* (Cape Town: Tafelberg Press, 1984).

Doxey, Margaret, *International Sanctions in Contemporary Perspective* (Basingstoke: Macmillan, 1996).

Ebrahim, Hassen (ed.), *The Soul of a Nation: Constitution-making in South Africa* (Cape Town: Oxford University Press, 1998).

Ellis, Stephen and **Sechaba, Tsepo,** *Comrades against Apartheid: The ANC and the SACP in Exile* (London: James Currey, 1992).

Evans, Graham, 'The International Community and the Transition to a New South Africa', *Round Table*, vol. 330, 1994.

Feinstein, Andrew, *After the Party: A Personal and Political Journey inside the ANC* (Cape Town: Jonathan Ball, 2007).

Gevisser, Mark, *The Dream Deferred: Thabo Mbeki* (Cape Town: Jonathan Ball, 2007).

Goldsworthy, D., *Colonial Issues in British Politics: 1945–1961*, (Oxford: Oxford University Press, 1971).

Goodwin, Geoffrey, *Britain and the United Nations* (London: Oxford University Press, 1957).

Gordin, Jeremy, *Zuma: A Biography* (Cape Town: Jonathan Ball, 2008).

Gumede, William M., *Thabo Mbeki and the Battle for the Soul of the ANC* (Cape Town: Zebra Press, 2005).

Hartshorne, Ken, *Challenges and Crisis: Black Education 1910–1990* (Cape Town: Oxford University Press, 1992).

Higgins, Rosalyn, 'Intervention and International Law', in Hedley Bull (ed.), *Intervention in World Politics* (Oxford: Clarendon Press, 1984).

Higgins, Rosalyn, *The Development of International Law through the Political Organs of the United Nations* (London: Oxford for the Royal Institute of International Affairs, 1968).

Hirsch, Alan, *A Season of Hope: Economic Reform under Mandela and Mbeki* (Scottsville: University of KwaZulu-Natal Press, 2005).

History of Discussions with the Union of South Africa, 1909–39 (London: HMSO, 1952).

Holden, Paul, *The Arms Deal in Your Pocket* (Cape Town: Jonathan Ball, 2008).

Hufbauer, G., Schott, J. and Elliott, K., *Economic Sanctions Reconsidered* (Washington, DC for the Institute of International Economics), quoted in Margaret Doxey, *International Sanctions in Contemporary Perspective* (Basingstoke: Macmillan, 1996).

Independent Electoral Commission, The, *An End to Waiting: The Story of South Africa's Elections – 26 April to 6 May 1994* (Johannesburg: IEC, 1995).

Jackson, R.H., 'International Legitimacy in Sub-Saharan Africa' (Paper presented to the British International Studies Association, Bristol, 1985).

Jeffery, Anthea, *The Natal Story: 16 Years of Conflict* (Johannesburg: South African Institute of Race Relations, 1997).

Jenkins, Carolyn, 'Economic Implications of Capital Flight', in Liz Clarke, Karen MacGregor and William Saunderson-Meyer (eds), *The Industrial Trade Union Guide* (Durban, 1989).

Joffe, Joel, *The Rivonia Story* (Bellville: Mayibuye Books, 1995).

Johnston, A.N., 'Domestic Concerns and International Pressure: The Evolution of the New International Relations', in F. McA. Clifford-Vaughan (ed.), *International Pressures and Political Change in South Africa* (Cape Town and New York: Oxford University Press, 1978).

Karis, Thomas and **Carter, Gwendolen** (eds), *From Protest to Challenge: A Documentary History of African Politics in South Africa 1882–1964* (Stanford, CA: Hoover Institution Press, 1977).

Keohane, Dan, *South Africa*, unpublished manuscript.

Leiss, Amelia, *Apartheid and Forceful Measures* (mimeo, 1963).

Lelyveld, Joseph, *Mind Your Shadow: South Africa, Black and White* (London: Michael Joseph, 1985).

Leon, Tony, *On the Contrary: Leading the Opposition in Democratic South Africa* (Cape Town: Jonathan Ball, 2008).

Lipton, Merle, *Sanctions and South Africa – The Dynamics of Economic Isolation* (London: Economic Intelligence Unit, 1988).

Lodge, Tom and **Bill Nasson,** *All, Here, and Now: Black Politics in South Africa in the 1980s* (Cape Town: David Philip, 1991).

Lodge, Tom, *Black Politics in South Africa since 1945* (Johannesburg: Ravan Press, 1983), p.235.

Luthuli, Albert, *Let My People Go* (London: Collins, 1962).

Lyman, Princeton M., *Partner to History: The US Role in South Africa's Transition to Democracy* (Washington, DC: United States Institute of Peace Press, 2002).

Mandela, Nelson, *Long Walk to Freedom: The Autobiography of Nelson Mandela* (Boston, MA: Little, Brown).

Mbeki, Moeletsi, *Architects of Poverty* (Johannesburg: Picador Africa, 2009).

Mbeki, Thabo, *The Time Has Come: Selected Speeches* (Cape Town: Tafelberg, 1998).

Meyer, Roelf, 'From Parliamentary Sovereignty to Constitutionality: The Democratisation of South Africa, 1990 to 1994', in Penelope Andrews and Stephen Ellmann (eds), *Post-Apartheid Constitutions: Perspectives on South Africa's Basic Law* (Johannesburg: Witwatersrand University Press, 2001).

Minty, Abdul, *South Africa's Defence Strategy* (London, Anti-Apartheid Movement, 1969) p.15.

Moss, Rose, *Shouting at the Crocodile: Popo Molefe, Patrick Lekota and the Freeing of South Africa* (Boston, MA: Beacon Press, 1990).

Mthombothi, Barney, 'Accidental Hero', *Financial Mail*, 17 April 2009.

Mzala (pseudonym), *Gatsha Buthelezi: Chief with a Double Agenda* (London: 2ed Books, 1988).

O'Malley, Padraig, *Shades of Difference – Mac Maharaj and the Struggle for South Africa* (New York: Penguin Books, 2007).

Paton, Carol, 'Things Fall Apart', *Financial Mail* (Johannesburg), 23 May 2008.

Pelzer, A.N. (ed.), *Verwoerd Speaks: Speeches 1948–1966* (Johannesburg: APB Publishers, 1966), pp.83–4.

Pienaar, S.W. (ed.), *Glo in U Volk* (Cape Town: Tafelberg Press, 1964).

Pienaar, Sara, *South Africa and International Relations between the Two World Wars: The League of Nations Dimension* (Johannesburg: Witwatersrand University Press, 1987).

Pityana, N. Barney, Ramphele, Mamphela, Mpulwana, Malusi and **Wilson, Lindy** (eds), *Bounds of Possibility: The Legacy of Steve Biko and Black Consciousness* (Cape Town: David Philip, 1991).

Pogrund, Benjamin, *Sobukwe and Apartheid* (Johannesburg: Jonathan Ball, 1990).

Pottinger, Brian, *The Mbeki Legacy* (Cape Town: Zebra Press, 2008).

Race Relations Survey 1985 (Johannesburg: South African Institute of Race Relations, 1986).

Race Relations Survey 1986 (Johannesburg: South African Institute of Race Relations, 1987).

Race Relations Survey 1987–8 (Johannesburg: South African Institute of Race Relations, 1988).

Race Relations Survey 1989–90 (Johannesburg: South African Institute of Race Relations, 1990).

Rand Daily Mail (Johannesburg), 15 April 1975.

Rand Daily Mail, 3 March 1976.

Rapport (Johannesburg), 22 June 2008.

Renwick, Robin, *Unconventional Diplomacy in Southern Africa* (Basingstoke and London: Macmillan Press, 1997).

Report from South Africa, December 1969.

Report of the Commission on Native Education, 1949–51 (Pretoria: Government Printer, 1951).

Report of the Committee for Constitutional Affairs of the President's Council on an Urbanisation Strategy for the Republic of South Africa: PC 3/1985 (Cape Town: Government Printer).

Report of the Truth and Reconciliation Commission (Cape Town, 1998), Vol. 2, p.221.

Richard, Dirk, *Moedswillig die Uwe,* (Johannesburg: Perskor, 1985).

Sachs, Albie, *Justice in South Africa* (London: Heinemann, 1973).

SASO, *Alice Declaration: Statement by SASO on the Boycott of Black Universities, May 14, 1972.*

Scholtz, J.J.J. (ed.), *Vegter en Hervormer* (Cape Town: Tafelberg Press, 1988).

Schuster, Lynda, *A Burning Hunger: One Family's Struggle against Apartheid* (London: Jonathan Cape, 2004).

Seegers, Annette, *The Military in the Making of Modern South Africa* (London: I.B. Taurus, 1996).

Seekings, Jeremy, *The UDF: A History of the United Democratic Front in South Africa 1983-1991* (Cape Town: David Philip, 2000).

Shepherd, George Anti-Apartheid – Transnational Conflict and Western Policy in the Liberation of South Africa (Santa Barbara: Greenwood Press, 1977).

Simons, H.J., *African Women: Their Legal Status in South Africa* (London: C. Hurst, 1966).

Sparks, Allister, *Tomorrow Is Another Country* (Johannesburg: Struik, 1994).

Spence, J.E., 'The High Commission Territories', *Journal of Modern African Studies,* vol. 2, 1960, pp.221–46.

Spence, J.E., *Republic under Pressure – A Study of South African Foreign Policy* (London: Oxford University Press, 1965).

Spence, J.E., *The Strategic Significance of South Africa* (Royal United Services Institute, 1970).

Spence, J.E., 'The Republic of South Africa: Proliferation and the Politics of the "Outward Movement" ', in R.M. Lawrence and Joel Larus (eds), Nuclear Proliferation *Phase II*, Lawrence/Manhattan/Wichita: University Press of Kansas for the National Security Educational Programme, 1974), pp.209–38.

Spence, J.E., 'The Most Popular Corpse in History', *Optima* (Johannesburg: Anglo-American Corporation, 1986).

Spence, J.E., 'Foreign Policy Retreat into the Laager', in J. Blumenfeld (ed.), *South Africa in Crisis* (London: Royal Institute of International Affairs, 1987).

Spence, J.E., 'The Cold War in Africa', *History Today*, vol. 49, no. 3, 1999, pp.43–9.

Stadler, H.D., *The Other Side of the Story* (Pretoria: Contact Publishers, 1997).

Summary of the Report of the Commission for the Socio-Economic Development of the Bantu Areas within the Union of South Africa (Tomlinson Report) (Pretoria: Government Printer, U.G. 61/55).

Sunday Express (Johannesburg), 27 July 1975.

Sunday Times (Johannesburg), 22 April 1975.

Survey of Race Relations 1975 (Johannesburg: South African Institute of Race Relations, 1976).

Survey of Race Relations 1976 (Johannesburg: South African Institute of Race Relations, 1977).

Survey of Race Relations 1987/88 (Johannesburg: South African Institute of Race Relations, 1988).

Survey of Race Relations in South Africa 1955/6 (Johannesburg: South African Institute of Race Relations, 1956).

Survey of Race Relations in South Africa 1964 (Johannesburg: South African Institute of Race Relations, 1965).

Survey of Race Relations in South Africa 1977 (Johannesburg: South African Institute of Race Relations, 1978).

Tambo, Adelaide (ed.), *Preparing for Power: Oliver Tambo Speaks* (London: Heinemann, 1987).

Temkin, Ben, *Buthelezi: A Biography* (London: Frank Cass, 2003).

Thomas, Scott, *The Diplomacy of Liberation: The Foreign Relations of the ANC since 1960* (London: I.B. Tauris, 1996).

van der Vliet, Virginia, 'South Africa Divided against AIDS', in Kyle D. Kauffman and David L. Lindauer (eds), *AIDS and South Africa: The Social Expression of a Pandemic* (Basingstoke: Palgrave, 2004).

van Rooyen, Johann, *Hard Right: The New White Power in South Africa* (London: I.B. Taurus, 1994).

Verslag van die Kommissie van Ondersoek oor die Oproer in Soweto en Elders van 16 Junie 1976 tot 28 Februarie 1977 (Cillié Commission) (Pretoria: Government Printer RP106/1979), vol. 1, paras 107–8, 126, 127.

Vigne, Randolph, *Liberals against Apartheid: A History of the Liberal Party 1953–1968* (London: Macmillan, 1997).

Visser, George Cloete, *OB – Traitors or Patriots?* (Johannesburg: Macmillan South Africa, 1976).

Waldmeir, Patti, *Anatomy of a Miracle: The End of Apartheid and the Birth of the New South Africa* (London: Penguin Books, 1997).

Walker, Eric, *History of Southern Africa* (London: Longmans, 1956).

Webb, Colin, 'Foreign Policy of the Union of South Africa' in J.E. Black and K.W. Thompson (eds), *Foreign Policies in a World of Change* (New York: Harper and Row, 1964).

Wight, Martin, *The Power Struggle within the UN* (London: Proceedings of the Institute of World Affairs, 1956).

Wilkins, Ivor and Strydom, Hans, *The Super-Afrikaners: Inside the Afrikaner Broederbond* (Johannesburg: Jonathan Ball, 1978).

Worden, Nigel, *The Making of Modern South Africa: Conquest, Segregation and Apartheid* (London, Blackwell, 1994).

Index